THE MISSING PIECE

To my wife, Kim, with love

THE MISSING PIECE

SOLVING SOUTH AFRICA'S ECONOMIC PUZZLE

KEVIN LINGS

MACMILLAN

First published in 2014
by Pan Macmillan South Africa
Private Bag X19
Northlands
Johannesburg
2116

www.panmacmillan.co.za

ISBN 978-1-77010-376-4
e-ISBN 978-1-77010-377-1

Editing by Lisa Compton
Proofreading by Sally Hines
Indexing by Sanet le Roux
Cover and text design by Karen Lilje, Hybrid Creative

Printed and bound by Creda

SEE THE WEBSITE WWW.THEMISSINGPIECE.CO.ZA
FOR FURTHER RESOURCES AND INFORMATION

CONTENTS

FOREWORD

In many ways the South Africa we inhabit in 2014 is totally different from the country delivered from minority rule in 1994. For a visitor from our past, this difference would perhaps be most obvious in the scale of our country's economic activity; in the faces and discourse of our political, business and social leaders; and, less tangibly, in the changed perceptions South Africans now have of their fellow citizens. While travelling through the country, our visitor would also not fail to notice the substantial changes in social infrastructure – the many houses, schools, hospitals and clinics that have been built and the networks delivering power to that infrastructure. But our visitor would also see that many of the problems that were evident under late apartheid have been magnified. The most obvious benefits of the growth in the economy and the provision of opportunities for advancement have not been evenly spread, and the gap between the most and the least advantaged has increased. The stubbornly high levels of unemployment would soon become evident when our visitor slipped off the highways into the urban townships, small towns and rural areas and spent some time with the many young people who have failed to find the economic opportunities they desire.

In this important contribution to the debate on how best to address the structural problems that have plagued the South African economy, Kevin Lings not only documents the many social and economic achievements of the post-apartheid government, but identifies the key areas in which the country has not performed adequately and suggests some potential solutions. However, no advanced training or expertise in economics is required to understand the scale of the problem – an average unemployment rate of 25% over the past ten years – nor are any special prognostic abilities required to predict the long-term consequences if this problem is not addressed. The value of Kevin's work lies in trying to understand why, despite a raft of policies and initiatives that have tried to deal with this fundamental problem, so little progress has been made.

As is often the case with complex systems, there is no simple 'magic bullet' that will resolve all our problems. Formulaic repetitions of entrenched ideological positions may provide good copy for politicians, newspaper columnists and regular writers of letters to the editor but are unlikely to produce any solutions. If the economic system is not creating the employment required, the solution will probably require interventions that address the low levels of investment in economic infrastructure; the lack of clarity and coherence in the development and implementation of economic policies; the perceived effects of corruption and anti-competitive behaviour; and the management and nurturing of our human resources.

Some of these aspects are reflected in the findings of the Global Competitiveness Index. In 2006/2007 South Africa was ranked 45th out of 125 countries, but has fallen to 53rd out 148 countries in 2013/2014.

This has occurred even though our absolute score on the index has remained relatively stable (rising very slightly from 4.36 in 2006/07 to 4.37 in 2013/14) – a clear indication that we are failing to match the progress made by our competitors. The relative stability in South Africa's score does, however, mask some significant movements within the components of the index: we have fallen from 49th to 66th with respect to infrastructure (4.04 to 4.13), from 46th to 95th with respect to macroeconomic environment (4.74 to 4.39), and from 103th to 135th with respect to health and primary education (5.07 to 3.89).

There is, however, one particular intervention that, while not sufficient to guarantee a positive outcome, is a necessary component of any successful economy today – increasing the level of investment by both the state and the private sector in research and development (R&D). There is little debate about the value of such investment. Studies have shown that the rate of return on R&D spending generally exceeds 40%. Innovation and technological change are fundamental inputs to economic growth through increased efficiencies, improved productivity and the creation of new industries, and these factors can only come into play as a result of directed investment to increase the stock of knowledge. Much of what we take for granted in the modern world has been the result of investments in technological innovation, including our systems of communication (radio, television, and more recently the Internet and mobile communications); the energy system (the internal combustion engine, and the centralised generation and transmission of electricity); and the many advances in health technologies.

In the South African context there are very specific conditions that provide further motivation for an increase in R&D investment, including the clear inability of the existing economic framework to provide the necessary growth, a sustained period of relative underinvestment in R&D, and the limitations of the current models of service delivery.

In the first instance, the specific failure to deliver on sufficient employment opportunities is, as indicated above, manifest. There is little reason to believe that the continued application of the same policies and frameworks will provide different outcomes. Significant and carefully targeted investment in R&D in emerging technologies provides us with one viable route to generate the growth we require.

The second issue concerns the systemic underinvestment in R&D in the South African economy, and has been well documented. The Centre for Science, Technology and Innovation Indicators (CeSTII) reported that in 2011/12 (the latest year for which this information is available), South Africa allocated 0.76% of GDP to R&D. Expenditure on R&D as a proportion of GDP has declined from a high of 0.95% in 2006/07, and has averaged approximately 0.77% since 1994/95. The CeSTII report further indicated that South Africa's R&D expenditure as a proportion of GDP was lower than the world average of 1.77%, the European Union average of 1.94% and the OECD average of 2.37%. Among the BRICS countries, the comparable figures were 1.84% in China, 1.16% in Brazil, 1.09% in Russia and 0.76% in India. The level of R&D spending in South Africa is also well below the target of 1.5% set in the National Development Plan. There is thus a substantial long-term deficit in support for R&D that needs to be addressed. A further complication is that, in addition to underspending on R&D, we have also failed to gather information on the effectiveness of the expenditure we have made. Meeting the target of spending 1.5% of GDP on R&D will not be very meaningful if that expenditure is poorly targeted or inefficiently allocated, and hence does not produce the expected returns. There is an urgent need to review and assess the impact of our R&D work to assist in identifying the optimal strategy for future investment.

One issue that invariably arises is what the role of the state should be in supporting this investment, particularly when this role, at least in the developed economies, is increasingly being assumed by the private sector. One part of this argument is relatively easy to make: even in developed economies the market will not produce the required R&D in certain areas. This is particularly true of fundamental research, where the economic value of the discovery is not likely to fall to initial discoverers. The track record of state involvement in this area is long and distinguished – the development of the infrastructure that underpins the Internet, for example, would not have been possible without significant state support. We can draw many similar examples from the health, agriculture and energy sectors. In South Africa there is an argument to be made that the long period of relative underinvestment in R&D has degraded, at least relative to the size of the economy, the R&D capacity (both people and infrastructure). A substantial investment from the state is required to rebuild our R&D capacity (in addition to further support for investment via the tax system), and we need to use this expanded capacity to stimulate further private sector investment.

There is also the question of national interest. Even in the era of globalisation there are unique benefits that may accrue to the local economy where the innovation takes place. These 'spillover' effects could include the development of skills and techniques that have application in other sectors, the development of support industries, and intangible benefits such as the promotion of a culture of innovation among the general population.

The third and final motivation for increased state investment in R&D concerns the problems facing service delivery in South Africa. During the first fifteen to twenty years of our democracy, there were a number of socio-economic challenges that could, in the main, be addressed through a substantial reallocation and transfer of resources. This was particularly the case in six key areas: housing, education, health, electricity, water and social security. However, we are now entering a stage where the additional allocation of resources will in all probability not translate into significantly improved outcomes. To take one example: our education system is not, by international benchmarks, delivering improved outcomes even while it is consuming an increasing proportion of the national budget. In the next fifteen to twenty years the focus will increasingly have to be on improving outcomes through improved system performance. Investing in R&D will be a key intervention to improve the performance of the health, education and electricity systems, for example. In the immediate post-apartheid period, there was a strong argument to be made for prioritising immediate reallocation and transfer of resources, and as a consequence strategic R&D expenditure was de-emphasised. The alternative argument is now more compelling: the allocation of substantial resources to improving the performance of our service-delivery systems is now necessary.

In conclusion, we want to ensure that, given the opportunity to visit our future selves twenty years from now, we again find ourselves in a very different country. Some of those differences will be due to the inevitable march of time and technology, but we should hope that some of those differences are more substantial – that we have made significant progress in addressing the problems of poverty and inequality, and that we no longer waste so much of our valuable human resources. Technological innovation will be an indispensable ingredient in attaining that goal, both by driving the economic growth and development that will deliver the much-needed increases in the quality of life of our citizens, but also by mitigating the environmental and social threats to that growth.

Dr Sibusiso Sibisi
CEO
Council for Scientific and Industrial Research

ABBREVIATIONS AND ACRONYMS

ANC	African National Congress
ARV	antiretroviral
BRIC	Brazil, Russia, India and China
BRICS	Brazil, Russia, India, China and South Africa
CPI	consumer price index
CPIX	consumer price index excluding interest rates on mortgage bonds
DBSA	Development Bank of Southern Africa
DTI	Department of Trade and Industry
EU	European Union
FDI	foreign direct investment
FET	future education and training
FIFA	Fédération Internationale de Football Association
FPI	foreign portfolio investment
G20	Group of Twenty
GDP	gross domestic product
GEAR	Growth, Employment and Redistribution strategy
GEM	Global Enterprise Monitor
HEI	higher education institution
ICT	information and communications technology
IMF	International Monetary Fund
JSE	Johannesburg Stock Exchange
Mbps	megabits per second
NDP	National Development Plan
NEET	Not in Education, Employment or Training
PPP	purchasing power parity
R&D	research and development
RDP	Reconstruction and Development Programme
S&P	Standard & Poor's
SAICE	South African Institution of Civil Engineering
SANRAL	South African National Roads Agency
SARS	South African Revenue Service
SEDA	Small Enterprise Development Agency

SEFA	Small Enterprise Financing Agency
SMME	small, medium and micro enterprises
Stats SA	Statistics South Africa
UK	United Kingdom
US	United States
VAT	value added tax
WGBI	World Government Bond Index

INTRODUCTION

At the time of South Africa's first democratic elections in 1994, everyone agreed that poverty had to be uprooted, inequality reduced and the conditions for sustainable economic growth established. It was clear that the structure of the country's economy had to change, and that land ownership, employment opportunities and access to essential services had to match more closely the needs of the entire population; otherwise it would be difficult to achieve lasting political and social stability.

In the twenty years since 1994, South Africa's economic growth rate has comfortably exceeded the country's average population growth. Income per person has increased meaningfully, and well in excess of South Africa's average annual inflation rate. Unfortunately, the distribution of income and wealth remains extremely unequal by global standards and has actually worsened since 1994, while the unemployment rate has remained exceedingly high, especially among the youth.

Achieving sustained high economic growth that included a meaningful rise in employment but also addressed the vast array of social and economic backlogs required the country to focus on four key pieces of economic policy. These comprised internationalising the country after years of isolation; instigating sound macroeconomic policy; vastly increasing the provision of social goods and services; and encouraging the modernisation and competitiveness of the business sector. In 1994, it was clear that South Africa's success in developing these four policy pieces would determine its progress in meeting the aspirations of the population.

Implementing the required policy changes was never going to be easy. The financial and trade sanctions imposed in the 1980s had done an effective job of isolating the country, while the extent of the socio-economic backlogs was massively underestimated, especially the lack of basic services. In addition, prior to 1994 government debt had ballooned alarmingly, while inflation had become entrenched at well above 10%.

Within a few years of the 1994 elections, it became abundantly clear that concerns about the management of South Africa's monetary and fiscal policy were largely unfounded. Inflation had been brought well under control and a policy of inflation targeting was successfully established. Furthermore, the government transformed a persistent and substantial fiscal deficit into sustained fiscal discipline and was able to radically improve the process of tax collection, which led to meaningful increases in tax receipts that regularly exceeded budget. Utilising the so-called democracy dividend, which included the benefits of dismantling an extremely expensive and highly inefficient apartheid system, the fiscal authorities reallocated government spending away from defence-related expenditure to key social services, including the provision of education, healthcare and welfare.

The process of internationalising the country was equally successful. Import duties were lowered to bring South Africa in line with the requirements of the World Trade Organization, and a number of important trade agreements were concluded. The government also embarked on a process of obtaining an investment-grade international credit rating, which quickly allowed South Africa increased access to the global capital markets, and ultimately facilitated the country's build-up of foreign exchange reserves.

In 1994 South Africa had an enormous shortfall of social goods and services, which needed to be redressed as quickly as possible. Remarkably, despite a number of constraints and glaring mistakes, the government made meaningful strides in addressing some of the key deficiencies. Among the achievements were the supply of electricity to millions of households, the subsidised provision of formal housing, increased access to water and sanitation, reduced levels of malnutrition, a substantial rise in welfare payments and increased access to free education.

This is not to say that the socio-economic backlogs have been completely eliminated, or that there are not significant numbers of people struggling to survive, or that service delivery is no longer a source of great frustration and unhappiness. Nevertheless, it seems fair to argue that the government has made significant progress in addressing some critical areas of historical social neglect, especially given the extremely low base of service delivery and the prevailing financial constraints.

The fourth and final piece of South Africa's economic puzzle – and the area of economic development that is of greatest concern – is the deficiency of support for the business sector. This is evidenced by a shortage of effective economic infrastructure, lack of infrastructure maintenance within many municipalities, the scarcity of critical technical skills, the over-regulation of business, increasing levels of corruption, insufficient access to finance by many small businesses and lack of competitiveness. These factors have been compounded by a somewhat inconsistent and relatively complicated and confusing industrial policy, as well as a highly disruptive labour market. In addition, the behaviour of certain sectors of the business community, especially collusion and uncompetitive pricing, has accentuated the problem.

Unfortunately, the distinct lack of progress in developing the fourth piece of the economic puzzle has meant that South Africa's economic growth has ultimately been below expectations and employment growth has been staid. More importantly, this constraint has now begun to undermine the other three pieces of the economic puzzle, creating a negative feedback loop. If left unchecked, this can derail the South African economy, leading to increased unemployment, an outflow of foreign investment and rising social tension.

South Africa urgently needs to focus on encouraging the development of the business sector in an effort to support job creation as well as grow the tax base. This will require a dramatic improvement in the country's basic economic infrastructure, more vocational skills development, a concerted effort to encourage small business, as well as easier and cheaper access to technology. In addition, the sub-Saharan African region has enormous potential, which South Africa should be actively helping to develop.

A country's most valuable asset is a sizeable and vibrant business sector. A large and growing business sector increases employment, reduces the social burden on the state and generates the revenue that underpins the tax base, providing government with the tax receipts to achieve its social and political objectives. While this may sound obvious, many governments, especially in Europe, have stumbled because they have found themselves overburdened by social demands, and have lacked the tax revenue to meet the aspirations of the electorate. In many instances, the growth in the size of government has come about because the authorities have been determined to direct the functioning of a large portion of the economy, which tends to crowd out or stunt the development of the private sector, thereby undermining the tax base. In contrast, much of the profitable growth in China over the past fifteen years has come about because of increased deregulation by the state. The message is clear: governments should spend as much time worrying about where their tax revenue will come from as they spend worrying about how to use taxpayers' money.

The book is divided into three parts. Part I examines the economic performance of the country over the past twenty years and discusses South Africa's position in the world economy (Chapter 1). The discussion then shifts to how the structure of the economy has evolved since 1994 (Chapter 2), highlighting that the services sector has easily outperformed the industrial sector, and that mining and manufacturing have become a far less significant component of the economy. Chapter 3 discusses the problem of persistent high unemployment, especially high youth unemployment. It highlights why it is important that young people gain work experience as quickly as possible and concludes that youth unemployment is South Africa's most important economic challenge. Chapter 4 analyses the performance of South Africa's financial markets over the past twenty years, in particular the stock, bond and property markets. It is evident that despite all the political and economic concerns facing the country, households that increased their savings and chose to invest the funds in the financial markets, including unit trusts and retirement products, have seen their investments easily outperform inflation since 1994.

Part II expands extensively on the idea that South Africa had to implement four key pieces of economic policy to become economically successful and devotes a chapter to discussing each puzzle piece. Chapter 5 discusses the first puzzle piece, which is the need to internationalise the country after years of isolation. South Africa's reintegration into the world economy since 1994 has been truly remarkable, and has included re-establishing trade links, attracting foreign investment and participating in global events. The country's success in this area easily exceeded most people's expectations, and it is difficult to suggest how this piece of the puzzle could have been better handled. Chapter 6 looks at the second puzzle piece, which is the need to implement sound macroeconomic policy, in particular the controlling of government's finances as well as bringing inflation under control. The introduction of an inflation target in 2000 was extremely successful and provided the framework to substantially reduce South Africa's inflation rate. Moreover, in the first fifteen years after the 1994 election, the government was able to dramatically reduce its debt position, which was applauded in the international financial community. Unfortunately, in the past five years the government's debt position has deteriorated, which has contributed to the downgrading of South Africa's credit rating. Overall, however, the second puzzle piece also exceeded expectations. Chapter 7 explores the third puzzle piece, which is the need to eliminate the extensive socio-economic backlogs that manifested during the apartheid years. Although many mistakes were made and large amounts of money wasted on unsuccessful projects, the government was able to make significant progress in providing access to electricity, water, social welfare, housing and schooling. Unfortunately, income and wealth inequality remains extremely high. Chapter 8 reviews the final puzzle piece, which is the need to support the business community, including small business, through the development of appropriate economic infrastructure, skills and technology. Unfortunately, this piece of the puzzle has fallen well short of expectations, which is now starting to undermine the successes achieved in implementing the other puzzle pieces.

Part III suggests a number of policy initiatives to help boost South Africa's gross domestic product (GDP) growth and job creation. Chapter 9 focuses on initiatives that can be implemented within a relatively short period, such as 'ready-to-go' projects. Longer-term policies that will take time to implement fully, such as a substantial increase in vocational training, are discussed in Chapter 10.

PART I

SOUTH AFRICA HAS NOT
REACHED ITS POTENTIAL

INTRODUCTION

A number of key indicators point to the remarkable success of South Africa's economy over the past twenty years. At the end of 2013 the South African economy was the biggest it has ever been, after adjusting for inflation. The economic growth rate has easily exceeded population growth on a sustained basis. Consequently, the average income per person of the country, once again after adjusting for inflation, is also the highest it has ever been. Furthermore, household wealth, which reflects the difference between household assets (mostly houses and financial investments) and household debt (mostly mortgage debt), is at a record level, helped by the outstanding performance of the domestic stock market.

Unfortunately, these facts mask the many structural economic changes South Africa has experienced over the past twenty years, not all of them favourable, as well as the many economic impediments and challenges the country faces. In addition, although household incomes and wealth are at a record high, the disparity between rich and poor remains extreme by global as well as historical standards, leading to a significant increase in social tension and political discord.

Part I of this book examines South Africa's economic progress since 1994, highlighting the country's position in the world economy. It also looks at how the structure of the economy has changed since 1994, including the increased role of financial services, and shows that despite numerous policy initiatives, South Africa has failed to meaningfully expand industrial production. The high level of unemployment has been a persistent theme in the country's economy for the past twenty years and remains South Africa's most important economic, social and political challenge.

1. SOUTH AFRICA'S ECONOMIC GROWTH HAS FALLEN SHORT OF TARGET

The South African economy is the second biggest in Africa despite the country having only the fifth largest population on the continent. South Africa is a member of the G20 as well as the BRICS, has an investment-grade credit rating, is classified as an upper-middle-income country by the World Bank, and has hosted a number of international mega sporting events. These are remarkable achievements for a country that endured significant racial segregation for most of the twentieth century. Unfortunately, during the past twenty years South Africa has not managed to meaningfully reduce its level of unemployment, especially among the youth; income inequality has worsened; and levels of corruption have risen. This is so despite the introduction of numerous policy initiatives aimed at lifting the economic growth rate on a sustained basis.

South Africa's economic potential is readily recognisable by many people who live in or visit the country. At a superficial level, this potential is reflected in the natural beauty of the landscape, the numerous nature and wildlife reserves, and the moderate climate. At a deeper level, this potential is evident in South Africa's extensive mineral resources, its considerable area of arable land, its relatively large but young population and its access to important shipping routes.

Economic potential does not automatically lead to economic success. Instead, success depends on harnessing the natural endowments of a country to create jobs and lift incomes while also ensuring that the population is able to satisfy its needs for housing, transport, security, education and healthcare.

During the past twenty years, South Africa has regularly demonstrated an ability to surpass even the most optimistic of expectations. Four events illustrate the country's ability to excel at the highest level.

The first event is the remarkable political transition South Africa was able to achieve in the April 1994 national elections, which marked the country's passage from apartheid to full democracy. Ahead of the event there were serious concerns that the elections would be marred by violence and civil unrest. Instead, it was an extremely peaceful and uplifting event for all those who voted, and is now regarded internationally as a political miracle.

Second, the country was invited to join the Group of Twenty (G20) when it was formed in 1999, together with eighteen other countries as well as the European Union (EU). The G20 was originally started as a meeting of finance ministers and central bank governors with a mandate to focus on measures to support global economic growth, with a strong emphasis on promoting job creation and open trade. In 2008 the meetings were extended to include heads of state. While South Africa is not one of the twenty largest economies in the world, it was included because it is the largest financial system within Africa and plays a meaningful role in the international financial system. In the *Global Competitiveness Report 2013–2014*, published by the World Economic Forum, South Africa was ranked an incredible third out of 148 countries in terms of financial market development, and second in terms of the availability of financial services. The inclusion of South Africa in the G20 has meant that the country has been able to influence global economic policy on a level that seemed completely unimaginable just five years earlier.

Third, the country has hosted numerous global sporting events since 1994, including the 1995 Rugby World Cup, the 1996 African Nations Cup, the 2003 Cricket World Cup and the 2009 FIFA Confederations Cup. However, it is the successful hosting of the 2010 FIFA World Cup that highlights South Africa's ability to plan, coordinate, build and organise a major international event. After the event, FIFA stated that 'hosting the event in South Africa proved to be a huge success'. Critics had feared that the country's high crime rate and lack of public transportation would undermine the soccer world championship, but these concerns simply never materialised. In an independent assessment, 83% of the visiting international soccer fans surveyed expressed an intention to return to the country, while 94% said they would happily recommend South Africa as a tourist destination to their friends and family. In the twenty years since the 1994 elections, the country's tourism proceeds have risen by over a staggering 1 100%, admittedly off an extremely low base.

Finally, in 2011, South Africa was invited to join the BRIC (Brazil, Russia, India, China) group of countries. BRIC was originally an informal grouping of four large developing countries that shared common interests and felt the need to increase economic cooperation among themselves, partly to rival the dominance of the United States (US). The first BRIC summit was held on 16 June 2009 in Russia. The group has since held four formal meetings, although the leaders have also met on the sidelines of other multilateral meetings. While South Africa's inclusion was questioned by many analysts, it highlighted the country's potential role within sub-Saharan Africa. Membership in the group opens up opportunities for more foreign direct investment and the expansion of trade relations.

Unfortunately, South Africa has also created headlines for the wrong reasons. The platinum-mining industry strike at Marikana, near Rustenburg, on 16 August 2012, when thirty-four people lost their lives at the hands of the police, is probably the country's worst post-apartheid tragedy. From an economic perspective, the event dented domestic and international investor confidence, and contributed to South Africa losing its A3 credit rating by Moody's Investors Service on 27 September 2012. Subsequently, both Standard & Poor's as well as the Fitch Ratings agency also downgraded the country's credit rating.

Social tension within the country has worsened in the past five years. According to the monitoring agency Municipal IQ, South Africa recorded 27 service-delivery protests against local government in 2008. Unfortunately, this number has risen considerably in almost every year since, and in 2012 the country recorded a worrisome and record-high 177 major service-delivery protests. The number of service-delivery protests eased to 155 in 2013, but then escalated dramatically ahead of the national elections in May 2014. In total, from 2009 to 2013 South Africa has experienced 628 significant protests, with around half of these occurring in informal settlements. Unfortunately, approximately 75% of these events turned violent.

Possible explanations for this increase in social tension include a combination of rising unemployment, especially among the youth; a worsening of income inequality; a high rate of urbanisation; large numbers of children leaving school before reaching Grade 12; increased illegal immigration; rising levels of corruption; and a relatively high level of crime.

SOUTH AFRICA HAS NOT ACHIEVED ITS GROWTH TARGETS

The GDP of a country measures the total monetary value of all goods and services produced during a quarter (three months) or a year. This is then compared with the preceding period to determine the rate at which the economy is growing. GDP is effectively the total output of the economy, which equates to the national income of the country. Although there are limitations with this form of measurement, especially the fact that it does not measure the welfare of the country, GDP remains the most important gauge of overall economic performance.

In June 1996, government's Growth, Employment and Redistribution (GEAR) policy document suggested that initiatives outlined in the report 'are expected to provide sufficient impetus for GDP growth to climb to the targeted 6% by the year 2000'. In reality, South Africa achieved a growth rate of 4.2% in 2000 and has not achieved 6% in any calendar year over the past twenty years. Subsequent policy documents have also highlighted the need to lift the country's growth rate to around 5% to 6% a year on a sustained basis. These growth targets are not randomly selected but largely reflect the sustained increase in economic activity that is required to create around 500 000 new jobs a year. While a job growth rate of 500 000 new jobs annually would still not be sufficient to significantly reduce the country's unemployment rate, it would be large enough to absorb many of the new entrants into the job market.

Unfortunately, South Africa's economic growth rate has mostly fallen short of the 5% to 6% target. In the past twenty years, the country achieved an average annual economic growth rate (GDP) of 3.2%. Fortunately, South Africa has experienced only one calendar year of negative economic performance since 1994. This occurred in 2009, when GDP declined by 1.5% compared with the previous year (after adjusting for inflation). The recession in 2009 was directly linked to the global financial market crisis and the subsequent global recession. The South African economy has since recovered, and is now larger than it has ever been.

The best annual growth rate the country has been able to achieve in the past twenty years occurred in 2006, when the economy grew by a respectable 5.6%. From 2005 to 2007, the growth rate averaged an impressive 5.5% per annum. However, this was not a sufficiently long enough period to lead to a meaningful improvement in employment. In addition, many other factors have tended to discourage job creation, including a shortage of skills, the increased use of technology, and a highly regulated and fairly disruptive labour market that was unable to achieve the productivity gains South African business needed to remain globally competitive. Consequently, despite the country maintaining a positive growth rate for most of the past twenty years, the growth in employment has lagged the overall performance of the economy.

South Africa's economic growth during the past twenty years has far exceeded the country's average population growth rate of 1.5% per annum. Furthermore, the population growth rate has slowed significantly in recent years, and was estimated at less than 1% in 2013. This is down from 2.4% in 1994. The fall-off in the growth of South Africa's population is mainly due to a sharp rise in the death rate rather than a decline in the birth rate. Sadly, the rise in the death rate largely reflects the rise in the incidence of AIDS-related deaths.

Because South Africa's economic growth has greatly exceeded the population growth over the past twenty years, the income per person of the country has increased meaningfully. For example, in 1994 the annual income per person was measured at R12 281 per year, or a mere R1 042 per month. By 2013 the income per person had risen to a much more respectable R62 676 per year, or R5 223 per month. This represents a total increase of 401% over twenty years, or a compound average annual rise of 8.9% per year, which is comfortably in excess of South Africa's average annual inflation rate of 6% over the same period. In dollars, the gain is equally impressive, improving from only $3 522 per year in 1994 to $6 428 in 2013, a rise of over 80%. South Africa is now classified as an upper-middle-income country by the World Bank, together with Turkey, Mexico, Brazil and China. As recently as 2003 South Africa was ranked as a lower-middle-income country.

Unfortunately, although South Africa's income per person has experienced inflation-beating growth in the past twenty years, the distribution of income remains extremely unequal by global standards and has actually worsened since 1994. An Oxfam report released in January 2013 concluded that South Africa is 'now the most unequal country on earth and significantly more unequal than at the end of apartheid'. In addition, the official rate of unemployment remains exceedingly high at over 24%, with youth unemployment at almost 50%.

SOUTH AFRICA'S POSITION IN THE WORLD ECONOMY

Despite a somewhat disappointing growth rate over the past twenty years, the country has been able to maintain its share of world GDP. For example, in 1994 South Africa comprised 0.50% of the world economy, measured in dollars at the prevailing market exchange rate. Twenty years later, South Africa represents 0.47% of the world economy. During this twenty-year period, the country's share of the world economy fluctuated from a low of 0.33% in 2002 to a peak of 0.57% in 2011. Most of this variation is explained by changes in the value of the rand. In other words, the stronger the rand is against the dollar, the larger South Africa's share of the world economy becomes when measured in dollars. The converse is also true.

The US remains the world's largest economy, comprising 22.7% of world economic output in 2013. As recently as 2001, the US represented almost 33% of the world economy. Meanwhile, Japan has slipped from a peak of 18% in 1994 to a mere 6.6% in 2013. In contrast, China has grown from less than 1.8% in 1990 to over 11% in 2013, making it the world's second largest economy. Assuming that China is able to continue to achieve a growth rate of around 7.5% on an annual basis, and the US achieves a sustained growth rate of 3% a year, then China would become the world's biggest economy by 2027. Clearly, however, a lot can change over the next ten to fifteen years.

Interestingly, the economic output of Brazil, Russia, India, China and South Africa (BRICS) combined is now almost equal to that of the US, although the BRICS represents 42.5% of the world's total population, whereas the US comprises only 4.5%. On this basis, it is easy to see how the large emerging economies such as China and India are likely to increasingly dominate the world economy. Equally, the phenomenal productive capacity and efficiency of the US has to be acknowledged, given what the country has been able to achieve with less than 5% of the world's population.

In 2013 South Africa was ranked as the 31st largest economy in the world, down slightly from 29th position in 1994. The country then fell to 32nd position in 2014, after Nigeria revised its GDP significantly higher (see further discussion in Chapter 10). While this is not especially impressive, it is striking that South Africa is included in a number of key global forums, including the BRICS and the G20. This effectively means the country has more influence in the formulation of global economic policy than the size of its economy would suggest.

There are no formal selection criteria that stipulate which countries are included in the G20. In practice, the Group of Twenty is generally composed of the largest economies in the world, together with countries that are considered significant within the international financial system. More specifically, South Africa was invited to be a member mainly because of its economic and financial importance within the African region.

South Africa's inclusion in the BRICS summit on 14 April 2011 signified an important evolution of BRICS into an organisation covering Asia, Europe, America and Africa. This breadth of representation deepens the voice and importance of emerging markets, and generally improves the circumstances for emerging economies within the global economy.

Some analysts and commentators were surprised that South Africa was invited to join the BRIC grouping, arguing that since the country was only the 12th largest emerging economy, it was not the most obvious choice to join a group that comprises the four largest emerging economies. At first glance, Indonesia would have been a more obvious candidate since it has a large population (over 250 million people) and the economy has been growing at more than 6% per year. In comparison, South Africa has around 52 million people and is growing at only 2% to 3% annually. However, South Africa leads the African continent in terms of mineral and industrial output, electricity generation, developed transport and communication infrastructure, and depth and breadth of financial markets, and also has a diversified services sector.

Clearly, although the inclusion of South Africa in the BRICS forum is still in its infancy, the relationship will be further strengthened should Africa move ahead with regional economic integration. This would open up opportunities for more foreign direct investment into Africa and the expansion of trade relations, including increased regional trade.

The BRICS forum is really a reflection of the rising importance of emerging economies in the world economy. Hence, it is only natural that the large emerging economies want to have a greater say on issues that impact world development. This includes trying to ensure that the current international economic system is more balanced, equitable and sustainable. Having access to the BRICS forum allows South Africa the opportunity not only to promote sub-Saharan Africa's development issues, but also to promote South Africa as an investment destination.

At the beginning of 1994, South Africa was the largest economy in sub-Saharan Africa, comprising a massive 50.7% of the region's annual economic output, despite having less than 8% of the region's population. Twenty years later, South Africa has less than 6% of the region's population and is the second largest economy in sub-Saharan Africa, after Nigeria. Since 1994, South Africa's share of the region's economic output has diminished to only 23%. This fall-off in relative economic size has largely come about because a number of key countries in the region have been able to significantly lift their economic growth rates on a sustained basis. In particular, Nigeria, Ghana, Tanzania, Ethiopia and Angola have all achieved an annual average growth rate of well in excess of 5% (after adjusting for inflation) over the past twenty years. Consequently, these five countries have taken their combined share of the region's total economic output from 16% in 1994 to over 50% in 2013. In particular, Nigeria now accounts for 33% of sub-Saharan Africa's total economic output, compared with a little less than 7% in 1994. Similarly, Angola has risen from less than 1.5% to over 9%, making it the third biggest economy in the region.

The outperformance of Nigeria relative to South Africa over the past fifteen to twenty years is off an extremely low base. However, there is a massive difference in population size between the two countries. In 2012 the population of Nigeria was estimated at a very substantial 170.1 million people (or nearly 20% of the entire sub-Saharan African population). This makes Nigeria the most populous country in Africa and the seventh most populated country in the world. In contrast, during 2012 South Africa's population was estimated at 51.1 million (5.7% of the population in sub-Saharan Africa).

POLICY AMBIGUITY HAS STUNTED GROWTH

Many reasons have been espoused as to why South Africa has not been able to achieve sustainably higher economic growth. From an economic policy perspective, the environment has been less than ideal as the country has seen a slew of policy initiatives over the past twenty years. These include the Reconstruction and Development Programme (RDP, 1994); the Growth, Employment and Redistribution (GEAR, 1996) strategy; the Accelerated and Shared Growth Initiative for South Africa (ASGISA, 2006); the New Growth Path (2010); and the National Development Plan (NDP, 2012). More recently, government has appointed a presidential task team to focus on accelerating economic growth in the country. There have also been numerous international studies that have been commissioned to provide advice on how to lift South Africa's growth rate, as well as policy pronouncements from within key government departments, including the National Treasury and the Department of Trade and Industry (DTI), on how to move the country forward.

Encouragingly, South Africa's policy studies have tended to be reasonably comprehensive and well researched, especially the recent NDP. The policy documents have all tended to highlight the need for higher sustainable growth that leads to increased employment. They have also all emphasised the need to redress the still extensive socio-economic backlogs, including the provision of low-cost housing, affordable healthcare, adequate water and sanitation, and better-quality education. They have also stressed the need for poverty relief. However, many of the documents have differed on how the key economic objectives are to be achieved and have actually diverged on core economic principles.

The regular introduction of new policy documents, coupled with changes to existing policy priorities, has led to confusion and uncertainty. There are at least four key limitations to the economic policy-formulation approach South Africa has adopted over the past twenty years.

First, by frequently switching from one policy agenda to the next, the business and household sectors quickly became unsure about which policies are relevant and applicable. This inconsistency dented confidence and limited the impact of any particular policy initiative. It would probably have been more beneficial to simply update the existing policy agenda. Second, the policy documents have tended to be extremely broad, lacking specific detail on how the policy is going to be implemented or the time frame for implementation. This lack of detail makes policy less 'real'. Third, while some of the policy documents have been extremely comprehensive, they have lacked a priority and/ or sequencing framework. For example, it is probably not advisable to actively promote exports without sufficient rail and port capacity, or to actively encourage the development of heavy industry without sufficient electricity supply. Simultaneously launching numerous growth strategies could undermine or limit the effectiveness of overall policy. A stipulated priority list allows the business and household sectors to focus resources and demonstrate success more quickly. Success rapidly builds confidence in future policy initiatives. Finally, the policy agenda has never been communicated cogently. To be effective, policy needs to become common knowledge. A clear and broad-based understanding of economic policy, within both the business and household sectors, is vital for its success. The clearest example in South Africa is the inflation target, which has been consistently and regularly communicated. It is now an accepted and well-understood feature of the country's economic landscape, and it is therefore effective.

Policy ambiguity has not been South Africa's only limiting factor. The country has struggled to improve the level of education and the availability of technical skills. Moreover, South Africa has neglected key areas of infrastructural development, including port and rail capacity, electricity generation, road maintenance and water supply. Private and public spending on research and development has dwindled. There has also been a tendency to introduce more and more business regulation, while corruption is on the rise and the labour laws remain cumbersome and relatively inflexible. Small- and medium-sized businesses struggle to gain access to finance, and have almost no say in the formulation of industrial policy.

2
SOUTH AFRICA HAS BECOME
A SERVICE-BASED ECONOMY

Over the past twenty years, South Africa has become a service-based economy, with agriculture, mining and manufacturing representing a much smaller portion of overall economic activity, and finance, shopping, communication and transport outperforming most other sectors. This fundamental shift in the structure of the economy was not intentional, but instead reflects a lack of global competitiveness in manufacturing, combined with the population's demand for increased access to credit, cellphones, transport and branded consumer goods. Looking forward, it seems clear that South Africa needs to actively encourage the development of the agricultural sector as well as some aspects of the mining and manufacturing sectors. Realistically, however, much of South Africa's future economic growth and employment is likely to come from the services sector, especially domestic-oriented services. This is not necessarily a bad thing as long as the economy can establish the right mix of services that will allow the country to prosper.

The structure of the South African economy has changed measurably in the twenty years since 1994. The primary sector (represented by agriculture and mining) and the secondary sector (which includes manufacturing, electricity and construction) have become a less significant portion of total economic activity, dropping from a combined 40% of GDP in 1994 to 30% in 2013, having already fallen from a peak of around 55% of total output in 1980. In contrast, the tertiary, or services, sector of the economy has increased from 60% of total output in 1994 to 70% in 2013. Essentially, South Africa has become a service-based economy. The bulk of these services are in the form of shopping, banking, insurance, real estate activity, transport and communication.

The breakdown of South Africa's formal sector employment, which normally refers to people working within registered businesses that have a fixed address and submit tax returns, also reflects this fundamental change in the structure of the economy. Back in 1994, 53% of total formal sector employment was in the services sector. In 2013, this had increased to an amazing 75%. The shift in the composition of South Africa's formal sector employment is due to the reduction in mining and manufacturing employment, combined with a sizeable increase in the number of people employed in the finance, business services and retail trade. The government has also systematically increased its own level of employment.

This fundamental shift in the structure of the economy was not intentional. In fact, over the past twenty years South Africa's industrial policy has consistently endeavoured to promote the development of both the primary and secondary sectors, most especially manufacturing activity. This is because manufacturing activity has a number of advantages. These include strong backward and forward linkages to other sectors in the economy, which means that a pickup in manufacturing activity typically boosts many other associated sectors. Manufacturing entities also have the ability to derive economies of scale (that is, the cost per item produced falls as the business expands), which means the return on investment (the profits derived from the money invested in the company) is potentially very large as long as capacity utilisation rates (the current output of the factory as a percentage of maximum output) remain high. Manufacturing can also be a valuable source of technological development and innovation, which can be applied in other sectors of the economy, thereby improving the country's overall level of productivity.

This is not to say that a country cannot be economically strong without a large manufacturing base. There are many highly successful economies that currently have a very small manufacturing sector, such as the US and the United Kingdom (UK). However, most of these economies had a strong manufacturing base during the course of their economic development. Typically, as an economy develops, the role of manufacturing diminishes relative to the services sector. This is largely because as household incomes rise, consumers tend to increase their demand for services relative to their demand for goods.

THE ROLE OF MANUFACTURING IS FADING

The policies employed by South Africa to promote manufacturing have varied considerably over time, but have included targeted measures to support specific industries (for example, direct incentives to help the motor industry); broader support measures applicable to all industries (for example, accelerated depreciation allowances on fixed investment, which means a company can derive a tax benefit by writing off the cost of machinery more quickly than would normally be allowed); preferential trade agreements to encourage industrial exports (for example, the Trade, Development and Cooperation Agreement between South Africa and the EU); and preferential financial support (for example, finance provided by the Industrial Development Corporation).

Unfortunately, with the exception of a few industries, these measures have not proved particularly successful. Manufacturing activity has diminished from around 21% of South Africa's total economic activity in 1994 (and a peak of 24% in 1981) to less than 12% in 2013. The key manufacturing industries that have managed to hold up reasonably well include food production (including beverages), basic industrial chemicals and motor vehicles. In contrast, some of the worst-performing manufacturing sectors have included clothing and textiles, footwear, printing and publishing, and iron and steel.

According to the South African Reserve Bank, since 1994 the capital stock (the value of machinery and equipment in a business) of the manufacturing sector as a whole has increased by an annual average growth rate of 1.3% a year (after adjusting for inflation), which is relatively modest but at least positive. This effectively means that the productive capacity of the manufacturing sector has actually expanded by a total of almost 29% since 1994, while production has risen by an annual average growth rate of 2.6%. Unfortunately, over the same period, the level of employment in the manufacturing sector has declined from 1.422 million workers to 1.147 million employees, a decline of 19% or 275 000 jobs. This effectively means that South Africa's manufacturing sector has become almost 63% more capital-intensive (the ratio of machinery to labour in a business) since 1994, even after adjusting for changes in capacity utilisation rates. While this trend is partly due to increased labour market difficulties, including strike activity, it also reflects a global trend towards the increased use of technology in the manufacturing process.

Over the past twenty years, numerous academic and industry-based studies have researched the performance of South Africa's manufacturing sector, trying to understand why the sector is relatively uncompetitive and how best to encourage an increase in output and an expansion of manufacturing capacity. It remains a complex issue, with debate focused on a number of key issues, including the role of government. However, it is worthwhile to highlight some pertinent issues that might help to put the performance of South Africa's manufacturing sector in context, and suggest areas for development.

During the apartheid years, especially the late 1970s and the early to mid-1980s, South Africa developed a number of strategically important industries that were relatively high-cost and uncompetitive in a global context. However, these industries were afforded a relatively high level of protection and to some extent were supported by the state. This formed a part of the government's policy of import substitution, a strategy aimed at increasing domestic production in place of importing foreign goods. During the 1990s, when South Africa started to more vigorously internationalise the economy, these industries were faced with increased foreign competition and dwindling government support. Consequently, they were unable to survive and prosper, and in many instances they either disappeared or have underperformed. This includes South Africa's armaments industry and the associated domestic suppliers.

The relatively rapid reduction in import duties in the 1990s also impacted another set of manufacturing industries that struggled to adapt to these reductions and the resultant flood of foreign competition. This included the textile, clothing and footwear manufacturing sectors. For example, in 1993 the clothing industry was afforded an effective import protection of around 100% of the import price. This meant that a shirt costing R120 to import would be charged an import duty of R120, pushing the total import price up to R240 before the garment reached the clothing store. However, after South Africa signed the World Trade Organization's Agreement on Textiles and Clothing in 1994, import duties began to be reduced. In fact, the South African government dismantled clothing and textile tariffs at a faster rate and over a shorter period than required by the agreement. By 2004 the typical import duty on clothing had fallen to 40%. At the same time,

China was in the process of accelerating its global trade and South Africa became an easy target.

Unfortunately, the country's clothing, textile and footwear sectors were unprepared for the rapid reduction in protection. Many of the clothing and footwear companies were relatively small family-owned businesses that did not have the expertise or financial capital to compete with a flood of imports. In addition, the South African customs authorities did not have the resources to guard against the illegal dumping of cheap goods in the country, which caused havoc with local producers. Not surprisingly, most of South Africa's clothing, textiles and footwear manufacturing companies went out of business, or were bought out and consolidated with other businesses.

Overall, the country's manufacturing sector has become increasingly concentrated, with many sub-sectors composed of a few large producers, leading to a general lack of domestic competition.

At times, labour has received a significant portion of the blame for South Africa's lack of manufacturing competiveness. This is an unfair generalisation. The labour unions have played an important role in improving working conditions within many key sectors of the economy, and have helped to narrow the historical wage divide that existed prior to 1994. It is also unfair to argue that South African labour is expensive without reference to the prevailing cost of living. Furthermore, low wages don't always determine the competitiveness of industry. A good example is Germany's ability to manufacture a broad range of industrial machinery and equipment for the export market, yet the industry does not enjoy the benefits of low wages.

Nevertheless, irrespective of the cost of labour or the type of product being manufactured, no manufacturing sector can prosper if there is constant labour market unrest. Unfortunately, key parts of South African industry have been hurt by regular bouts of labour unrest that typically result in a protracted industry-wide strike and many days or weeks of lost production. In many instances these actions appear to have a political undertone. While labour unions have an important role to play in the development of the economy, it appears that in some sectors the decision to strike has become a first-choice option as opposed to a last-resort course of action. Ideally, the focus needs to shift away from the current pattern of destructive engagement between labour and management, where no one gains, to a constructive interaction that is focused on skills development, productivity incentives, greater transparency about the remuneration of executives, and a common desire to expand and grow the business.

It is also critical that South Africa develops the appropriate infrastructure to meet the needs of the industrial sector. The most obvious example is electricity, given the severe supply constraints experienced by Eskom and the resultant power outages. It is unrealistic to expect manufacturing companies to expand their operations when they are unsure about continued power supply. Electricity is not the only critical infrastructure in need of improvement. South Africa's port and rail capacity is also in urgent need of renewal and expansion. Fortunately, in 2012 Transnet embarked on a R300-billion investment upgrade over the next seven years, which should relieve the constraints. In addition, adequate roads, water supply, public transport and other municipal services are crucial for a vibrant manufacturing sector.

While the DTI and institutions such as the Industrial Development Corporation, which provides finance to help develop South Africa's industrial sector on behalf of the government, have formulated a number of very useful policies to support and encourage industrial development over the years, most of these have been extremely poorly communicated, far too complex in design, inconsistently implemented and in many instances prematurely scrapped. Over the past twenty years, many existing and potential industrialists have simply been unaware of key components of South Africa's industrial policy. This is not because they have been uninterested, but because the policy approach has appeared complex, bureaucratic and erratic. In order for policy to be effective, it needs to be extremely simple, repeated on a regular basis (especially in the early stages of its introduction) and demonstrably very accessible. This applies especially to small- and medium-sized manufacturers that cannot afford a team of business analysts or consultants to advise management on how best to utilise various policy initiatives. In addition, small- and medium-sized manufacturers are certainly not in a position to lobby government for special consideration. In contrast, it seems fair to argue that if a company can afford to pay its executives millions of rand in remuneration and bonuses each year, then that company is probably not in need of government support.

South African industry appears to have become increasingly highly regulated. In the World Bank's *Doing Business 2014* report, based on an annual global survey, the country was ranked 41st in the world in terms of the ease of doing business. This ranking is unchanged from 2013, but is significantly worse than the 2006 ranking of 28th and the 2010 ranking of 34th. While it can be argued that 41st in the world is not a disaster, the global rankings of key sub-components of the survey are a significant concern, including the ease of starting a business (South Africa is ranked 64th in the world), ease of enforcing contracts (ranked 80th), ease of registering property (ranked 99th), ease of trading across borders (ranked 106th) and ease of getting electricity (ranked 150th). In contrast, South Africa ranks an impressive 28th in the world in terms of the ease of paying taxes.

This does not mean that the country should scrap all business regulation. Many components are vital for a stable, predictable and prosperous business environment. However, it is critical that the agencies that enforce the regulations see their role as enabling business to become more successful rather than simply trying to police business through the use of bureaucratic legislation or as a process to derive additional income for the state.

Competitiveness is not determined merely by the cost of labour or the value of the exchange rate. Clearly, these components can be a benefit, but they are not a panacea for local industry success. This is because the price of an item is not the sole determinant of its competitiveness. How many times does a customer walk into a shop and simply buy the cheapest watch, irrespective of its design, or the cheapest dress, or the cheapest television, or the cheapest pair of shoes? The purchase decision takes many factors into account, including design, functionality, availability, quality of workmanship, brand and other variables. Price is just one consideration. This means that the manufacturer does not have to concern itself purely with price, but should rather take into account a combination of factors that make a particular product attractive to the customer at the price offered. That is how German manufacturing is able to be competitive.

Hence, a key component of a successful manufacturing sector, which receives very little attention in South Africa, is the need for industry to constantly develop its technological capability. This, combined with the managerial capability of the company, ultimately determines the manufacturer's industrial capability and therefore its competitiveness.

Technological capability does not refer only to innovation, and it certainly does not mean that each and every manufacturing company has to be at the frontier of innovation. Innovation is just one component of a company's technological capability. The core of a company's technological capability is represented by its technical and operational skills. It must be able to use the prevailing technology, albeit imported, effectively and efficiently. This requires constant updating of skills; a recognition that the learning process for complex technologies can be expensive and time-consuming, and that there are elements of technology that have to be taught and cannot merely be gleaned from the instruction manual; an understanding of the need to improve productivity; and ultimately a commitment to develop a technology culture that leads the company to invest in its own R&D. The process of becoming and staying efficient and competitive is very demanding, and requires the full attention of management.

All of this suggests that South African manufacturing should be aiming to compete in the mid-market or medium-tech production for most goods (as opposed to high-tech or low-tech industries). A good example is footwear. South Africa would struggle to compete against high-end footwear from Italy. This is because footwear manufacturers in Italy have been developing and enhancing their technological capabilities for many years, including their process of design, choice of material and manufacturing techniques. Consequently, they have been able to develop powerful brands, which customers are willing to pay a small fortune to own. Equally, South Africa would probably also struggle to compete against entry-level footwear made in East Asia. The manufacturers of these types of shoes typically focus on achieving a low cost of production through a combination of high volume and relatively low cost of labour. Design and the quality of materials used are less critical. However, South Africa might be able to compete in mid-level shoe production, where the elements of design, choice of materials and quality of workmanship allow the company to charge a higher price than the East Asian producers, but not nearly as high as the fashion houses in Italy. This price-point targets middle-income earners who are looking for everyday shoes that have an element of style but that don't cost a fortune.

GOLD MINING IS NOW LESS THAN 2% OF THE SOUTH AFRICAN ECONOMY

The country's worst-performing industry over the past twenty years has undoubtedly been the mining sector. In total, mining production has fallen by 4.8% since 1994, which equates to an average annual decline of 0.3%. The fall-off in mining activity has been largely due to reductions in gold production. According to Statistics South Africa (Stats SA), gold production has fallen by a shocking 73% since 1994, reflecting a combination of lower grades per ton of ore mined as well as the difficulty of mining gold-bearing rock at increasingly extreme depths. Although the decline in gold production over the past twenty has been dramatic, the fall-off is largely understandable given the maturity of the sector. Gold output now represents only around 18% of total mining production in South Africa and less than 2% of the country's entire economy. Other areas of mining have also struggled over the past twenty years, including copper (down 57% over twenty years) and diamonds (down 36%).

Fortunately, it has not been all bad news for the mining industry. Production of coal has risen by 31% since 1994, platinum-group metals by 54% (despite the widespread strikes in late 2012 and early 2013), iron ore by 114% and manganese by an incredible 233%. Most of the gains in mining output reflect the staggering increase in demand for base metals from China.

Excluding gold, mining production in South Africa has actually risen by a total of 36% since 1994, which is equivalent to an average annual growth rate of 1.6%. This is still relatively modest, but not disastrous. However, there is little doubt that had South Africa's rail and port capacity been better developed, the growth in mining production would have been significantly higher over the past ten to fifteen years, given the relatively robust global demand. In other words, the mining sector could have exported more had there been increased infrastructure capacity to do so.

AGRICULTURE HAS ENORMOUS POTENTIAL

The performance of South Africa's agricultural sector over the past twenty years has been extremely disappointing. Not only has the overall growth rate been mediocre (the sector has grown by a modest average annual rate of 1.6% since 1994, making it the country's second worst-performing industry since 1994), but the number of commercial farms has declined and employment levels have fallen at a time when global food demand is at a record high, the country urgently needs to enhance its rural development, and job creation is critical.

Data on South Africa's agricultural sector has improved in recent years but remains patchy. According to the Department of Agriculture, there were an estimated 60 938 commercial farming units in the country in 1996. This fell to 45 818 units in 2002 and 39 666 units in 2007 (latest data available), a total decline of almost 35%. At the same time, the number of people employed in the agricultural sector has dropped from around 922 000 in 1994 to 720 000 at the end of 2013. Meanwhile, total farm debt, which is money owed by farmers to financial institutions, has risen from R18.18 billion in 1994 to R88.78 billion at the end of 2012, and in 2012 the value of agricultural imports surpassed the value of agricultural exports for the first time in at least five decades. The government's NDP recommends that South Africa aim to maintain a positive trade balance in agriculture. That goal is clearly already under pressure, after having been achieved each year for at least the previous fifty years. It is also another example of how significantly economic circumstances can change while plans are being formulated and debated.

The farming sector has been plagued by a number of difficulties over the years, including a shortage of suitable irrigation in some parts of the country, sharp fluctuations in produce prices, an escalation in crime (including livestock theft and farmhouse murders), a lack of infrastructure (including export infrastructure), very low wages for many farm workers, erratic weather patterns, and ongoing land claims that have still not yet been fully resolved. This combination of factors has made farming less attractive.

Not all areas of farming have struggled. In fact, many types of agricultural activity have experienced very impressive growth over the past twenty years. This is most evident in fruit farming, especially the production of apples, grapes, oranges, lemons, bananas and avocados. In contrast, sheep, dairy and pig farming have stagnated, while wheat farming has declined. Fortunately, poultry activity has soared, while maize and cattle farming remain large and relatively stable.

Looking forward, it seems clear that South Africa needs to actively encourage the development of the agricultural sector. This includes a significant increase, probably in the order of 25% to 30%, in the amount of farmland under irrigation. This will take many years to achieve, but it is important to launch the process as soon as possible, highlighting successes that have been achieved and constantly reiterating the intended development path.

Other initiatives are also critical, including improved education and training in the broader agricultural industry; an enhancement of scientific research to support the local agricultural sector; a massive expansion of new farm entrants by institutions such as the Land Bank; an improvement in infrastructure to support the distribution and export of farm produce; incentives for exiting commercial farmers to encourage new farm entrants, including mentorship, skills transfer and voluntary access to under-utilised land; and a more effective resolution of outstanding land claims, with a clear understanding of the prevailing fiscal constraints.

During the mid-1990s, the government allowed residents to submit land claims if they felt that had been wrongly dispossessed of their land. This is a crucial process in addressing the ills of apartheid. The cut-off date for land-claim submissions was 31 December 1998. Unfortunately, not all of the land claims have since been resolved. Furthermore, in early 2014 the government reopened the land-restitution process and set a new deadline of 31 December 2018 for any additional land claims to be submitted. The government argued that many people had not been able to submit their claims before the initial cut-off date and should be given another chance. While this remains an important process in addressing the wrongs committed during the apartheid years, it effectively makes ownership of land, especially farmland, very uncertain since many farmers are not sure whether a land claim will be lodged against their farms. The NDP outlines a number of recommendations on how best to proceed with land reform, which remains an extremely contentious issue in South Africa. Many of the proposals in the NDP are logical but not necessarily easily achieved and would require existing farmers to contribute significantly to the process. In particular, the NDP proposes that once suitable farmland has been identified for possible redistribution (including land in the market, land held by farmers under financial pressure, land held by absentee landlords and land in a deceased estate), 'the land would be bought by the state at 50% of the market value. The shortfall would be made up by contributions from farmers in the area. In exchange for contributing the remaining 50%, commercial farmers will have their land protected and will gain black economic empowerment status', which would, presumably, allow them to bid on various government tenders to supply food. The choice of words by the NDP is very unfortunate, since most existing landowners would assume that their land is already protected under the rule of law, while the wording in the NDP suggests this might not be the case under all circumstances. In order for this type of land reform to work, there would have to be a clear indication of the extent of the reform proposed, a finite timeline offered and an assurance that the process will not be altered. More than ever, the agricultural sector requires certainty about the path of land reform.

It would also be sensible to try to advance two other associated developments. The first is the encouragement and expansion of downstream agricultural processing industries, such as fruit juice, wine, cheese and vegetable oils, but also leather and wood products. The government has already identified the potential growth in this form of manufacturing activity, which could be extremely effective given the backward linkage to an already developed agricultural sector as well as a large consumer market within southern Africa. The second is a regional agricultural development plan. South Africa has a fundamental shortage of water, and the building of infrastructure to store and distribute fresh water is extremely expensive. However, the countries to the immediate north, especially Zimbabwe and Zambia, have an abundance of fresh water and extremely fertile land. It is far more cost-effective to develop farming around the available water supply than to take vast amounts of water to arid areas that have large numbers of farmers. Obviously, in order to be effective, this type of initiative would require much closer regional cooperation than currently exists.

CELLPHONES AND TAXIS LEAD THE PACK

Perhaps not surprisingly, the best performer in the South African economy over the past twenty years has been the transport and communications sector, which has grown by an annual average of almost 5.5% a year since the beginning of 1994 (after adjusting for inflation). However, most of this growth occurred in the first ten years after democracy, with the sector growing by an average of 7.7% a year from 1994 to 2003. It has since slowed to an annual average growth rate of 2% in the past five years.

This high growth partly reflects the amazing performance of the cellphone industry, which has seen the number of cellular users in South Africa growing by around 20% a year for the past thirteen years. It also reflects the phenomenal growth of the minibus taxi industry, which has mushroomed to at least 150 000 minibus taxis compared to a few thousand in 1994. While the cellphone industry is now considered to be relatively mature and unlikely to show anywhere near the same growth over the next ten years as it did over the past twenty, the taxi industry has enormous potential, given the underdevelopment of the public transport sector. Unfortunately, the taxi industry continues to struggle with a poor safety record and has not managed to transform itself from a largely informal set of taxi operators into an innovative, service-oriented and respected industry. Consequently, it is vulnerable to the current growth initiatives in the public transport sector, including the development of the bus and rail transport system.

FINANCIAL SERVICES ARE HIGHLY DEVELOPED

The second best-performing industry in South Africa since 1994 has been the finance and business services sector, which has grown by an impressive 5.2% a year on average for the past twenty years. Consequently, the industry now represents 22% of total economic activity, up from 16% in 1994, making it the biggest sector of the economy.

As economies develop, it is likely that their financial markets and financial companies will also evolve. Well-functioning capital markets, where shares and government bonds are issued to raise finance, and financial companies, such as banks, make it easier for households, corporations and governments to borrow money and raise funds for investment purposes. Increased investment translates into greater economic output, which means higher incomes that can be invested back into capital markets or deposited in banks in order to finance even more productive economic activity.

There is also a natural tendency for a responsible banking sector to outperform most other sectors of the economy over time, especially if real economic activity remains relatively volatile. This is because almost all sectors of the economy (both corporate and household) require access to finance and financial products during both good times and bad. For example, the banking sector may be in a position to provide loan finance to a troubled sector of the economy, and at the same time provide expansion finance to a growing sector of the economy. Alternatively, the domestic banking sector may become involved in financing offshore expansion at a time when the domestic economy is slowing. This ability to diversify business activity during the course of the business cycle means the banking sector can achieve a relatively consistent level of income and growth. If, at the same time, the real economy is extremely volatile, which has been the case with South Africa's agriculture, mining, manufacturing and construction sectors, then the financial services sector will outperform other sectors.

Unfortunately, there is a tendency by some analysts in South Africa to assume that the entire financial and business services sector is represented by the financial companies, especially banks. This superficial analysis is then used to conclude that South Africa's financial community is extremely large by global standards and that it plays a disproportionately large role in the country's economy, which is harmful to the other sectors. This is simply not true.

The finance and business services sector actually comprises three key sub-industries: finance and insurance; real estate activity; and business services. The finance and insurance sector (mostly banks and insurance companies) accounted for only 9.9% of South Africa's economic activity in 2013, and has averaged 9.6% of total economic activity over the past ten years. In comparison, the real estate sector (mainly property developers and estate agents) constituted 5.9% of total economic activity in 2013, while business services (an extremely broad sector including legal, advertising, audit, accounting and architectural services) makes up a further 5.4%. Based on this breakdown, South Africa's finance and insurance sector is not especially large by global standards, nor has it become especially large over the past ten years.

In many countries, especially emerging economies, the development of the financial system reduces transaction costs, raises investment levels, and improves the distribution of capital and risk across the economy. In addition, it can be argued that despite rapid growth in financial market activity in emerging economies over the past decade, there is still ample room for further growth. This is because the financial depth (financial market activity as a proportion of GDP) in most emerging economies is between 50% and 250% of GDP, with South Africa at 350%, compared with 300% to 600% of GDP in developed countries.

The degree to which financial deepening (a rising share of financial market activity in the country) occurs in an economy will depend on whether the country has the right regulatory and institutional framework to channel funds into their most productive use. South Africa has been consistently applauded for its financial market regulation, and in the World Economic Forum's *Global Competitiveness Report 2013–2014*, South Africa was ranked first out of 148 countries in terms of 'regulation of securities exchanges' and third out of 148 countries in terms of 'soundness of banks'.

Furthermore, no South African financial institution required assistance during the global financial market crisis in 2008/09. This largely reflects the conservative nature of the country's banking system and its unwillingness to become involved in leveraged financial market activity. The 2013 Annual Report of the Reserve Bank's Bank Supervision Department indicated that the banking sector remains adequately capitalised in terms of the current minimum regulatory requirements. The report also raised no significant concerns about profitability, liquidity risk (risk that the bank cannot sell some of its assets), credit risk (risk that debt cannot be repaid), impaired advances (clients are not able to meet their regular loan repayments), market risk (risk to the bank should the equity and bond markets weaken appreciably) or off-balance sheet activities (which tend to be complex, making the assessment of risk more difficult).

Credit-rating agencies have consistently applauded the strength of the financial system in South Africa. Over the past ten years this helped to improve the country's credit rating, thereby lowering the cost of international finance.

Crucially, this does not mean that everyone has access to credit and banking services. In particular, the structure of the banking system, as well as the array of products offered and the areas of expertise on hand, is not especially geared towards helping start-up or small businesses. Yet it is clear that to be successful in creating the necessary employment opportunities to meet the needs of the population over the next ten years, South Africa will have to find a way to fund a very significant increase in new business development, including small- and medium-sized businesses.

SOUTH AFRICANS LOVE TO SHOP

The retail sector has been a consistent and strong performer over the past twenty years, achieving an average annual growth rate of almost 4% since 1994. This consistently high growth rate has meant that the sector – which includes retail and wholesale trade, the accommodation industry as well as the motor-vehicles trade – has increased from a little over 14% of total economic activity in 1994 to 16.5% in 2013. This makes it the third largest sector in the economy, after business services and the government.

The sustained high growth in South Africa's retail activity largely reflects the household sector's high propensity to shop, coupled with a willingness to take on additional debt and to perpetually maintain a low savings rate. This is not an ideal combination, unless most of what is bought by households is made locally. Unfortunately, this is not the case. The vast majority of what South Africans buy in the shops is imported, with the exception of food. Consequently, there is a tendency for the growth in shopping to translate into sustained high imports.

Initiatives to encourage consumers to buy locally produced goods have largely failed to achieve any significant change in spending patterns. This is partly because consumers have become very brand conscious and are willing to pay the premium required to own branded goods, and partly because local manufacturers simply do not make the array of merchandise that local consumers now demand.

A breakdown of consumer spending over the past twenty years reveals some fascinating spending patterns. The standout feature is the South African consumer's love of clothing and shoes. The household sector's spending on clothing and shoes has achieved a remarkable average annual growth rate of 8.8% over the past twenty years, after adjusting for inflation. In addition, the sector has not experienced a decline in consumer spending in any of the last twenty years, even during the global financial market crisis in 2008/09. It is no surprise that most large shopping centres in South Africa are inundated with clothing and footwear stores. Unfortunately, a significant percentage of this increased spending is satisfied through imports.

Other fast-growing areas of consumer spending over the past twenty years include the purchases of cellphones, household furnishings and appliances, sporting equipment and, more recently, computer-related equipment, including computer tablets. In contrast, there are a number of areas of consumer spending that have clearly lagged the overall increase in consumer activity. These include petrol (as the price of petrol increases, households tend to use their cars less on weekends), security services (which is a typical grudge purchase), newspapers and magazines, and domestic services, including domestic workers (who appear to have been negatively impacted by the introduction of a minimum wage, albeit an extremely low one).

Crucially, there remains an extremely close relationship between household income growth and consumer spending. This means that a sustained rise in household income, which includes increases in salaries and wages, quickly translates into a sustained rise in household spending, including shopping. At times, consumer spending is boosted by a surge in the use of credit, including store credit, credit cards, personal loans and overdrafts. However, the use of credit tends to be cyclical in nature, heavily impacted by changes in interest rates and the household sector's ability to afford additional debt.

Unfortunately, personal savings remains an extremely low priority in South Africa, with many individuals not undertaking any form of savings on a regular basis. This reality is actually not easy to explain other than by arguing that the country has not developed a widespread culture of savings, despite having a highly developed contractual savings, asset and wealth management industry. Many ideas have been put forward to broaden the base of domestic savings. These include increasing the incentive to save (for many years, South Africans had only modest tax incentives to save), increasing access to further education and introducing a forced level of contractual savings administered by the government. While some of the suggestions have merit, it seems reasonable to argue that in South Africa a higher level of household savings is extremely dependent on an increase in household income. The solution lies not in consistently increasing wages well in excess of the inflation rate, but rather increasing the level of employment so that more people have regular income. Under these circumstances, even if everyone saved very little, the pool of national savings would rise, which would lift the aggregate level of savings available in the country. While this would not significantly benefit individual households, it would mean that the country is less reliant on attracting foreign savings in order to supplement the low level of domestic savings. It also has to be recognised that during the apartheid years, many households were not in a position to accumulate household goods (due to a lack of income, housing, electricity and running water). Consequently, for many years to come numerous South African households will still be engaged in a process of effectively catching up, which makes increased savings less likely.

A REALITY CHECK

In South Africa, there is a disconnection between the reality of how the economy has actually developed over the past twenty years versus the stated intention of industrial and trade policy since 1994. This is due to a broad range of factors, some of which have been outside the control of policy officials, including the effects of moving rapidly from an isolated, inward-focused economy that had import substitution at the core of its industrial policy to an open economy that tried to encourage exports, including manufactured goods. Unfortunately, this process of trying to reorient the economy was not accompanied by the necessary increase in skills development (including the retraining of workers impacted by the effect of increased imports), the development and enhancement of the country's economic infrastructure, the deregulation of industry to provide room for small-business development, and the consistency of policy needed to create investor confidence. In addition, through years of isolation, many manufacturing businesses never really understood the need to constantly develop and upgrade their technological capabilities, and consequently they lost competitiveness.

All this has meant that a range of other factors started to dominate and shape the development of the economy, including the introduction of cellular technology, the need for low-cost transport (taxi industry) in the absence of widespread public transport, and the need for the majority of citizens that had been effectively isolated from the economy through years of apartheid to start to catch up in areas such as banking, shopping, sport, education, travel and the rate of urbanisation. Consequently, the growth of the services sector easily overtook the growth of the productive sector.

Looking forward, South Africa should be trying to develop some aspects of the mining and manufacturing sectors. This applies especially to manufacturing products to meet the basic needs of the country, such as food, as well as items that are difficult or uneconomic to transport over long distances, or products that are in high demand in the rest of Africa. The country should also be looking to establish niche manufacturing industries that make economic sense. For example, it is still baffling as to why South Africa has not managed to develop a much larger jewellery manufacturing sector.

However, much of the country's future economic growth and employment is likely to come from the services sector, especially domestic-oriented services such as banking, shopping, insurance, healthcare, education, security and transport. This is not necessarily a bad thing as long as South Africa can establish the right mix of services that will allow the economy to prosper.

3

UNEMPLOYMENT IS SOUTH AFRICA'S MOST IMPORTANT ECONOMIC CHALLENGE

South Africa has a relatively young population, with the average age estimated at 25 years. The country also has a very high level of youth unemployment, estimated at around 50%. If the number of discouraged work-seekers is included, the unemployment rate for people younger than 25 jumps to a shocking 63%. It is clear that reducing the level of unemployment, especially among the youth, requires a bold solution that has the role of the private sector firmly at its core, supported by appropriate infrastructural and new business development. A three- to five-year policy-induced boost in employment could lead to a self-reinforcing rise in private sector investment and employment if the initial boost in jobs is large enough, if the plan is well articulated and simple, and if the business environment is relatively employment-friendly.

SOUTH AFRICA HAS A YOUNG AND GROWING POPULATION

In mid-1994, South Africa's population was estimated at 40.54 million people. By mid-2013, the population grew to 52.98 million. This equates to an average population growth rate of 1.6% per annum, which is relatively high by world standards. Over the past twenty years, the global population has risen by an annual average of around 1.2%.

Crucially, South Africa's population growth rate has slowed from 2.1% per annum in 1994 to 0.7% per annum in 2013. This is largely due to a substantial rise in the death rate, which has doubled over the past twenty years from slightly less than 300 000 deaths per year in the early 1990s to an estimated 610 000 deaths per year in 2004/05. Consequently, the life expectancy at birth in South Africa fell from 62 years in 1994 to a low of 52 in 2005. This decline is mostly a result of the AIDS epidemic. Fortunately, the widespread introduction of antiretroviral (ARV) drugs in recent years has slowed the country's death rate measurably. Consequently, life expectancy at birth has been on the rise in the past few years and has increased to 57 years in 2013, according to the United Nations Department of Economic and Social Affairs. The life expectancy at birth for the world population is 70 years; for Japan, it is an amazing 84 years.

Despite the demise of apartheid, there is still a huge focus on the racial composition of the South African population. This is partly because a number of employment-related government policies are based on race, especially affirmative action. In 2013, almost 80% of the population was classified as black African, 9% coloured, a little less than 9% white, and 2.5% Indian or Asian. An interesting aspect of the country's racial composition is that the white population is in significant decline, falling by a total of almost 4% over the past ten years, while growth rates among the other race groups have been fairly similar, at between 1.05% and 1.72% per annum. Consequently, among children aged 0 to 4 years old, the white population represents only 4.7% of the total, Indian or Asian 1.6%, coloured 8.3% and black African 85%.

A breakdown of the population by age reveals that South Africa has a relatively young population. In 2013, almost 30% of the population were younger than 15 years and almost 75% younger than 40. In contrast, a mere 5% were 65 years or older. The average age of South Africa's population was estimated at a little over 25 years in 2013. However, this is up from an average age of 21 years in 1994.

In comparison, the average age of the world population is 29 years, with Japan and Germany at around 45 years, the US and Russia at around 39 years, China 35 years, and India and Brazil 26 years. In contrast, the average age of the population in Kenya and Nigeria is around 19 years.

UNEMPLOYMENT REMAINS EXCEPTIONALLY HIGH

Stats SA is responsible for surveying, compiling and disseminating the country's official employment and unemployment data. From 1993 to 1999, unemployment data was calculated only once a year in South Africa, using the October Household Survey. From 2000 to 2007, Stats SA introduced a biannual Labour Force Survey (LFS), and in 2008 the LFS was expanded to become a quarterly survey, renamed the Quarterly

Labour Force Survey (QLFS). The QLFS is a household-based sample survey of roughly 30 000 households, including the informal sector, which typically reflects unregistered forms of economic activity such as street traders, craft market stalls and parking attendants as well as small-scale subsistence farmers and domestic workers. The survey is specifically designed to measure the dynamics of employment and unemployment in the country. Importantly, the survey complies with the standard definitions of the International Labour Organization. In addition, in 2006 Stats SA launched the Quarterly Employment Statistics, which is an industry-based survey that estimates the number of people employed in the formal sector of the economy.

Unfortunately, the various surveys of unemployment in South Africa are not strictly comparable for a variety of reasons, including differences in the questionnaire designs. This means that the unemployment data over the past twenty years is not necessarily an accurate reflection of the country's labour market dynamics. Instead, the employment data should be viewed as a broad indication of labour market trends.

In addition, some analysts have questioned many aspects of the country's labour market data, reaching significantly different conclusions from those of Stats SA, including the notion that South Africa's unemployment rate is actually significantly lower than currently reported. Some of these criticisms have substantial merit and need to be explored in far more detail.

Moreover, there is meaningful difference between the 2011 Census results and the QLFS data. According to the 2011 Census, 29.8% of South Africa's labour force was unemployed in October 2011, yet for the same period Stats SA's QLFS recorded the official unemployment at 23.9%. While there are significant technical differences between the two estimates, especially relating to the reference period, this divergence is large and adds to the confusion about the country's unemployment data. Hopefully, all these differences will eventually be resolved, as it is critical that policy authorities are able to accurately gauge South Africa's progress in reducing the unemployment rate.

According to the final QLFS survey for 2013, there were 35 million people aged between 15 and 64 years in South Africa. Among these people, 20 million were economically active, which means they are actively looking for work, but only 15.18 million were employed. Of these, 10.8 million people were employed in the formal sector of the economy, 713 000 in agriculture, 1.24 million in private households and 2.45 million in the informal sector. Consequently, 4.83 million people were unemployed, which is an all-time record high, and equates to an unemployment rate of 24.1%.

Back in 1994, the unemployment rate was estimated at 20%, with around 7.97 million people employed and almost 2 million unemployed. That means that South Africa has created an estimated 7.21 million jobs in the past twenty years, which equates to an average of 360 000 jobs per year. It also means, unfortunately, that the rate of job creation has not kept up with population growth. Consequently, the number of people unemployed has risen by 2.83 million in the past twenty years, at an average of 235 000 additional unemployed people each year.

South Africa's labour market has not always lacked vibrancy. During the five-year period from 2004 to 2008, the country was able to create a total of 2.6 million jobs, which is an impressive average of 520 000 jobs a year. This partly reflected the infrastructural development ahead of the 2010 Soccer World Cup, with construction employment growing substantially over the five years. It also reflected a boom in mining employment buoyed by strong growth in China and record high commodities prices. Not surprisingly, over the same period South Africa's economic growth rate averaged almost 5% a year, after adjusting for inflation. Unfortunately, this impressive growth phase was thwarted by the onset of the global financial market crisis in 2008.

Between the final quarter of 2008 and the third quarter of 2010, South Africa lost an incredible 1.05 million jobs as a direct result of the global recession. Fortunately, the economy has since recovered, and at the end of 2013 the labour market had regained all of the jobs lost during the past recession, ending the year at an all-time record high of 15.177 million people employed.

SOUTH AFRICA HAS A LARGE NUMBER OF DISCOURAGED WORK-SEEKERS

According to the definition of unemployment, a person is considered unemployed if he or she is economically active at the time of the interview but did not work in the previous calendar week, had taken active steps to look for work or to start a business in the last four weeks, and wants to work and is available to start work within the next week. However, in South Africa there are a large number of people who have simply stopped looking for work for a variety of reasons, including the high cost of travel or the lack of available transport. In terms of the strict definition, these people are classified not as unemployed, but as discouraged work-seekers.

At the end of 2013, there were an estimated 2.2 million discouraged work-seekers in South Africa. If these people are included as being unemployed, then the unemployment rate at the end of 2013 jumps from 24.1% to 34%, which is exceedingly high by global standards and a major concern. This high level of discouraged work-seekers is not unusual within the South African context. Over the past twenty years, there has been a consistently large number of people who want to work but have simply stopped looking for work.

YOUTH UNEMPLOYMENT IS URGENTLY IN NEED OF ATTENTION

A noticeable feature of South Africa's labour market is the high rate of youth unemployment. At the end of 2013, the unemployment rate for people aged 15 to 24 was officially recorded at 48.9%, with young people accounting for 70% of the total unemployment in 2013. If the number of discouraged work-seekers is included, the unemployment rate jumps to a shocking 62.6%. In fact, 36% of all the discouraged work-seekers in the country are younger than 25.

While South Africa has lived with especially high youth unemployment rates of 50% for many years, this has become a feature of the labour market in numerous countries that have previously enjoyed consistently low levels of unemployment for decades. In fact, since the economic crisis began in 2008, the number of disengaged youth has been on the rise globally. This is particularly true in southern Europe, especially Greece, Spain, Portugal and Italy.

While it is generally the case that unemployment rates among younger people tend to be higher than for the rest of the working-age population, the rapid rise in global youth unemployment since 2008 is alarming given the risk of high youth unemployment leading to widespread social disorder.

Germany is a key exception, having managed to systematically reduce its youth unemployment rate over the past seven years, from 15.8% in 2005 to an average of 7.8% in 2013, a record low. Germany's experience highlights that if a country is willing to adopt specific economic policies targeted at dealing with youth unemployment, the employment needs and aspirations of young people can be met successfully. In particular, it is critical that education and training institutions impart employable and relevant skills to young people entering the labour market.

A few years ago Stats SA started to report on the number of young people (below the age of 25) who are not employed nor attending an educational facility or undergoing formal training. The individuals in this group are categorised as NEET (Not in Education, Employment or Training), which has become an internationally accepted term after first being used in the UK in 1999. In mid-2013, there were an estimated 3.3 million NEETs in South Africa, representing 31% of youth aged 15 years to 24 years and highlighting the vulnerability of the country's young people. These youths are considered to be disengaged from both work and education, and should be of particular interest to policymakers as most NEETs will presumably face extreme difficulties in finding employment. In South Africa the NEET rate is much higher among women (36%) than among men (27%).

A large number of disengaged youths can lead to severe and adverse social, economic and political consequences. Since NEETs cannot generate sufficient income to cover their basic necessities, they may choose to disengage from society and participate in risky or socially disruptive behaviour. Interventions that help young people into jobs or to stay on in education are vital, given the massive costs associated with social exclusion.

The depth and breadth of the youth employment crisis, along with the social unrest that could unfold, highlights how much is at stake in this country. South Africa urgently needs a national young-adult education and training programme focused on imparting technical and practical skills aligned to the country's industrial policy initiatives. In addition, there should be an opportunity for secondary school learners to embark on a more technical training programme rather than follow an academic matric. In order to have a meaningful impact, these education and training initiatives need to be supported by policies that actively encourage self-employment and the formation of small business. Policymakers need to broaden their understanding of the economic benefits accruing from encouraging and assisting young people into the labour market.

HELPING YOUNG ADULTS GET THEIR FIRST JOB IS CRITICAL

In November 2013, Stats SA released their annual *Labour Market Dynamics* report, which highlighted two fairly obvious but important aspects of South Africa's labour market that have significant implications for policymakers.

First, Stats SA found that having previous work experience significantly increases an individual's chances of finding employment, regardless of age and level of education. Work experience is especially important for young people. Young adults (below the age of 25) with previous work experience were six times more likely to find a job than their counterparts with no work experience.

Second, the length of unemployment is also a relevant factor for young work-seekers. Young people who have been unemployed for less than a year (short-term unemployment) are more than twice as likely to find a job than those who are unemployed for more than a year (long-term unemployment).

Overall, the conclusions contained in the Stats SA report argue overwhelmingly that the country should be doing a lot more to help young adults find their first job, especially in the formal sector. This could include, for example, actively promoting the Employment Tax Incentive Act, which is better known as the youth wage subsidy that was signed into law at the beginning of 2014. The Act provides a tax incentive for companies to employ young adults aged 18 to 29 over a period of two years. Youth education and skills development needs to be better suited to the workplace as well as the needs of the country. It also seems logical that there should be a much closer link between educational institutions and work opportunities. Equally, there needs to be much more support in helping those people who have lost their jobs to find additional work, especially if this requires retraining.

Unfortunately, other than sweeping statements of intent, there are very few effective policy responses currently being initiated in South Africa to deal with the high rate of youth unemployment. Yet it is obvious that the longer the high levels of youth unemployment prevail, the greater the risk to social stability – a situation that will increasingly have to be addressed by policy officials.

WHY JOB CREATION IS IMPORTANT

Like many other developing countries, South Africa faces numerous economic and social challenges. Among these are a low savings rate, a high level of income inequality, lack of retirement provision, a narrow tax base, meagre unemployment insurance, limited access to tertiary education, lack of housing, an overburdened public healthcare system and high crime levels.

Through its departmental allocations in the national budget, the government endeavours to address all these issues simultaneously as they all require urgent attention. Unfortunately, this means that government's expenditure is spread relatively thin, and is under constant pressure. It also means that as government introduces policies to deal with each major socio-economic challenge, its actions lead to many unintended consequences, which in turn require another set of policy measures. While the government has made some progress in addressing the country's major socio-economic challenges over the past twenty years, the task ahead remains enormous.

Job creation, unlike any other economic, social or political policy, has the ability to positively impact all of South Africa's major socio-economic challenges simultaneously. In other words, each formal sector job created has multiple benefits for society. For example, a young, unemployed and relatively uneducated man living in Diepsloot in northern Johannesburg would directly experience many of the country's major economic challenges. These include minimal unemployment benefits, limited access to further education, a lack of adequate housing and sanitation, and a high risk of crime. He would be highly reliant on family and friends for survival, and perhaps some informal income. However, if this young man was formally employed, his income would rise immediately, his on-the-job training would enhance his skills development, and his access to healthcare benefits would broaden. Perhaps he could afford better accommodation, and start to contribute to a retirement account and pay more tax. Multiply these benefits by the number of jobs created and the impact on society could be enormous. It would also reduce the burden on the state, while at the same time boosting tax revenue.

In trying to satisfy a wide range of highly demanding growth, development and welfare objectives, there is a perpetual risk that policymakers repeatedly articulate a large and unwieldy set of economic priorities in the hope that these will lead to an overall improvement in economic and social conditions. In truth, it is extremely difficult for any government, given its limited resources, to satisfactorily deliver on more than one or two key national policy objectives within a fiscal year. But by making job creation the single most important and overarching national economic objective, all other growth, development and welfare issues are systematically addressed.

The benefits of employment are so fundamental and substantial that job creation needs to be South Africa's number one economic, social and political objective. This means that the government should set a realistic and achievable employment target, and that every policy initiative should be reviewed in order to determine its impact on job creation, with a view to scrapping policies that significantly reduce or endanger employment. In contrast, initiatives that actively promote job creation, such as the Jobs Fund (a government-funded programme administered by the Development Bank of Southern Africa [DBSA] that helps to create jobs by financing labour-intensive business initiatives), the youth wage subsidy and small-business development should be vigorously promoted.

HOW TO CREATE JOBS

Job creation is not merely a function of the cost of labour. In other words, companies don't simply expand employment because wages are low. Moreover, lifting the level of employment in a market-based economy on a sustained basis cannot be simply legislated or coerced without a destructive increase in inefficiency. Forcing companies to increase employment would result in the business having to charge higher prices to pay for the additional labour or would ultimately lead to the failure of the business due to a lack of competitiveness. Instead, South Africa's high unemployment requires a far more complete and bolder solution that has the role of the private sector firmly at its core, supported by appropriate infrastructural and new business development.

The level of fixed investment activity – which is spending related to the construction of roads, railways, harbours, factories, bridges, shopping centres, hospitals and schools, for example – determines the level of employment. The expansion of private sector business or public sector infrastructure will lead to an increase in employment. Stated more simply, building a factory, a railway, a harbour, an airport, a power station or a hotel, for example, will lead to job creation.

South Africa does not spend enough of its national income expanding the capital stock (mostly machinery, equipment and buildings) of the country. In 2013, South Africa spent a mere 19.3% of its national income on fixed investment activity. That is far too little given the country's extensive infrastructure backlogs. Ideally, South Africa should be spending a minimum of 25% of GDP each year on fixed investment activity, and maintaining it at that level for more than a decade. This was the stated policy objective contained in the 1996 GEAR document, and remains a core policy objective in the 2012 NDP. Internationally, there is a clear and strong correlation between increased investment spending and sustained higher GDP growth, with the level of investment ultimately determining the level of employment.

Consequently, a concerted and sustained effort to lift the level of public and private sector fixed investment activity would help enormously to alleviate the high level of unemployment in the country. Realistically, this would have to start with an increase in public sector investment that aims to alleviate many of the country's infrastructural bottlenecks, including electricity supply, port capacity, rail capacity, road-network enhancement and water provision.

A sustained increase in private sector fixed investment requires a high level of business confidence. Business confidence itself is a function of many variables, including the cost of capital (interest rates), access to finance, tax rates, the ease of doing business, adherence to the rule of law, the availability of skills and technology, and appropriate infrastructure. Although business conditions fluctuate significantly over time, it is critical that the framework in which business is able to operate remains reasonably consistent and predictable.

Besides the development of appropriate and critical infrastructure, there are a number of policy initiatives that government can introduce or expand in order to enhance job creation. These suggestions are discussed more fully in Part III of this book, but they include the active implementation of the youth wage subsidy, the expansion of the existing Jobs Fund, the promotion of new business, skills development and training directly linked to specified industries, and a national programme to implement 'ready-to-go' projects, which are small infrastructure projects that can be initiated and completed relatively quickly, such as the improvement of storm-water drains or the repair of road-safety barriers.

Each year, South Africa's labour force expands by roughly 500 000 people. This represents a reasonable target for job creation, even though creating 500 000 new jobs each year would not significantly reduce the current number of unemployed people. However, it is clear that meeting even this job-creation target cannot be achieved without a commensurate and sustained increase in investment activity by all sectors of the economy.

There is a tendency among South African policymakers to try to develop an economic plan that articulates how millions of jobs will be created over many years. This approach is somewhat unrealistic, highly interventionist and unlikely to succeed because South Africa is a small open economy, heavily impacted by global economic developments. Instead, a three- to five-year policy-induced boost in employment could lead to a self-reinforcing rise in private sector investment and employment if the initial boost in jobs is large enough, if the plan is simple and well articulated, and if the business environment is relatively employment-friendly.

For example, assume that government continues with its current infrastructure development programme aimed at alleviating some key infrastructure bottlenecks (power, port and rail capacity), but at the same time implements a 'ready-to-go' infrastructure development programme over an 18- to 24-month period. Then assume that this coincides with a boost in the Jobs Fund, the active implementation of the youth wage subsidy, and initiatives to encourage new business development and industry-related skills training. This policy-induced boost in employment could be very meaningful, leading to a broad-based pickup in economic activity, which in turn would encourage an increase in private sector fixed investment spending and a natural expansion of the productive capacity of the country.

In conclusion, many of South Africa's social and economic difficulties, such as income inequality, high levels of crime, service-delivery protests and a deficiency of retirement savings, would all be significantly reduced if the level of unemployment was systematically reduced. However, sustained job creation can only happen if business confidence is elevated and the necessary skills are available.

4

INVESTING IN SOUTH AFRICA HAS BEEN EXTREMELY REWARDING

South Africa's financial markets have delivered exceptional investment returns on a consistent basis in the twenty years since 1994. This is especially evident in the performance of the bond, equity and commercial property markets. These markets have all easily outperformed inflation since 1994 and compare extremely favourably with most investment returns around the world, even measured in dollars. These strong returns have been achieved despite an array of negative news about South Africa, and a somewhat disappointing economic performance, especially in the past five years.

INVESTING IN THE GOVERNMENT HAS BEEN PROFITABLE

The South African bond market, which is mostly represented by government bonds, has provided investors with a total return of 908% over the twenty years from 1994 to 2013. This means that had someone invested R10 000 in the government bond market on the first trading day of 1994, and had simply left the money invested until the last trading day of 2013, the investment would have been worth R100 800. This translates into a compound average annual return of 12.2%, and compares with an average annual inflation rate of 6.8% over the same period, and an average annual return of 10.5% had the money been placed on deposit at the bank.

Moreover, the South African bond market has declined in only two of the last twenty years, with the largest decline occurring back in 1994, when the market lost 9.1% of its value. On the upside, the market achieved its highest annual return of 30.2% in 1995, and has recorded a total return of 15% or more in eleven of the last twenty years.

The consistently strong performance of the South African bond market reflects a combination of factors, including a noticeable improvement in the government's financial position over most of the past twenty years, a sustained lowering of inflation and interest rates, a general upward trend in the country's international credit rating (at least until a few years ago), and the benefits of a consistently well-regulated market environment that has actively sought to give investors easier access to the bond market as well as the ability to move in and out of the market as required.

The bond market has also been boosted by a steady inflow of foreign investment. In total since 1994, foreigners have invested roughly R186 billion in the South African bond market. Most of this has occurred since the beginning of 2010, coinciding with the dramatic reduction in global interest rates in the aftermath of the 2008/09 financial market crisis, as well as the extensive 'quantitative easing', which is simply the systematic injection of money into the financial system, undertaken by many of the major central banks, especially the US Federal Reserve. This had the effect of creating a global investment culture that became referred to as a 'search for yield', which effectively meant that many investors in the developed world – including the US, the UK and the EU – opted to increase their investments in other countries that offered a significantly higher return (yield) on their government bonds, and other directly related investments, than what they could achieve in their own markets. In 2010, the yield on a South African ten-year government bond averaged around 8.5%, compared with 3.2% on a US ten-year government bond.

Foreign investment into South Africa's domestic bond market received a further substantial boost when the country was included in the Citibank World Government Bond Index (WGBI) on 11 June 2012. This, combined with the ongoing global search for yield, meant that foreign investors bought R88 billion in South African bonds in 2012, which is a record high. In addition, over the three years from 2010 to 2012, foreigners invested a total of R182 billion in South African bonds, which far exceeds foreign bond purchases during any other period since 1994.

THE STOCK MARKET HAS OUTPERFORMED THE ECONOMY

The South African equity market has also provided investors with an impressive return over the past twenty years. The South African All Share Index has yielded a total return (which includes dividend payments) of an amazing 1 728% from the beginning of 1994 to the end of 2013. This equates to a compound average annual return of 15.6% a year, which is clearly well in excess of inflation. An investment of R10 000 made in the beginning of 1994 would have been worth an incredible R182 816 at the end of 2013. Furthermore, the equity market has declined in only four of the last twenty calendar years, with the largest decline occurring in 2008, when the total return from equities fell by 23.2%. In contrast, during 1999 the equity market recorded its best annual growth of 70.8%, and has risen by more than 20% in nine of the last twenty years, including a 21.4% total return in 2013.

For many observers, the performance of the South African equity market is hard to reconcile with the performance of the domestic economy. In particular, the strong equity performance can seem at odds with sustained high unemployment, worsening levels of income inequality, a skills shortage or electricity outages. However, there are two important factors that have helped South African listed companies maintain a relatively high level of earnings and profitability.

First, over the past twenty years an increasing number of South African companies have been able to derive a significant portion of their income from outside the country. This has not always been the case. Between 1994 and 1997, as much as 90% of profit (after tax) earned by South African companies listed on the Johannesburg Stock Exchange (JSE), excluding gold- and platinum-mining entities, was derived from inside South Africa. However, in more recent years, especially since 2001, many large industrial companies have successfully expanded their operations internationally. For example, back in 1994, South African Breweries (SAB) was essentially a locally based brewery earning most of its income from selling beer and soft drinks in South Africa. Twenty years later, SAB is the second largest brewing company in the world, with around 200 beer brands, some 70 000 employees and a presence in 75 countries. SAB now earns a massive 85% of its revenue outside of South Africa. Many other companies, such as MTN, Naspers, Aspen and Richemont, also derive a substantial portion of their income from outside the country, including from within the rest of sub-Saharan Africa, yet they are listed on the JSE.

This increase in the diversification of earnings has meant that many South African companies listed on the JSE are no longer entirely dependent on the performance of the local economy to remain profitable, and are regularly able to offset a slump in domestic revenue with offshore earnings. This has become a very attractive feature for investors, both domestic and foreign. In total during 2013, an estimated 50% of the earnings of the South African companies listed on the JSE (excluding gold- and platinum-mining companies) were derived from outside the country.

Second, many of the somewhat larger South African companies have been able to consistently maintain relatively high profit margins. This is due to a combination of factors, including a general lack of competition in many sectors of the economy. For example, in some industries two, three or four companies dominate domestic output, leading to a highly concentrated market environment, limited consumer choice and sustained high operating margins. In addition, some companies have benefited from favourable pricing agreements, including, for example, the price of electricity. Most of these agreements are historical in nature, but they have nevertheless contributed favourably to earnings.

Finally, despite many companies acceding to relatively high wage increases (in many instances well above inflation), the cost of labour in South Africa has fallen significantly as a percentage of GDP since the highs of the early 1990s. This is in line with the global trend and reflects a combination of factors, including an increase in capital intensity, which is effectively a rise in the use of machinery and equipment at the expense of labour, in the workplace; increased use of technology; and improvements in system/process design. This means that many companies have become relatively more capital-intensive, which has benefited profitability due to the fact that production has risen faster than the cost of doing business. Unfortunately, this has not always come about through an actual increase in fixed investment spending. Instead, in many instances companies have systematically and consciously stunted employment growth even though business activity has expanded.

There is an ongoing risk that the policy authorities feel compelled to intervene in various markets to try to legislate against high profit margins by introducing some form of price control. But price controls have significant unintended consequences. In particular, they discourage innovation and are likely to lead to a drop in service levels or the quality of production. Instead, there needs to be an active deregulation of industry, with a focus on trying to encourage new entrants into the market. This would have the benefit of increasing competition, thereby eradicating super-profits, as well as increasing investment and employment.

Critically, under current circumstances there is little incentive for some business leaders or boards of directors to take risk. Numerous business executives are handsomely rewarded for a 'business as usual' approach to management, either through a good salary, spectacular bonuses or lucrative share incentive schemes. In their view, why should they undertake a new and somewhat risky investment that requires a sizeable expansion of employment when they are already extremely well paid? Instead, simply managing costs becomes a viable business strategy. However, an increase in competition means that in order for any business to achieve a significant and sustained increase in profits, and consequently pay large bonuses or reward senior management, the executive has to be far more entrepreneurial, innovative, dedicated and passionate about the business and its employees in order to profitably expand the business. This would naturally lead to an increase in research and development, advancement in technology, and higher levels of investment, job creation, skills development and staff motivation.

The South African equity market has also been boosted by a steady inflow of foreign investment. Amazingly, since the beginning of 1994, foreigners have invested an estimated R420 billion in the South African equity market, and at the end of 2013 owned around 35% of the shares on the JSE. More impressively, despite numerous suppositions to the contrary, foreign investors have sold South African equities in only five of the last twenty years, suggesting that most of them are not as fickle as many people assume.

One of the reasons for the steady increase in foreign equity investment into South Africa over the past twenty years has been the desire on the part of the foreign investor to gain an increased exposure to mining companies. Most other equity markets around the world have a relatively small number of listed mining companies. In comparison, South Africa has historically offered foreigners the opportunity to invest in a diverse range of relatively large mining entities. However, in recent years, many mining companies have struggled with rising costs and falling or stagnant commodities prices, making them less attractive as an investment. Fortunately, instead of disinvesting from South Africa, many foreigners opted to switch their exposure from mining companies to industrial companies, especially businesses that have managed to successfully increase their sales to other emerging markets, including the rest of Africa. Although most of sub-Saharan Africa is still considered a 'frontier market', there is an increased global recognition that many economies in Africa have been able to sustainably lift their economic growth and have steadily improved their economic fundamentals, including achieving a much more manageable level of government debt.

THE COMMERCIAL PROPERTY MARKET TAKES FIRST PLACE

Although investing in the South African bond and equity markets has been extremely rewarding over the past twenty years, these investment returns pale in comparison to investments in commercial property.

The listed commercial property sector, essentially comprising companies that own a wide range of commercial property and are listed on the JSE, has provided investors with spectacular returns since 1994. This mainly includes investments in shopping centres, office parks, industrial hubs and warehousing. Listed commercial investments in residential property are relatively small as most houses and flats are privately owned. Since the beginning of 1994, the listed commercial property sector has provided investors with an almost unbelievable total return of 3 171%, which is equivalent to a compound average annual return of 19.1%. This included the gains in income as well as capital, and is clearly well in excess of inflation, making listed commercial property one of the best investments in South Africa since 1994.

These outstanding returns reflect a combination of factors, including the fact that most commercial property was substantially undervalued ahead of the 1994 elections and that South Africa has had a fundamental shortage of commercial developments for many years. In addition, the systematic reduction in inflation and interest rates over the past twenty years has boosted property values through a lowering of the cost of capital. There also has to be an acknowledgement that these returns reflect an underlying confidence in the South African economy.

SOUTH AFRICAN INVESTMENTS HAVE BEATEN MOST GLOBAL MARKETS

There is a tendency simply to dismiss the performance of the South African financial markets, since the returns are derived in a relatively weak currency.

However, the country's investment returns have also been impressive in dollar terms. Over the past twenty years since 1994, the domestic bond market has yielded an average annual dollar return of 6.1%, while the equity market has gained 9.3% a year in dollars and the listed commercial property market has risen 12.5% a year. In comparison, an investment in the US equity market (S&P 500) over the same period would have provided investors with an average annual total dollar return of 9.2%, which is almost identical to the dollar return of South African equities.

This comparison can be extended to other equity markets around the world. For example, investing in developed-market equities collectively (MSCI Developed Market Index) provided a total average annual return of 7% a year since 1994, considerably less than the comparable investment in South Africa, while investing in emerging markets (MSCI Emerging Market Index) yielded a total average annual return of only 5.1%. In other worlds, South Africa's investment returns have been extremely impressive since 1994 irrespective of which currency is used for comparison purposes, and they have performed well against most other investment markets.

MOST SOUTH AFRICANS HAVE MISSED THE INVESTMENT WAVE

Sadly, instead of reaping the benefits of these impressive investment returns, many South Africans have either reduced their level of savings since 1994 in order to increase their level of consumption, or have not been in a position to undertake any form of investment, especially into the financial markets, due to a relatively low level of income or to simply being unemployed. This is the case despite various tax incentives to encourage investments and a broad range of awareness programmes highlighting the importance of investing sufficient money to provide for retirement. These awareness campaigns have been initiated by both the private and public sectors over the past twenty years to explain the importance of planning for retirement or investing to meet a specific goal, such as education, but they have achieved little success. This means that the vast majority of individuals in South Africa have not saved nearly enough money to be able to meet their monthly expenses when they retire, nor have they enjoyed the benefits of inflation-beating investment returns, which could have allowed them to retire much more comfortably.

An interesting element of the South African savings industry is the massive difference between contractual savings and discretionary savings. Contractual savings, which refers mostly to pension funds, retirement annuities and unit trusts, is relatively large in relation to the size of the economy, especially when compared with many other emerging markets, and is extremely sophisticated by global standards. This level of development reflects a combination of factors, including the legacy of relatively high levels of personal savings in the 1960s and 1970s, a significant level of mandatory pension contributions within the formal sector of the economy, the development of a wide range of innovative investment products that have become increasingly accessible, and a rigorous set of regulations that ensure the industry remains highly professional. Consequently, South Africa's asset management industry is world-class.

In contrast, the level of discretionary savings, which reflects mainly cash deposits in the bank netted off against overdrafts and personal loans, is extremely negative, reflecting the fact that many individuals live from month to month and are not able to build up any safety net for emergency purposes, much less invest in unit trusts or retirement annuities. This means the financial position of many households is extremely precarious and vulnerable to an unexpected shock.

DO DAILY PRESS REPORTS MATTER?

Over the past twenty years, South Africa's political, economic and social environment has attracted a great deal of negative press, both domestically and internationally. This negative news flow has covered a significant array of topics, including the tardy approach to AIDS treatment; high levels of crime, especially the murder rate; increased corruption; electricity outages; labour unrest, including the shootings at Marikana; poor levels of education; high unemployment; significant income inequality; and recent credit-rating downgrades.

All of these events tend to negatively impact consumer and business confidence. For example, in 2013 consumer confidence in South Africa was recorded at its lowest level in more than ten years. However, as many chapters in this book highlight, these news items don't tell a balanced story about the country's economic and social progress over the past twenty years. Fortunately, there is very little correlation between the daily flow of South African news items and the performance of many components of the investment markets. This is highlighted by the incredible performance of the commercial property market since 1994. This does not mean that negative news is irrelevant. Rather it highlights that investment decisions need to be made with a broader perspective than that provided by simply reading the daily newspaper.

PART II
SOUTH AFRICA'S FOUR
ECONOMIC PUZZLE PIECES

INTRODUCTION

In 1994, after years of international isolation and economic malaise, South Africa had to start to substantially broaden and completely overhaul the political, economic and social structure of the economy. This required the country to focus on four key elements of economic policy in order to deal with the vast array of social and economic backlogs, as well as to lift the level of economic growth, employment and competitiveness.

These four policy pieces comprised the internationalisation of the country; the implementation of sound macroeconomic policy, especially monetary and fiscal policy; a vast increase in the provision of social goods and services; and the revamp and modernisation of microeconomic policy, which includes improvements in the country's economic infrastructure, skills development, access to finance, and increased competition and competitiveness. South Africa's success in developing these four policy areas will determine its progress in meeting the aspirations of the population.

It was important that South Africa made substantial progress in implementing all four pieces of the country's economic puzzle. This is because a significant underperformance in one key area of economic development would eventually undermine the progress in other pieces of the puzzle, creating a negative feedback loop. Achieving the right balance between addressing the country's enormous socio-economic backlogs while at the same time managing the country's financial position was never going to be easy, especially considering the already high level of unemployment that prevailed at the start of 1994, and the structural impediments to growth that had been established in the preceding decades. However, the overwhelming success of the 1994 election demonstrated that the country had an inherent desire to succeed to the benefit of all its citizens.

Part II looks at each of the four policy pieces of South Africa's economic puzzle, assessing the progress the country has made in transforming the key building blocks of the economy. Each puzzle piece is scored, subjectively, on a scale of 0 to 5, in order to identify areas of strong or exceptional performance, as well as areas that require significantly more policy support. Crucially, outperforming in two or three of the policy pieces is not as beneficial as not underperforming in any one key policy piece.

5
THE FIRST PIECE OF SOUTH AFRICA'S ECONOMIC PUZZLE

OVERVIEW

The process of internationalising South Africa after years of isolation and sanctions has been extremely successful. The country managed to lower import duties in line with the requirements of the World Trade Organization, and to conclude a number of important trade agreements, especially with the EU and the US. Although the rapid increase in imports since 1994 disrupted and undermined a component of South Africa's industrial sector, it also provided vital access to enhanced technology and crucial machinery and equipment needed to modernise key sectors of the economy, including mining, manufacturing, healthcare and telecommunications. The government embarked on a process of obtaining an investment-grade international credit rating, which quickly allowed South Africa increased access to global capital markets. This provided the government, as well as the corporate sector, with a diversified source of funding to potentially expand capacity, including key infrastructural development. It also allowed the South African Reserve Bank to steadily build up its holding of foreign exchange reserves from less than one and a half months of imports in 1994 to over six months of imports in 2013.

The process of internationalising the country was not confined to economic integration, but included establishing strong political links with numerous other countries. These links are reflected in South Africa's membership of the Southern African Development Community in August 1994, the establishment of the African Union in May 2001, South Africa becoming a member of the G20 when it was first convened in September 1999, and being asked to join the BRICS in 2010. The country also actively integrated its sporting activities with the rest of the world, which has become an important part of South African culture and social identity. Over the past twenty years, South Africa has successfully hosted a truly impressive array of global sporting competitions and international conferences. These and other events helped to lift domestic and international confidence in the country, showcasing South Africa's social, political and economic transformation since 1994.

RELATIONSHIP WITH THE REST OF THE WORLD HAS BEEN TRANSFORMED

South Africa's relationship with the rest of the world has changed dramatically over the past twenty years. The country has become progressively more import-intensive, which has eroded a portion of the manufacturing base. Exports continue to be dominated by mining commodities, although there has been some diversification in manufactured exports and the destination of South Africa's exports has changed significantly. Unfortunately, a combination of increased import intensity, missed export opportunities, and an increase in foreign interest and dividend outflows means that the country's current account deficit has widened uncomfortably. Fortunately, South Africa has done remarkably well at attracting a steady inflow of foreign investment over the past twenty years, albeit mostly foreign portfolio investment, and the level of foreign exchange reserves has improved enormously. Nevertheless, the recent credit-rating downgrades, coupled with a fall-off in international competitiveness, highlight that the rand is at risk of weakening and indicate that the policy authorities need to do more to encourage direct foreign fixed investment.

AN OPEN ECONOMY

South Africa has become a relatively open economy since 1994, as measured by the ratio of imports and exports to GDP. Back in 1994, the value of South Africa's imports and exports represented only 41.9% of the country's total economic activity, having risen from less than 40% in 1992. In 2013, the ratio had risen to a substantial 65.5%, having peaked at almost 75% in 2008, highlighting the growing importance of international transactions relative to domestic transactions and South Africa's increased integration into the world economy.

A country with a ratio of international trade to GDP of less than 50% is normally considered a relatively closed economy. For example, in Japan the ratio is typically around 25%, while in the US it is at about 30% and in Australia 45%. In contrast, some countries, especially small European economies such as Ireland, have a ratio that is well above 100%.

Many factors can impact the relative openness of an economy, including the extent of international trade restrictions, the size and structure of the economy, and the geographic remoteness from potential trading partners. Typically, smaller countries, such as South Africa, are generally more open than larger economies. This is because exports in smaller countries tend to occur in a limited number of sectors and, in comparison to larger countries, more goods and services need to be imported to satisfy domestic demand.

The escalation in the degree of openness of the South African economy over the past twenty years is understandable since it largely reflects the increased internationalisation of the economy after years of isolation, which included extensive trade and financial sanctions as well as relatively extensive import duties. Interestingly, South Africa's share of world trade is around 0.5%, which is largely in line with the country's share of world GDP, suggesting that the overall level of international trade is not especially pronounced relative to the size of the South African economy.

BECOMING MORE IMPORT-INTENSIVE

South Africa's growth in imports has easily outstripped the growth in exports over the past twenty years. From 1994 to 2013, South Africa's merchandise exports grew by a total of 123% in volume terms, which equates to an average annual growth rate of 4.3%. In contrast, over the same period, merchandise imports increased by a total of 220% in volume terms, or an average of 6.3% a year. Consequently, the country has gone from recording regular trade surpluses on a monthly basis in the early 1990s to frequent and increasingly larger trade deficits. For example, in the ten years from 1994 to 2003, South Africa achieved an average trade surplus of 2.7% of GDP. However, in the ten years from 2004 to 2013, the international trade balance averaged a deficit of 0.5% of GDP, with the deficit in 2013 at a massive 3% of GDP, the worst recorded since the data series began in 1960.

The South African economy has become much more import-intensive over the past twenty years. This is because the growth in imports has easily outpaced the growth in overall economic activity (GDP). This trend would be considered very acceptable, even desirable, if it mostly signified a systematic increase in imports of machinery and technology needed to enhance the competitiveness of domestic industry that ultimately leads to an increase in exports, especially manufactured exports. It would also be acceptable if the bulk of the imports were being used to upgrade and expand the economic infrastructure of the country. Unfortunately, this has not always been the case.

In the three-year period from 2010 to 2013, South Africa's single biggest import has been crude oil, representing roughly 14% of total imports. In fact, oil, combined with refined fuel, has been the country's single biggest import for many years, despite the various initiatives to reduce South Africa's reliance on imported oil (for example, the development and expansion of Sasol and Mossgas). Other significant and regular imports include motor vehicles and motor-vehicle parts, cellphones, various types of medicines, computer equipment, clothing, and at times large items of machinery and equipment as well as a range of intermediate goods that are used within the mining or manufacturing sectors.

In some instances, the increase in imports has simply eroded the domestic manufacturing base of the country. This applies especially to the importation of textiles, clothing and footwear. In other instances, the increase in imports has merely fed a rise in consumer spending, based on a surge in demand for branded goods, as well as a proliferation of consumer spending on electronic items, especially cellphones.

There is a danger that if the composition of South Africa's imports becomes much more consumption-based rather than representing predominately machinery and equipment, it could evoke an unwelcome policy response that endeavours to curtail consumer spending on relatively high-priced items. This could take the form of increasing taxes on luxury goods, most of which are imported, in an effort to reduce the overall level of imports. This would be difficult to implement effectively, partly because it can be challenging to define a luxury item and partly because it can be costly to administer the process. In addition, there would most likely be significant unintended consequences, including the development of an underground market for luxury items as well as a possible rise in the incidence of theft. Instead, policy officials should focus on encouraging the South African business community to enhance their industrial capacity in order to become more export-competitive, or at least able to compete more effectively in the domestic market.

MISSED EXPORT OPPORTUNITIES

Not surprisingly, South Africa's export performance improved significantly following the lifting of trade sanctions in the early 1990s. This was especially evident in the three-year period from 1995 to 1997. Consequently, by 2001, South Africa's exports of goods and services, measured as a share of GDP, had risen to a little over 30%, compared with a mere 22% of GDP in 1994. This is an exceptional performance after years of sanctions.

In 2001, the share of exports in the economy was still well below the record high of 36% of GDP achieved in 1980. However, in 1980 South Africa's exports were helped by a surge in the gold price, which rose from an average $306 per ounce in 1979 to a peak of $850 per ounce in January 1980, with an average of $612 per ounce for 1980 as a whole.

Since 2001, South Africa's exports in volume terms have recorded a mixed performance. After struggling in 2002 and 2003, exports rose strongly over the four-year period from 2004 to 2007, reaching a record high of 37% of GDP in the first half of 2008. However, the onset of the global financial market crisis in late 2008 and 2009 had a devastating impact on the country's export performance. From the third quarter of 2008 to the third quarter of 2009, merchandise exports fell by an incredible 32.3% in value terms, pushing the South African economy into recession. While global trade has since recovered, ending 2013 at a new record high, South Africa's exports are still below the pre-crisis high. The most recent lacklustre performance in the country's exports is reflected in the fact that as a percentage of GDP, exports fell back to less than 32% in 2013, which is relatively unchanged compared with 2001.

In reviewing South Africa's export data over the past ten to fifteen years, the lasting impression is that the overall performance was ultimately undermined by a combination of at last three unfortunate sets of circumstances.

First, there was a dramatic decline in the volume of gold exports. According to the South African Reserve Bank, the volume of the country's gold exports fell in sixteen of the last twenty years to 2013, and in nine of the last ten years. In total, the volume of the country's gold exports has declined by an incredible 75% since 1994. Fortunately, the combination of a higher gold price (which has risen by a total of 268% since 1994) coupled with a weaker exchange rate (which has declined by a total of 63% since 1994) has meant that the value of gold exports has risen by 163%. While this sounds impressive, the position would have been considerably better had South Africa managed to maintain a consistent volume of gold production over the twenty-year period. In 1994, gold represented 25% of the country's total exports, but fell to only 7% in 2013.

Second, the phenomenal economic growth in China over the past fifteen years, as well as strong growth in other emerging markets, meant that the international demand for commodities rose strongly, as did the price of commodities. Given that South Africa remains largely an exporter of commodities, including iron ore, coal and manganese, this represented an ideal opportunity for the country to prosper through higher export earnings. Unfortunately, because the country has not expanded its rail and port capacity for many years, and much of the associated infrastructure has aged, South Africa was not able to fully exploit the commodities boom. Instead, growth in key mining sectors was dampened by rail and port capacity constraints, regular breakdowns in transport infrastructure and delays in goods being loaded onto waiting ships. Fortunately Transnet, together with the government, has initiated a significant upgrade and expansion of the country's port and rail capacity over the next seven years.

Third, many of South Africa's largest exporters, including gold- and platinum-mining companies as well as motor-vehicle manufacturers, have been plagued by regular, widespread and prolonged labour market unrest. These labour disruptions resulted in significant work stoppages, leading to lost production that has retarded the country's overall export performance over many years. In addition, the uncertain labour environment has also contributed to the general lack of expansion investment in many of the country's productive sectors, which ultimately is reflected in lost export opportunities.

Despite these shortcomings, exports have contributed an impressive 25% of the country's overall economic performance over the past twenty years, and there have been a number of compelling success stories.

In particular, South Africa's exports of motor vehicles and parts have achieved an annual average growth rate of more than 13% in the past ten years, despite the devastating impact of the global financial market crisis.

South Africa remains predominately a commodities exporter despite various industrial policy initiatives to encourage manufactured exports. In fact, in April 2014 the DTI launched the sixth iteration of its Industrial Policy Action Plan, which aims, once again, to promote the country's productive industries, especially mining beneficiation and manufacturing. The beneficiation of raw materials refers to the further processing of metal and mineral products, such as turning iron ore into steel and then into a window frame, or transforming gold into jewellery, or manganese ore into specialised steel products. The advantage of beneficiation is that each stage of additional processing adds enormous value, which can lead either to reduced imports into South Africa or to a growth in value-added exports.

Over the past twenty years, South Africa's largest exports have comprised gold, platinum, iron ore, coal, manganese, diamonds and motor vehicles. This means that the economy is very vulnerable to changes in demand and prices in international commodities markets. Fortunately, the country's commodities exports have become somewhat more diversified, with each major commodity representing less than 10% of total exports over the three years from 2010 to 2013. (Back in 1980, gold exports comprised just over 50% of total exports.) Unfortunately, manufactured goods represent only 52% of South Africa's total exports, which is down from a peak of 63% in 2003 and little changed from 54% in 1998. High-technology exports, or items with high research and development (R&D) intensity and typically found in computers, the airline industry, pharmaceuticals, scientific instruments and electrical machinery, comprise less than 5% of total exports. This is unsurprising, since the South African private sector spends less than 1% of GDP on R&D annually.

There have been significant changes in the destination of South African exports over the past twenty years. The most obvious development has been the massive increase in exports to emerging and developing economies. Back in 1998 (which is the earliest year a full data series is available), South Africa's exports to emerging and developing economies comprised a mere 21% of total exports. In 2013, this had increased to an impressive 58.5%, representing the expanded role of emerging economies, especially Brazil, Russia, India, Indonesia and China, in the world economy. In particular, exports to China, India, Russia and Indonesia have increased dramatically in the past twenty years. On the other hand, relative to other countries, South Africa has underperformed in terms of exports to South America.

South Africa has also experienced a very impressive increase in exports to other parts of Africa, especially sub-Saharan Africa, including Nigeria, Ghana and most of the southern African states. In fact, during 2013 South Africa's exports to the rest of Africa represented almost 29% of total exports, making it the second largest export destination after Asia (32% of total). This means Africa is a more important export destination than Europe (21.5% of total), which was for many years South Africa's major trading region. It is also means that exports to the rest of Africa are almost three times the size of the country's exports to North and South America combined (9.6% of total).

Importantly, South Africa's exports to the rest of Africa include countries within the Southern African Customs Union. These exports are effectively a rand-revenue export given the one-to-one currency convertibility between the South African rand and the currencies of Namibia, Lesotho and Swaziland. (Botswana, which is also part of the Southern Africa Customs Union, has not directly pegged its currency to the rand.) Consequently, the gain in trade with the rest of Africa over the past twenty years is somewhat less impressive when measured in dollars. Nevertheless, South Africa's trade with Africa is substantial and, crucially, comprises mostly manufactured goods. This means Africa is by far South Africa's largest export destination for manufactured goods, and represents a vital opportunity for the country if the continent is able to sustain its current high growth rate.

TRAVEL RECEIPTS AT A RECORD HIGH

The 2010 Soccer World Cup was the largest event of any kind ever held in South Africa, and on the African continent. Ahead of the event, the South African government spent around R30 billion on a wide range of related infrastructural developments, including stadiums, extensive information and communications technology (ICT) upgrades, an elaborate media centre and wide-ranging security measures. There were also upgrades to the transportation system, including most major airports as well as components of the rapid bus transport systems. The private sector also increased investment activity ahead of the event, especially the accommodation sector.

In May, June and July 2010, the number of foreign visitors to South Africa (specifically people arriving by air) amounted to an impressive 1.062 million. Obviously, not all of these people arrived in the country to attend the Soccer World Cup. However, in the same three-month period a year earlier, South Africa attracted only 555 000 foreign visitors. Even adjusting for the fact that world travel had slumped significantly in 2009 due to the global recession, it is fair to conclude that the World Cup significantly boosted South African tourism at the time of the event. Grant Thornton, a consulting firm contracted by government to assess the economic impact of the World Cup, estimated that the country attracted up to 350 000 foreign tourist arrivals specifically for the event. While this is less than the number of visitors that attended the previous World Cup events in Germany and the US, the 2010 event is still regarded as very successful by global standards.

Ahead of the event, the South African finance minister, Pravin Gordhan, as well as many private sector analysts, estimated that the World Cup would add an additional 0.5% to the country's 2010 GDP growth. While this estimate probably overstated the impact, the event certainly provided a boost to the accommodation industry, retail sales, employment levels and tax revenue. The investment activity ahead of the World Cup, coupled with the increased activity during the event itself, helped offset some of the weakness in the South African economy due to the prolonged impact of the global financial market crisis. It is also possible that had the event occurred during more buoyant global economic conditions, the economic impact would have been more significant. Ultimately, the World Cup provided the country with a vital long-term infrastructure boost.

Although some analysts have been critical about the economic benefits of hosting the World Cup, the event demonstrated to all South Africans that the country was capable of successfully organising a major global event. In addition, it raised the profile of the country as a business and tourist destination and probably contributed to South Africa being included in the BRICS.

Although tourism inflows fell away sharply in the year following the World Cup, no doubt partially impacted by the still weak global economic environment, they have since improved dramatically. At the end of 2013, the country's foreign travel receipts were recorded at an annualised and impressive R90 billion. This is easily the highest level ever recorded, and far exceeds the level of travel receipts achieved during the year of the Soccer World Cup, which was R66.4 billion. More impressively, over the past twenty years South Africa's travel receipts have risen by an annual average of 14.1%, reflecting an increase in tourists from most parts of the world, attracted by the spectacular game parks and the natural highlights of the Cape province. In November 2011, Table Mountain in Cape Town was voted as one of the New Seven Wonders of Nature. Despite these successes, the overall level of tourism in South Africa remains far below the world average and well below its potential.

CURRENT ACCOUNT A MAJOR CONCERN

The current account of the balance of payments reflects a country's interaction with the rest of the world in terms of its trade in goods (which is normally the largest component of the current account), but also international transactions in services (for example, airline services), income (for example, investment income) and transfers (for example, transfers related to international cooperation between governments). Typically, this is measured over a period of three months or a year.

A negative balance on the current account (more generally referred to as a deficit) indicates that a country is spending more offshore than it is earning from transactions with other countries. More simply stated, the country is consuming more than it is producing.

In general, the larger the current account deficit, the more problematic it can be for the country involved. This is simply because the larger the deficit, the more pressure the country is under to finance the deficit through foreign capital inflows. As a basic guideline, most countries are advised by the International Monetary Fund (IMF) to try to keep their current account deficit below 5% of GDP, and ideally less than 3% of GDP.

From 1985 to 1993, South Africa's policy officials did everything in their power to ensure that the country recorded a persistent and at times fairly substantial surplus on the current account. This was necessary simply because the country was not in a position to finance a current account deficit due to the impact of financial sanctions. In particular, the financial sanctions imposed on South Africa meant that many foreign banks and international financial institutions, effectively including the IMF, were prohibited by law from providing South Africa with finance. (In the 1980s, financial sanctions had more of a crippling effect on South Africa than trade sanctions.) After 1994, South Africa was in a position to allow the current account to go into deficit on a regular basis as foreign finance became more readily available and progressively cheaper.

In the ten years from 1994 to 2003, South Africa's current account averaged a deficit of only 0.7% of GDP, and at no point did the deficit increase to much more than 3% of GDP. However, a combination of increased import intensity, missed export opportunities, and an increase in foreign interest and dividend outflows meant that the country's current account deficit systematically increased to well over 3% of GDP in the ten years from 2004 to 2013, and on many occasions rose to well over 5% of GDP. In fact, since 2004, the current account has averaged a deficit of 4.5% of GDP, recording a massive shortfall of 6% of GDP in 2013.

The larger the current account deficit, the more reliant the country is on attracting foreign finance, essentially to pay for the fact that the economy is consuming more than it is producing. Rather than constantly evaluating South Africa's current account as a ratio of GDP, it is sometimes useful to quantify exactly how much foreign finance the country has to attract on a monthly basis. Using 2013 as an example, a current account deficit of 6% of GDP equates to an annual (savings) shortfall of R180 billion. This means that South Africa has to attract at least R15 billion in foreign finance each month; otherwise, the rand exchange rate will tend to weaken. That is extremely demanding, especially considering that the country no longer has an A credit rating, and is at risk of having its credit rating downgraded further.

On reflection, South Africa has done remarkably well at attracting a steady inflow of foreign investment over the past twenty years. This is despite the impact of the emerging market financial crisis in 1997/98, the global financial market crisis in 2008/09, recent credit-rating downgrades and regular spates of negative press and scepticism among many local investors.

In terms of foreign investment, it is well documented that South Africa has largely been unable to attract a steady and meaningful inflow of foreign direct investment (FDI), which typically involves a foreign investor either starting a business in South Africa using foreign finance or acquiring more than 10% of an existing company. This type of foreign funding can be relatively stable and is unlikely to be quickly withdrawn. Instead, the country has relied heavily on attracting foreign portfolio investment (FPI), which normally entails a foreigner investing in South Africa's equity or bond market. These inflows of finance can be relatively volatile from month to month and can be withdrawn within a few days should the foreigner wish to disinvest from South Africa. For example, in 2012 net FDI amounted to a mere R12.9 billion, while net FPI totalled R54.7 billion. Incredibly, since the beginning of 1994 to end 2013, foreign investors have bought a net $67 billion of South African equities and a net $29 billion of South African bonds.

Unfortunately, a very large portion of South Africa's foreign capital inflows cannot be fully explained and is simply recorded either as 'net other investment' or as 'unrecorded transactions'. In 2012 and 2013, this amounted to a combined R280 billion, which equates to 67% of total foreign capital inflows over the two years. Clearly, South Africa's ability to accurately and comprehensibly access the composition of foreign capital flows remains less than ideal. This means that economists are not able to accurately monitor why money is arriving in or leaving South Africa, which makes forecasting changes in the value of the rand exchange rate much more difficult.

The inability to attract significant FDI on a consistent basis reflects a general lack of foreign confidence in many aspects of the country's business environment. This appears to include concerns about high levels of crime, rising levels of corruption, infrastructural bottlenecks in the form of electricity shortages, and a general lack of adequate port and rail capacity. Foreign companies also express concerns about the regularity of strike activity in some of South Africa's key industries as well as the shortage of skills.

In contrast, the relatively high level of FPI reflects foreign confidence in the regulation of South Africa's securities trading, including both the equity and the bond markets. This includes the adoption of international rules and regulations, efficient electronic trading and clearing systems, and an excellent dispute-resolution process. Ironically, the historical growth of South Africa's equity and bond markets, which are relatively large by global standards, is not due to a high domestic savings rate or a systematic increase in FPI, but is the consequence of decades of exchange control regulation.

For a number of decades, especially the 1980s and 1990s, South African investors (both households and corporates) had to invest most of their savings in the local financial markets, as they were largely prohibited from investing offshore. This 'trapping' of domestic savings led to the formation of a relatively large and vibrant domestic contractual savings industry. Over time, the securities industry became increasingly sophisticated and well regulated, encouraged by the existence of a captive market. Although there has now been a significant relaxation of exchange control, the legacy effect remains, making the country's equity and bond markets attractive to global investors and relatively large in relation to the size of the South African economy.

A complete relaxation of South Africa's exchange controls, which would mean lifting all controls on the amount of money that can be taken out of the country, is desirable. However, the contractual savings industry in South Africa, which comprises mostly pension funds and unit trusts, provides a ready source of money to finance the government's budget deficit. This deficit arises because each year the government budgets to spend more money than it receives in tax revenue. This deficit has to be funded. Domestic savings also provides relatively inexpensive funding for the capital expansion programmes of numerous public corporations, including Transnet, Eskom and SANRAL (the national roads network). It also seems appropriate for South Africa to maintain prudent limits on offshore investments by pension funds and unit trusts, since most of the members of these funds live and work in South Africa and will eventually need the money to be available in this country.

The significant and sustained increase in South Africa's current account deficit in recent years poses two major risks.

First, there is the risk that foreign private investors will simply stop investing in South Africa's financial markets or even start to withdraw their current investment holdings. This could be sparked by a number of scenarios, including a major change in domestic economic policy, but a more likely impetus would be a shock to the global financial system that leads to a massive increase in global risk aversion. This could be extremely harmful to the South African economy as it might lead to significant currency weakness, a rapid increase in inflation, higher interest rates and a slump in domestic economic activity. Interestingly, these scenarios have largely been tested in recent years, and the country has actually faired relatively well. This was partly due to a combination of an undervalued and flexible exchange rate, adequate foreign exchange reserves, modest levels of foreign debt, sensible fiscal and monetary policy, a strong and stable financial sector, and a relatively attractive investment yield.

Second, the longer South Africa runs a substantial current account deficit, the greater the level of foreign debt and foreign investment that has to be committed to the country. Already foreign investors own an estimated 35% of the South African government bond market and around 37% of the South African stock market. It is unrealistic to expect this type of funding to rise indefinitely. At some point this type of investment is likely to plateau, in which case the currency is at risk of weakening significantly. In addition, this level of foreign investment and debt has to be funded, which means a steady increase in interest costs as well as dividend and investment income payments that have to be transferred back to the foreign investors. South Africa's foreign interest and dividend payments have increased from R2.7 billion in 1994 to R88.9 billion in 2013. The 2013 outflows represented 2.6% of GDP, which is substantial. All of this implies an increasing strain on South Africa's balance of payments and underscores the need to increase exports.

SOUTH AFRICA'S MOST IMPORTANT FINANCIAL CONSTRAINT

Although the balance on the current account largely reflects the difference between the value of exports and imports, it can also be expressed as the difference between national savings and investment. In South Africa's case, rather than suggesting a high level of fixed investment spending, the current account deficit reflects a lack of domestic savings.

A key component in achieving healthy and sustainable economic growth is the level of fixed investment activity, which typically involves the building of roads, railways, harbours, factories, bridges, shopping centres, hospitals, schools, and so on. At the end of 2013, South Africa's level of fixed investment represented only 19.1% of GDP. However, for the economy to grow in the 4% to 6% range on a consistent basis, the ratio of fixed investment spending to GDP would certainly have to approach 25% of GDP on a sustained basis.

Crucially, the savings-investment identity dictates that the level of savings equals the level of investment. At the end of 2013, South Africa's savings amounted to only 13% of GDP, which is essentially the lowest ever recorded in the country, yet fixed investment spending amounted to 19% of GDP. This means the country is running a massive domestic savings shortfall equivalent to 6% of GDP, or R180 billion. Correspondingly, while South Africa's perpetual and relatively large current account deficit may be indicative of a lack of international competitiveness and industrial capacity, it also implies a shortage of domestic savings. In addition, it signifies that South Africa has become highly dependent on attracting foreign savings to supplement its poor level of domestic savings in order to fund a relatively low level of investment activity. Sadly, this position is likely to worsen as the country embarks on an expanded infrastructural development programme.

It is not unusual for a country that is going through a period of rapid development and expansion to rely in part on foreign capital to modernise and expand the capital stock and infrastructure. Conversely, using foreign savings to fund a domestic consumption binge can prove disastrous. In any case, a large savings shortfall leaves the country more exposed to possible episodes of turbulence in international financial markets, such as the recent global financial market crisis. It also means that any policy changes that effectively deter foreign investors could prove disastrous.

A REMARKABLE BUILD-UP OF FOREIGN RESERVES

One of the most remarkable economic successes South Africa has achieved over the past twenty years is the build-up in foreign exchange reserves, despite the increase in the current account deficit and the lack of domestic savings.

Essentially, foreign exchange reserves are foreign financial assets controlled by the monetary authorities (South African Reserve Bank) that can be used, if necessary, to regulate foreign payment imbalances that could potentially destabilise the economy (for example, a dramatic and uncontrolled weakening of the rand exchange rate). Under ideal circumstances, the Bank's holdings of foreign reserves should never be utilised, but rather remain within the hands of the monetary authorities as a perpetual safety net.

The level of foreign exchange reserves can rise only if the money that flows into the country is greater than the amount of money that leaves the country over any given period. Back in 1994, the Reserve Bank's gross holding of foreign reserves amounted to a paltry $2.4 billion. At the time, that amount represented a mere 1.3 months of imports, which is considered extremely low by global standards. Most international guidelines suggest that a country such as South Africa should have a minimum of three months of imports in foreign reserves, and ideally more than six months, but after years of international isolation South Africa had almost fully depleted all available foreign assets.

Remarkably, within five years of the first democratic elections, South Africa's official holdings of foreign exchange reserves had more than doubled to $5.7 billion, and within ten years foreign reserves were up to almost $8 billion. However, this remained far too low by global standards, and became a key risk identified by all the major global credit agencies. It was the most important factor holding back any chance of South Africa's international credit rating being upgraded.

Nevertheless, the country's monetary and fiscal authorities continued their efforts to attract a steady inflow of foreign investment, including the raising of offshore finance. At the end of 2005 the level of reserves had climbed to over $20 billion, and by the end of 2007 they were up to $33 billion.

Amazingly, the Reserve Bank was able to keep the country's foreign reserves position relatively unchanged during the worst of the global financial market crisis, and by the end of 2013 the reserve position had climbed to $50 billion, equivalent to almost six months of imports.

RECENT CONCERNS

In April 1994, South Africa's balance of international payments was in a very precarious position. The authorities had been forced to choke off imports through high import duties in order to engineer a surplus on the current account. The country had been unable to attract any meaningful foreign capital inflows, and instead had imposed significant foreign exchange controls in order to restrict the outflow of local capital. The level of foreign exchange reserves had been almost depleted; moreover, the country had no international credit rating and was still in the process of repaying foreign debt on an accelerated basis as agreed to under the partial debt standstill agreement of the mid-1980s between South Africa and its major creditors in the US and Europe. (The last payment under this agreement was finally made on 15 August 2001.)

Remarkably, the South African monetary, fiscal and trade authorities were able to dramatically improve the country's position within a reasonable period. This involved complying with the rules of the World Trade Organization; signing a number of significant international trade agreements, especially with Europe and the US; and even being invited to join the BRICS. The country systematically began to attract foreign investment, albeit mostly foreign portfolio investment, and in 2012 was included in the Global Bond Index, which represents a combination of the largest and most well-regarded bond markets in the world, including the US, the UK and Germany. At the same time, foreign exchange controls on local residents were gradually relaxed, and they now provide little hindrance to local investors who wish to undertake offshore investments. The level of foreign exchange reserves rose from the equivalent of one month's imports to over six months in 2007, and the country's international credit rating was eventually raised to an A3 status by Moody's Investors Service in July 2009.

Unfortunately, a number of concerns have emerged in the past three years. In particular, import intensity has risen and the current account deficit has widened appreciably without a concomitant increase in economic growth, fixed investment or employment. South Africa's global competitiveness ranking has worsened. Capital inflows are still dominated by portfolio investment, and there appears to be little effort to attract more foreign direct investment. In addition, South Africa's international credit rating has been downgraded for the first time since 1994, and at the end of 2013 South Africa remained on a negative outlook from both Moody's Investors Service as well as Standard & Poor's (S&P) and was eventually downgraded one notch by S&P on 13 June 2014. Consequently, the risk of a significant weakening of the rand exchange rate has risen appreciably.

INTERNATIONAL CREDIT RATING TELLS A STORY

Initially, the international credit-rating agencies were sceptical about South Africa's political, economic and social transition following the 1994 elections. It took the rating agencies more than six years before they had all assigned South Africa an investment-grade international credit rating. Fortunately, the country made steady progress in implementing and maintaining sound monetary and fiscal policies, and by 2005 South Africa's credit rating had risen to only one notch below an A rating. Finally, in 2009 South Africa was assigned an A3 credit rating by Moody's Investors Service, reflecting the country's remarkable success in a number of key areas, including its astute management of public sector debt. However, within just four years of receiving an A rating, South Africa had been downgraded and placed on a negative rating outlook. This deterioration partly resulted from the impact of weak and troubled global economic conditions, but it also reflected the country's increasingly constrained public finances as well as the lack of progress in dealing with rising socio-economic challenges, including extreme income inequality, high unemployment, poor education outcomes and heightened labour market unrest. A further ratings downgrade, especially by Standard & Poor's, would have dire implications for the country.

When the African National Congress (ANC) was elected to power in April 1994, the South African economy had just emerged from three years of severe recession. The economic downturn from 1990 to 1992 was the worst the country had experienced in decades. It was characterised by an extreme lack of business and consumer confidence, a dearth of investment activity, rising unemployment, and a rapidly deteriorating fiscal position that had become burdened by years of excessive military spending and international isolation.

Shortly after the 1994 elections, the government embarked on a process of internationalising the economy. This included re-establishing important foreign trade agreements, engaging more actively with key multilateral organisations such as the IMF and the World Bank, and embarking on a process of obtaining an international credit rating.

THE IMPORTANCE OF A CREDIT RATING

There are numerous credit-rating agencies around the world, but three tend to dominate the business of rating a country's international credit risk: Standard & Poor's, Fitch Ratings and Moody's Investors Service. Unfortunately, they don't all use the same rating system. Standard & Poor's and Fitch Ratings use a fairly intuitive method in which AAA is the best possible rating, followed by AA and A. The ratings then move to BBB, BB, B, followed by CCC, CC, C and ultimately D, which denotes a default. A further differentiation of + and – is made for each rating. For example BBB+ is higher than BBB, which in turn is higher than BBB–.

Moody's Investors Service uses a slightly more complex system of letters and numbers. According to their process, Aaa is the best rating possible, followed by Aa1, Aa2 and Aa3. The rating then drops to A1, A2 and A3, which is followed by Baa1, Baa2 and Baa3, all the way down to a default rating.

All rating agencies emphasise that credit ratings are not a guarantee of debt repayment or an investment recommendation. Instead the rating is purely an indication or measure of credit quality, and reflects the rating agency's opinion about the relative creditworthiness of the entity issuing the debt. For example, a government bond that is rated AA is viewed by the rating agency as having a higher credit quality than a bond with a BBB rating. But the AA rating is not a guarantee that the government will not default; it indicates only that, in the agency's opinion, the government is less likely to default on an AA bond than on a BBB bond.

All three rating agencies apply a crucial cut-off between an 'investment grade' rating and a 'non-investment grade' or 'speculative grade' rating. The term 'investment grade' generally refers to debt issued by an institution or government that is considered to have a relatively high level of creditworthiness or credit quality. In contrast, the term 'speculative grade' refers to debt issued by entities that have the ability to repay the debt, but face significant uncertainties that could affect their creditworthiness. In terms of the Standard & Poor's and Fitch Ratings systems, entities that are assigned a credit rating of BBB– or above are considered by regulators and market participants to be 'investment grade', while those that receive a rating of BB+ or lower are generally considered to be 'speculative grade'. For Moody's Investors Service, 'investment grade' is considered a credit rating of Baa3 and above, while Ba1 or below is deemed to be a 'speculative grade' rating.

In general, the higher the credit rating, the more willing investors are to own the debt and hence the more demand there is for that debt.

This means that a government with a relatively high rating, say AAA, is generally able to issue debt at a much lower interest cost than a government with a BBB credit rating. Furthermore, many large investors around the world are legally prohibited from investing in government debt that does not have an investment-grade rating, especially when that investment involves the use of pension funds.

Importantly, the higher the international credit rating of the government, the easier it is for local public corporations or large private businesses and banks also to obtain a somewhat higher credit rating. Correspondingly, as the government improves its own credit rating, the broader economy is systematically able to benefit from an increasingly lower cost of capital as well as access to diversified sources of long-term finance. This is crucial in helping businesses remain competitive.

In September 1994, Fitch Ratings assigned South Africa its first international credit rating of BB, which is regarded as a speculative-grade rating and is two levels below investment grade. Standard & Poor's rating services confirmed this rating in October 1994 by also assigning South Africa a BB international credit rating, which they increased to BB+, one level below investment grade, in November 1995. Fortunately, Moody's Investors Service adopted a more positive view of South Africa, assigning the country its first investment-grade credit rating of Baa3 at the end of May 1995.

It is understandable that the credit-rating agencies were initially reluctant to assign South Africa a relatively high credit rating. During late 1994 and early 1995, the country was still in the early stages of trying to cope with the lingering effects of extensive trade and financial sanctions that had been vigorously applied over the preceding fifteen years. For example, it is estimated that from 1985 to 1990, more than 200 US companies cut all ties with South Africa, resulting in a loss of more than $1 billion in direct investment. In addition, the level of foreign exchange reserves held by the South African Reserve Bank amounted to a meagre $3.13 billion, mostly in gold, at the end of 1994. This was hopelessly insufficient to protect the exchange rate and safeguard the country against even modest capital outflows.

However, within three years of the ANC being elected, the economic growth rate of South Africa had climbed to over 4% a year, business confidence had soared, international financial and trade sanctions had been lifted, and foreign investment had started to return. The government dramatically scaled back spending on military activity in favour of much-needed social service, including education, healthcare and housing; initiating the Truth and Reconciliation Commission in 1995; and promulgating the country's internationally acclaimed Constitution in 1996. In terms of economic policy, the government had started to transition from the relatively socialist RDP to the more business-friendly GEAR strategy. A miraculous political, economic and social transition had begun to take shape.

Despite these and other significant monetary and fiscal policy improvements, it took Fitch Ratings and Standard & Poor's more than five years to raise South Africa's international credit rating to investment-grade status. Finally, in February 2000, Standard & Poor's assigned South Africa a BBB– investment-grade international credit rating, while Fitch Ratings followed in June 2000 with a BBB– rating. During this five-year period, Moody's Investors Service simply kept South Africa's rating unchanged at Baa3.

Remarkably, from 1994 to 2000, the South African government had managed to moderate its level of debt from a high of 49.5% of GDP in 1995/96 to 42% of GDP in 2000/01. In addition, the interest cost of servicing government's debt had started to fall from a peak of more than 21% of total government spending in 1998/99. Although the level of foreign exchange reserves held by the Reserve Bank had more than doubled to $7.4 billion, the level of reserves was still considered extremely low by international standards and the country remained very vulnerable to a sudden outflow of foreign capital.

In the ten years prior to the 1994 democratic elections, South Africa's foreign debt barely exceeded 2% of GDP. In fact, at the end of the 1993/94 fiscal year, foreign debt totalled a mere 2.7% of total debt, or 1.2% of GDP. That was considered extremely low by global standards, and suboptimal given the government's need to diversify and expand its sources of long-term funding.

The attainment of an international investment-grade credit rating from all three major credit-rating agencies, coupled with the apparent low cost of foreign debt, inspired the South African government to expand its offshore borrowing, off a very low base. Consequently, by 2001/02, the government's foreign debt had increased to a worrying 18.9% of total debt, or 7.8% of GDP.

This dramatic increase in South Africa's foreign debt to GDP ratio was not due entirely to a rise in foreign currency debt. It also reflected the impact of a weaker rand exchange rate on the valuation of the country's foreign debt.

Although South Africa's economic fundamentals had systematically improved from 1994 to 2000, the rand exchange rate had proved to be extremely volatile. This volatility contributed to a ballooning of the country's offshore debt in rand terms, and the minister of finance quickly became concerned that if foreign loans rose too quickly and the rand kept weakening, the government would rapidly become burdened with an ever-larger foreign debt repayment schedule that would quickly prove unmanageable. Furthermore, during times of economic uncertainty, a large holding of foreign debt would exacerbate South Africa's economic vulnerability given the still extremely low level of foreign exchange reserves. Correspondingly, the government scaled back its offshore borrowing ambitions, and set its own internal guideline that foreign debt should ideally not exceed 20% of total government debt.

Since 2001/02, the government's level of foreign debt has eased to a much more manageable 7.4% of total debt (2013/14), or 3.2% of GDP. This is, once again, considered extremely low by global standards and appears unlikely to increase significantly over the coming years.

RATINGS ON THE RISE

From 2000 to 2005, South Africa experienced a number of credit-rating upgrades, and by the end of August 2005 all three major rating agencies had increased the country's international credit rating to three notches above the minimum investment-grade rating, which meant South Africa was only one notch below receiving an A rating.

These upgrades reflected a steady improvement in many of the country's economic parameters, including ongoing fiscal discipline, the successful introduction of inflation targeting, and a further strengthening of the country's foreign exchange reserves position, which had risen to a more respectable $20.65 billion by the end of 2005.

The rating agencies also pointed to several other factors that supported the upgrades. These included somewhat faster economic growth, increased investor optimism about the country's future prospects, stable prices and low real interest. All these factors, the rating agencies argued, reflected the benefits of a decade of macroeconomic reforms that generated greater prosperity, reconnected and enhanced South Africa's financial and trade linkages with the rest of the world, and improved the government's capacity to respond to the still large social and infrastructure needs of its population. It was also argued that the Reserve Bank's healthier level of foreign exchange reserves and its commitment to a floating exchange rate should allow the Bank to more easily manage episodes of capital account volatility.

The rating agencies also highlighted some concerns. These included South Africa's rapid growth in imports, which pushed the trade balance and current account into an increasingly larger deficit despite a pickup in commodities prices. This made the country increasingly vulnerable to a change in foreign investor sentiment. South Africa also faced formidable long-term challenges including chronic poverty and unemployment, which was aggravated by the rapid spread of HIV/AIDS. It was argued that the government's response to HIV/AIDS had been frustratingly inadequate.

Despite these concerns, Moody's Investors Service surprised South Africa in July 2009 by upgrading the country's sovereign credit rating to A3. This was the first time the country achieved an A rating in the international financial markets. In announcing the decision, Moody's Investors Service highlighted a number of key positives about the South African economy, including the further build-up in official foreign currency reserves, which at the time had risen to over $35 billion, the astute debt management of government, and the ongoing portfolio and investment inflows. Moody's was also encouraged by the fact that South Africa's growth rate had been more resilient to the global crisis than many other countries with the same credit rating had been, and that the domestic banking system felt little of the direct impact of the global financial crisis due to its prudent regulatory environment and low levels of financial leverage.

Achieving an A rating in 2009, coupled with the general improvement in the country's credit rating over the preceding eight years, was instrumental in South Africa being included in the Citibank World Government Bond Index (WGBI) on 11 June 2012. According to Citibank, the country had satisfied all three inclusion criteria – namely, the size of the bond market exceeded $50 billion, the country had a minimum credit rating of A– or A3 by either Standard & Poor's or

Moody's Investors Service, and there was a lack of barriers to entry, which means the government being considered for inclusion in the index should actively encourage foreign investor participation. South Africa thus became the first African government bond market to be included in the WGBI, which was immediately reflected in an increase in foreign investment, especially into the government bond market. It also raised the country's profile as a viable investment destination, and helped to differentiate South Africa from the many other developing countries that were not eligible for inclusion in the WGBI. At the time of inclusion, there were eleven South African government bonds eligible for the index. The market value of these bonds totalled $83 billion, which represented a market weight of 0.41% in the WGBI.

RATINGS ON THE DECLINE

In the first fifteen years following the 1994 elections, South Africa made remarkable progress in improving its macroeconomic parameters, even exceeding some of the most optimistic estimates of what was achievable. This included a systematic improvement in the government's financial position, including a radical improvement in tax collection, a much-improved budget allocation, a sizeable reduction in the ratio of government debt to GDP, and a meaningful decline in the cost of servicing public sector debt. Moreover, the South African Reserve Bank introduced an inflation target of 3% to 6% in February 2000 and was able to achieve and maintain the target in a relatively short period. In addition, the level of foreign exchange reserves held by the central bank increased from almost nothing to well over $35 billion. South Africa's progress in implementing sound fiscal and monetary policy under relatively difficult socio-economic conditions was applauded on the global stage.

Unfortunately, over the past twenty years the country has barely dented many of the other key economic challenges it faces, including rising income inequality, entrenched high unemployment and poor educational outcomes. In addition, policy differences have escalated within the government's Tripartite Alliance, which includes the ANC, the Congress of South African Trade Unions and the South African Communist Party.

Economic growth has been hampered by substantial infrastructural bottlenecks (supply-side constraints), and labour market tensions have spilled over into violence, leading to a further loss of competitiveness of South African industry. The government appears to be increasingly conflicted between maintaining investor confidence and appeasing the demands of the politically powerful labour movement. A substantial proportion of the government budget is already absorbed by wages, social support and debt service, limiting the room for new growth-supportive spending. There has been a decline in the government's institutional strength amid increased socio-economic stresses, resulting in the government's diminished capacity to manage the growth and competitiveness risks of the country. This has aggravated the population's growing frustration about the lack of job creation and poor public sector service delivery.

The lack of progress in addressing South Africa's socio-economic difficulties, coupled with constrained public finances, was a key factor influencing the decision by Moody's Investors Service and by Standard & Poor's to downgrade the country's international credit rating one notch, to Baa1 and BBB respectively, in late 2012. Fitch Ratings also decided to downgrade South Africa to BBB in January 2013. This was the first time that the country has been downgraded since the rating process began in 1994.

Unfortunately, in June 2014, Fitch Ratings decided to place South Africa's international credit rating on a 'negative rating outlook', which means that if conditions don't improve, there is a real risk that the country's credit rating will be revised lower again. In addition, Standard & Poor's decided to downgrade the country's foreign currency credit rating one notch, to BBB– from BBB. The downgrade reflected S&P's expectation of lacklustre GDP growth in South Africa, against a backdrop of a relatively high current account deficit, rising government debt, and the potential volatility and cost of foreign finance. In particular, S&P highlighted that the prolonged strike in the platinum sector during the first half of 2014 led to a meaningful deterioration in GDP growth. Furthermore, while S&P thinks that President Jacob Zuma's second administration, which was elected in May 2014, will continue the policies of his first administration, which controlled fiscal expenditure, the agency does not believe it will manage to undertake major labour or other economic reforms that will significantly boost GDP growth.

Worryingly, although S&P placed South Africa's credit rating on a 'stable outlook', which means the agency doesn't expect to adjust the ratings within the next year, S&P did indicate that it could lower the ratings if South Africa's business and investment climate weakens further (for instance, if labour disputes fester). S&P could also lower the ratings if external imbalances continue to increase, or if funding for South Africa's current account or fiscal deficits becomes more difficult or costly. In contrast, S&P could raise the ratings if an improvement in investment and economic growth prospects produces a stronger government and external debt position.

Overall, the June 2014 assessment of South Africa by S&P was extremely negative, highlighting numerous constraints and risks. South Africa's foreign currency rating is now only one notch above speculative grade and back to the rating that prevailed in 2000, which suggests that the country has undone many of the economic improvements achieved since 2000. Fortunately, because S&P assigned South Africa a stable ratings outlook, it suggests the country has a reasonable opportunity to implement important reforms and policies in order to lift confidence and rebuild the credit rating.

A further credit-rating downgrade, especially if S&P takes South Africa back below investment grade, would have very important and dire implications for the country. In particular, it would send an important signal to domestic and foreign investors that the country has become a high-risk investment destination. This could lead to a significant increase in the cost of raising capital offshore, as well as bring into question South Africa's inclusion in the WGBI. It could also reduce the country's access to foreign capital at a time when a steady inflow of foreign capital has become vital for economic stability and success. At the same time, a further ratings downgrade could lead to an unwelcome and fairly rapid outflow of foreign investment. This would weaken domestic financial markets, leading to a higher cost of capital and a significantly weaker rand exchange rate. Although the weaker exchange rate could be viewed as beneficial for South Africa's export competitiveness, it could also simply translate into higher domestic inflation, undermining the purchasing power of most households.

It has to be acknowledged that South Africa's initial credit-rating downgrade occurred at a time of weak and troubled global economic conditions, and that credit-rating agencies have been heavily criticised for their reactive approach to credit-rating adjustments during the height of the global financial market crisis. Nevertheless, the downgrade in June 2014 was largely self-inflicted, reflecting the fact that South Africa's political, social and economic conditions have deteriorated meaningfully in the past couple of years and the risks are still weighted to the downside.

THE RAND ACTS AS SOUTH AFRICA'S SHOCK ABSORBER

The rand is one of the most volatile currencies in the world, experiencing at least five separate episodes of extreme weakness in the past twenty years. These substantial swings in the value of the rand do not always reflect the underlying economic fundamentals of the country, but may result from the vagaries of global financial market capital flows. The currency volatility is extremely disruptive for businesses and households, as well as frustrating for policy officials and institutions such as the South African Reserve Bank. Some analysts argue that South Africa should try to maintain a structurally weak currency in order to boost exports and discourage imports, but this may prove counterproductive and difficult to implement in practice.

THE RAND IS EXTREMELY VOLATILE

The exchange rate of any currency is the value at which that currency can be exchanged for another currency. In other words, the exchange rate is the price of a currency expressed in terms of the value you would receive in another currency.

The exchange rate of the rand is determined by millions of transactions undertaken daily by South African consumers, corporates, foreign exchange dealers, institutional investors and an equivalent array of foreign participants. The rand is essentially free to find its own level, depending on the supply of and demand for the currency. At the risk of stating the obvious, an excess supply of rand in the foreign exchange market is usually associated with a depreciation of the exchange rate. Conversely, a shortage of rand can be expected to cause an appreciation of the exchange rate.

In general, as interest rates rise in a particular country, the exchange rate of that country will tend to strengthen. This is because money will flow into that country because it can earn higher interest. Of course, this does not always prove true, because at the same time there may be other changes in the economy that result in money leaving the country, such as a downgrade of the country's international credit rating.

Over the years, policy officials have argued about whether it is a good idea to try to fix a country's exchange rate by guaranteeing that all currency transactions will take place at the same rate of exchange. In order to do this, the central bank needs to have sufficient foreign exchange reserves to ensure that there is always enough foreign currency available to meet the demands of people wanting to take money out of the country. It is not unusual for countries that have fixed their exchange rate to also restrict the amount of money that can be taken out of the country. There is also no guarantee that the central bank will be able to maintain the fixed exchange rate indefinitely, and in many countries, such as Argentina, this policy approach has had disastrous economic consequences, resulting in a very rapid depreciation of the exchange rate. While a fixed exchange rate has some appeal, especially if the currency is fixed at a level that encourages exports, the reality is that in the current global economic environment, where capital can move fairly easily around the world, it is difficult for countries to keep their exchange rates from fluctuating. This is because millions of rand move through the currency market every day, influenced by a multitude of factors, most of which cannot be forecast.

Floating or flexible exchange rates can also be problematic, especially when the currency becomes extremely volatile and unpredictable. This volatility poses significant problems for businesses, negatively impacting budgeting, profitability and pricing. In fact, for many businesses, especially in South Africa, managing the exchange-rate exposure can represent a more significant component of their business than their actual production. This is because profit margins on international trade are typically very small due to international competition. This means that even a small change in the exchange rate can make the difference between the company making or losing money on its exports or imports. This implies that substantial changes in the value of the rand have a large and potentially damaging impact on the South African economy.

In the days leading up to the April 1994 national elections, the rand was trading at around R3.60 per dollar. This was slightly weaker than at the start of 1994, when the rand was trading at R3.40 per dollar, and about 10% weaker compared with a year earlier. In the days after the elections, the rand strengthened marginally to R3.52 per dollar. Overall, this was considered a remarkable performance given the magnitude of the event and the uncertainty surrounding the acceptance of the outcome.

In the twenty years from April 1994 to April 2014, the rand has weakened by a total of 66%, which equates to an average annual decline of only 5.25% per year. Unfortunately, this statistic masks the path of the currency's decline. Instead of depreciating steadily each year, the rand has experienced numerous and fairly regular bouts of extreme volatility – for example, in 1996, 1998, 2001, 2008 and 2013. During each of these episodes, the rand weakened by more than 20%, and the currency was regularly regarded by market participants to be one of the most volatile in the world.

It is difficult to establish the specific cause of each of these episodes of extreme currency weakness. In fact, following the 2001 currency crisis, when the rand weakened by a massive 42% from 1 September to 31 December 2001, the government initiated a commission of enquiry into the rapid depreciation of the rand. After an extensive investigation, the commission published its final report in August 2002, stating that it could not establish any definitive reason for the rand's extreme weakness. In particular, the commission indicated that 'there is not sufficient evidence to conclude whether unacceptable speculation was a cause or contributing factor to the rapid depreciation of the rand in 2001'. The report also noted that 'South Africa has an open economy (with import and exports representing a combined 55% of GDP) and it is inevitable that from time to time there will be currency turbulence. The events of late 2001 were one of the times.'

It is naive to believe that the rand can, or should, maintain its value against the major global currencies, such as the dollar, over time. This is because South Africa's inflation rate tends to be higher than the inflation rate in the major developed countries, such as the US. The simplest economic model used to explain the movements of any exchange rate over time is the idea of purchasing power parity (PPP). In essence, the PPP model argues that the value of one currency will depreciate against another currency in line with the difference in inflation between the two countries. So, for example, if South Africa's inflation rate is 6% and the inflation rate in the US is 2%, then the rand should fall by 4% a year against the dollar to maintain the currency's relative purchasing power. In theory, this would ensure that R100 buys as much in South Africa as R100 worth of dollars buys in the US.

Consequently, in order for the rand to remain stable against the dollar, South Africa's inflation rate would have to fall to around 2%, and then be maintained at that level for a considerable period. This is highly unlikely given that South Africa's fiscal authorities have set an inflation target of 3% to 6%, and appear willing to manage the inflation rate around the top end of the target range, mainly through changes in interest rates. Significantly reducing the inflation rate to 2% would probably, at least at the outset, entail much higher interest rates.

While the theory of purchasing power parity is supported by sound economic logic, the PPP model has proved almost useless in forecasting the rand exchange-rate movements with any acceptable degree of accuracy. This is mainly because the value of foreign capital flows (which largely reflect foreign buying or selling of South African government bonds and shares on the stock market) are far more important than trade flows (imports and exports of goods and services) in determining the value of the rand, especially over the short term (less than a year).

Capital flows in and out of South Africa are influenced by a broad range of factors. These include the interest-rate differential between South Africa and other countries, as well as economic growth, the extent of the deficit on the current account of the balance of payments, the fiscal balance (the difference between government's tax revenue and government's expenditure), changes in the country's international credit rating, political and social stability, and global sentiment towards emerging markets. Unfortunately, the magnitude of the foreign capital flows into and out of South Africa can easily move the rand well away from its point of equilibrium (or fair value) for an extended period. It is also nearly impossible to gauge the nature of these capital flows in advance. This is because foreign investors are at times willing to move their funds from low-yielding assets offshore to higher-yielding assets in South Africa, but equally they may choose to move their money out of South Africa and into faster-growing economies, or to look for safety in developed-market currencies.

THE RAND IN A GLOBAL CONTEXT

The Bank for International Settlements, headquartered in Switzerland, undertakes a triennial survey of the size and structure of the global foreign exchange markets. This survey has been conducted every three years since 1989 and is probably the world's most comprehensive assessment of the global foreign exchange market. The latest survey took place in April

2013 and is based on data obtained from 53 central banks, and about 1 300 commercial banks and other foreign exchange dealers.

The global foreign exchange market achieved an average daily turnover of $5.3 trillion in April 2013. This is up from $4 trillion in April 2010 and $3.3 trillion in April 2007. Amazingly, foreign exchange trading with corporations actually contracted between the 2010 and 2013 surveys, reducing its share of global turnover to only 9%. Stated differently, the vast majority of the daily trade in the world's foreign exchange market is related to currency transactions undertaken by the large financial institutions.

Foreign exchange trading is increasingly concentrated in the largest financial centres. In April 2013, sales desks in the UK, the US, Singapore and Japan represented 71% of the world's foreign exchange trading, with the turnover in the UK (London) market more than twice that of the US. London is still the centre of the world's financial markets. In fact, foreign currency trading in the UK is larger than the currency markets in the US, Singapore, Japan, Hong Kong, Switzerland and France combined.

The currency composition of global foreign exchange trading shifted notably between 2010 and 2013, not only among the world's most actively traded currencies, but also among important emerging market currencies. The growth in the role of emerging market currencies reflects their rising importance in the world economy, which was accentuated during the 2008/09 financial market crisis.

The US dollar easily remains the world's dominant globally traded currency, represented in 87% of all foreign exchange trades in April 2013, up a substantial 2.1 percentage points from 2010. The euro is the second most traded currency, but its share fell sharply to 33% in April 2013 from 39% in April 2010. The international role of the euro has shrunk significantly since the beginning of the Euro Area sovereign debt crisis in 2010. (The Euro Area, also known as the Eurozone, comprises the member states of the EU that have adopted the euro as their currency. The Euro Area consists of 18 countries, while the EU has 28 member states.) In April 2013, the euro's share of the foreign exchange market reached its lowest value since the introduction of the common currency. In contrast, the turnover of the Japanese yen increased significantly between the 2010 and 2013 surveys, from 19% to 23%. Most of the rise in yen trading occurred between October 2012 and April 2013, a period characterised by expectations of a fundamental change in Japanese monetary policy, which then took place in April 2013.

Growth in the role of emerging market currencies has been impressive. In particular, the Mexican peso is now the 8th most traded currency in the world (2.5% of world trade, or $135 billion a day), up from 14th in 2010, while the Chinese renminbi entered the list of the top ten most traded currencies for the first time, with 2.2% of world trade (currently ranked 9th), mostly driven by a significant expansion of offshore renminbi trading.

As recently as 2004, the renminbi was only the 29th most traded currency in the world. It improved to 20th position in 2007, 17th in 2010 and now 9th in 2013. Clearly, the Chinese currency has got a long way to go before it can be considered a major currency by global standards, but it has gained significant traction in the past three years, with the value of global trade in the renminbi jumping by a staggering 249% from $34 billion a day to $120 billion. This compares with a gain of 38% in dollar trade.

The South African rand is ranked as the 18th most traded currency, with 1.1% of world trade, up from 20th in 2010. However, back in 1998 the rand was ranked 10th in the world. It then dropped to 13th in 2001, 16th in 2004, 15th in 2007 and 20th in 2010, and is now 18th. This does not mean that the trade in the rand has dwindled. In fact, the growth in the value of rand traded globally has been very impressive, rising a massive 108% in the past three years. However, the trade in a number of other emerging market currencies has simply grown at a faster pace, especially the large emerging markets such as China, Russia, Mexico and Turkey. The Brazilian real is the 19th most actively traded currency, while the Indian rupee is in 20th position.

Interestingly, South Africa (represented mostly by foreign exchange trading in Johannesburg) accounts for only 0.3% ($27 billion) of the world's daily foreign exchange market turnover, yet the rand accounts for 1.1% ($60 billion) of world's daily currency trading. This difference in percentage is due to the fact that 55% of all the daily trade in the rand takes place outside of South Africa, mostly in the UK between non-residents of the country. This is partly because there are almost no foreign exchange control restrictions applied to foreigners when dealing in the rand, yet numerous foreign exchange controls remain effective for South

African residents. The extent of trade in the rand outside the country also highlights the difficulties the South African Reserve Bank faces in trying to significantly and consistently influence the value of the rand.

SHOULD SOUTH AFRICA ENCOURAGE THE RAND TO WEAKEN?

The economic debate regarding the merits or demerits of South Africa maintaining an artificially weak exchange rate surfaces from time to time. Conceptually, a significantly undervalued rand will tend to encourage South African exports, and at the same time hinder the importation of goods into South Africa. This is because a weak rand will improve the price competitiveness of South African goods in foreign markets, but will also encourage domestic companies to source their inputs locally (import substitution) in order to avoid more expensive imports. The combination would tend to boost South African industry, encouraging domestic companies to expand their businesses and increase employment.

Conversely, as the rand strengthens, the prices of imports into South Africa fall and inflationary pressures abate. A relatively strong rand also means companies can more easily afford to import critical technology as well as machinery and equipment needed to expand existing businesses and remain competitive.

Nevertheless, the argument in favour of maintaining a relatively weak exchange rate in order to boost local industry is supported by a number of international examples. The most obvious is China, which has maintained a significantly undervalued exchange rate for decades and has clearly achieved great export success. The South African government's 2008 policy document titled *The New Growth Path* repeatedly emphasises the need for a weaker exchange rate, arguing that the monetary policy should 'do more to support a more competitive exchange rate', and that measures should be undertaken to counter the appreciation of the rand as a result of significant capital inflows.

However, before one automatically assumes that South Africa should adopt a weak exchange-rate policy, there are a number of factors to consider.

First, the historical evidence does not support the argument that a weaker rand is beneficial for the country. South Africa has experienced a number of episodes of currency weakness over the past twenty years, yet these events have not led to a sustained rise in exports or an increase in import substitution. This is partly because the bouts of currency weakness have tended simply to lead to higher domestic inflation, including higher wages. The higher inflation rate has then undermined or eroded the competitiveness of industry through an increase in the cost of production (including rents), offsetting the competitive benefit of a weaker exchange rate. In order to avoid this happening, the South African economic system needs to be much more flexible and competitive to ensure that any currency weakness does not automatically translate into a higher cost of doing business. If this can achieved, then some currency weakness could prove beneficial.

Second, it is almost impossible for the South African monetary and fiscal authorities (the South African Reserve Bank and the National Treasury) to accurately and consistently control the value of the exchange rate for any meaningful length of time. While the Reserve Bank can and does intervene in the rand exchange-rate market, by either buying or selling rand in return for either dollars or euros, it exercises this right with extreme caution and only under exceptional circumstances. This is because the value traded in the rand exchange-rate market comfortably exceeds $15 billion a day. In addition, an estimated 55% of all trade in the rand takes places outside of South Africa. Correspondingly, the Reserve Bank would have to transact millions of dollars in order to meaningfully influence the direction of the rand. Moreover, given the cost of intervening in the exchange-rate market, it is unlikely that the Reserve Bank would want to try to influence the value of the rand over an extended period. Stated more simply, currency intervention is very expensive with no guarantees, and is practically not feasible. The global nature of the rand exchange-rate market and South Africa's limited ability to control the rand's value was highlighted by the 2002 commission of inquiry mentioned earlier in this chapter. In particular, the commission's work was limited to transactions between South African residents, and between South African residents and non-residents. Transactions between non-residents were excluded because there is no record of those transactions in South Africa and the commission had no power offshore to investigate those transactions. Through the Reserve Bank, the commission requested the Bank of England to supply it with information on transactions between non-resident banks. However, the Bank of England responded that due to practical problems in obtaining transaction details from the non-resident banks, no meaningful information could be provided.

Third, the price at which a business offers its products to the market does not alone guarantee success. There are many other factors that determine the competitiveness of a product, including its design, function, availability, quality, consistency of supply, and product support. While a weaker rand would improve the price competitiveness of products made in South Africa, it would not necessarily lead to an increase in export volumes unless the overall competitiveness of the product is assured. Currently this seems somewhat unlikely, given the extremely low level of R&D undertaken by most South African industry.

Finally, over the past twenty years a significant portion of South Africa's industrial capacity has been either shut down or curtailed. This is due to a combination of factors, including increased international competition, changes in consumer tastes and preferences, advances in technology and changes in domestic legislation. In 1994 the manufacturing sector represented 24% of the South African economy, but by the end of 2013 its share had fallen to 12%. Correspondingly, there is currently less industrial capacity available to take advantage of a weaker rand. Hence, in order for South Africa to derive the potential benefits of a weaker currency, the country would have to expand its industrial capacity, including the formation of new manufacturing businesses. However, it is simply not prudent to start a business that requires an undervalued exchange rate to be profitable, unless the country has a fixed exchange rate that the authorities are willing and able to defend, or the authorities have a demonstrable ability to consistently control the value of the currency. This is certainly not the case in South Africa.

Instead, it makes economic sense for the monetary and fiscal authorities to try to ensure as best as possible that the rand is relatively stable, and that its value neither prejudices nor harms both exporters and importers.

SCORING THE FIRST PUZZLE PIECE

Back in 1994, very few analysts would have expected South Africa to overachieve in terms of reintegrating itself back into the world economy; but that is exactly what happened. This reintegration included increasing trade in goods and services, achieving an international investment-grade credit rating after initially being regarded as highly speculative, increasing the foreign exchange holdings of the South African Reserve Bank by more than $45 billion, attracting $90 billion in net foreign buying of South African government bonds and equities, and being included in the Global Bond Index. It can always be argued that the country should have achieved more success in the international markets, especially with regard to exports as well as attracting FDI. However, the process of internationalising South Africa after the 1994 elections started from an extremely low base, hurt by years of isolation.

The country's success in establishing important global connections is even more impressive considering that South Africa is now a member of the G20 as well as the BRICS, conforms to the rules of the World Trade Organization, and is a fully paid-up member of the IMF as well as a founding member of the African Union. South Africa has also managed to establish important sport and cultural links with many countries, hosting a number of key international events, including the Soccer World Cup in 2010.

Overall, it seems fair to conclude that South Africa overachieved in its endeavours to internationalise. This piece of South Africa's economic puzzle is assigned a subjective score of 4.5 out of 5, with the lack of FDI being the country's single biggest drawback. This is an important aspect of the economy that needs significant attention. Realistically, FDI can be expected to improve only once economic growth is somewhat higher on a sustained basis, economic policy is more consistent and key infrastructural backlogs are eliminated.

6

THE SECOND PIECE OF SOUTH AFRICA'S ECONOMIC PUZZLE

OVERVIEW

In the early 1990s there were many concerns about how South Africa's economic policy would evolve once the political transition was effected. Some of these concerns focused on the implementation of fiscal and monetary policy. In particular, would the incoming government manage to institute fiscal discipline given the already extremely poor state of government finances that included a huge budget deficit? For many economic and political analysts, this seemed unlikely given the huge socio-economic backlogs in areas such as basic sanitation, health, education and housing, as well as the socialist policies advocated by many members of the ANC. In terms of monetary policy, there was a deep concern that inflation would not be controlled, and that the country would not be able to attract the necessary foreign capital to build up foreign exchange reserves.

These uncertainties were highlighted in 1996, when Trevor Manuel was appointed minister of finance and the rand exchange rate weakened by around 22% against the US dollar. At the time, the IMF argued in their Article IV consultation (which is an economic analysis of the country required by Article IV of the IMF's Articles of Agreement) that this weakening in the currency 'mainly reflected concerns about the future course of financial and structural policies and represented a stark change in investor sentiment'.

However, within a few years fiscal discipline had clearly been achieved. Inflation had been reined in, and an inflation-targeting policy had been set. Since 1994 the country's inflation rate has averaged 6%, and then 5.3% once the inflation target was introduced in 2000. The sustained lower inflation rate allowed for a systematic reduction of interest rates, and a lowering of the cost of capital for both households and business. The government was able to radically improve the process of tax collection, which led to significant increases in tax receipts in eleven of the last fifteen tax years.

Utilising the so-called democracy dividend, which included the benefits of dismantling an extremely expensive and highly inefficient apartheid system, the fiscal authorities were able to reallocate government expenditure to key social services, including the provision of education, healthcare and welfare. At the same time, the government transformed a persistent and substantial fiscal deficit into a budget surplus in the period from 2006 to early 2008, and ensured that the fiscal deficit remained at less than 3% of GDP for most of the past fifteen years. The improvement in fiscal discipline allowed government debt to ease from almost 50% of GDP in 2006 to a low of 27% of GDP in 2009, while at the same time more than halving the government's debt service ratio. This is a truly astounding set of policy achievements. Not surprisingly, the minister of finance from 1996 to 2009, Trevor Manuel, and the governor of the South African Reserve Bank from 1999 to 2009, Tito Mboweni, received numerous international awards for their outstanding work.

FISCAL POLICY DEFIED THE ODDS

The South African government was highly successfully in achieving fiscal discipline from 1996 to 2009, despite populist demands to increase spending on the provision of social goods and services. This was achieved through a combination of improved tax collection, controlled increases in expenditure and a more appropriate allocation of the budget. The reduction in the fiscal deficit over a sustained period meant that government was able to reduce its debt from almost 50% of GDP in the early 1990s to a low of 27% of GDP in 2009. Unfortunately, the onset of the global financial market crisis in 2008/09, combined with a highly expansionary fiscal policy, meant that the government's budget deficit increased sharply. Ideally, the expansionary fiscal policy should have focused on developing South Africa's much-needed infrastructure. Instead, it facilitated a dramatic increase in government salary payments. Consequently, government debt has increased sharply, and if left unchecked will quickly become a major hindrance to the development of the country.

Government expenditure in South Africa had risen dramatically in 1992 and 1993, ahead of the first democratic elections, reaching an alarming 40.9% of GDP in 1993/94. At the same time, tax revenue was somewhat subdued due to a protracted economic recession in the early 1990s, although the government was still able to collect the equivalent of 30.7% of GDP. Consequently, the government's fiscal deficit (the difference between government's tax revenue and government expenditure) rose sharply from a little over 4% of GDP in 1990/91 to a staggering 9.6% of GDP in 1992/93 and a massive 10.4% of GDP in 1993/94. The deficit has subsequently been reduced somewhat, but at the time its rapid deterioration shocked the financial markets and lead to significant concerns about the state of government finances. Although a portion of the increase in government expenditure was blamed on the additional expenses incurred in preparing for the first democratic elections in 1994, there was little doubt that the outgoing government had abandoned any resemblance of fiscal discipline.

In 1994 many analysts concluded that South Africa's fiscal position was highly vulnerable with little scope for revenue growth. Furthermore, it was anticipated that government expenditure would be under enormous pressure. These pressures included the huge socio-economic backlogs in areas such as sanitation, water services, healthcare, education and housing, as well as numerous socialist and redistributive policies advocated by members of the ANC and their alliance partners. This view was aggravated by the fact that the interest cost of state debt (which has to be paid every six months to holders of government bonds, most of whom are based in South Africa) had risen to over 15% of total government expenditure in 1993/94 and was rising rapidly, leading to fears about a possible debt trap, which is when the interest cost of government debt gets so large that it starts to overwhelm the government's budget, thereby limiting the effectiveness of the state.

Although the interest cost of state debt eventually rose to well over 20% of total government expenditure in 1998, it soon became abundantly clear that concerns about the management of South Africa's fiscal policy were completely unfounded. This was due to a combination of factors, including improved tax revenue collection.

Shortly after Trevor Manuel was appointed minister of finance in 1996, the National Treasury together with the South African Revenue

Service (SARS) embarked on a comprehensive and extensive process of improving tax revenue collection. This included upgrading computer systems, allowing for the submission of tax returns online, recruiting skilled personnel and incentivising senior managers based on the amount of revenue collected. This process was supported by a simplification of the tax system, including substantially reducing the number of income tax brackets for individuals, thereby limiting the impact of fiscal drag (the effect of an increase in wages pushing the person into a higher tax bracket), and dramatically raising the threshold at which individuals start to pay tax as well as substantially reducing the number of people who are obliged to submit a tax return.

The process of improving tax revenue collection was greatly assisted by the findings of the Katz Commission, which was formed in June 1994 to investigate the structure, relevance and efficacy of South Africa's tax system. Over the next few years, the Katz Commission produced a number of reports and recommendations on how to reform the tax system. Many of these recommendations were adopted by the minister of finance, which helped to simplify, modernise and improve the efficiency of tax revenue collection.

Furthermore, as revenue collection improved, the minister of finance was able to reduce the tax rates applicable for individuals and corporates, which arguably helped to further improve revenue collection. This included lowering the top marginal tax rate for individuals, from a peak of 45% on an annual income of R122 000 or more in 1999/2000 to 40% on an annual income of R241 000 or more in 2002/03. The top marginal tax rate has since remained unchanged at 40%, although the income threshold at which this is reached has been systematically increased to around R673 000 in 2014/15.

Consequently, individual income tax has eased from 40% of total government revenue in 1996/97 to 34.9% of total revenue in 2013/14. In addition, the company tax rate has been lowered from 40% in 1993 to 28% in 2014, although the government has made use of various forms of dividend tax (tax on income received from shares held in a company) over the years. The value added tax (VAT) rate, which was introduced to try to expand the tax base since it is based on what people spend and not on what they earn, has remained unchanged at 14% since 1993, partly due to concerns that any increase in VAT would anger the ANC's alliance partners. VAT hurts poor households more than rich households since low-income earners tend to have to spend all of their income to survive, while high-income earners are able to save more of their money, which means they pay proportionally less VAT than poorer households. Despite the reduction in the company tax rate, revenue collected from companies in 2013/14 comprised 20% of total government revenue, which is well up from less than 15% of total revenue in 1996/97. This was helped by somewhat stronger economic growth, a commodities boom and improved tax compliance by the corporate sector.

In addition, although the VAT rate has remained unchanged for the past twenty years, the proportion of revenue collected through VAT has also increased, from 24.2% of total government revenue in 1996/97 to 27% in 2013/14, reflecting South Africans' increased propensity to go shopping as well as the effectiveness of the tax.

This process of improving revenue collection meant that tax receipts exceeded budget in at least fifteen of the last twenty tax years, which contributed enormously to government's success in controlling the overall fiscal deficit during most of the past twenty years. In addition, government revenue as a percentage of GDP was reduced from over 30% in 1993/94 to less than 25% of GDP in the late 1990s and early 2000s.

Unfortunately, the incidence of tax in South Africa has lately crept higher, reaching 29.2% of GDP in 2013/14. This has been aggravated by the introduction of some additional taxes, such as a capital gains tax and the skills development levy in recent years. While the incidence of tax is relatively high by South African standards, it is only marginally above the 2013 average for emerging economies of 27% of GDP, and well below the 2013 average for developed economies of 37.3% of GDP.

In 1994/95, total tax revenue amounted to R113.8 billion. This has since grown to R899 billion in 2013/14, which equates to a compound annual growth rate of 10.9%. In comparison, nominal GDP grew at 10.4% over the same period. This suggests that tax collection has kept pace with the growth in the economy. It also suggests that over the past twenty years, the overall burden of taxation has not grown substantially, although the tax base remains extremely narrow, mainly as a result of high unemployment. Data provided by the National Treasury in the 2014/2015 national budget shows that less than 5% of South Africa's labour force pays more than 50% of total income tax. In addition, the same individuals pay a significant portion of South Africa's indirect taxes, including VAT, the fuel levy, excise duties, capital gains tax, transfer duties and numerous local government taxes.

UTILISING THE DEMOCRACY DIVIDEND, BUT WASTING AN OPPORTUNITY TO DEVELOP THE ECONOMY

In the two years prior to the 1994 elections, the government spent almost 10% of the national budget on defence activity, having already reduced defence spending from around 14% of total government expenditure in the late 1980s. However, by 2000, defence spending had been cut to only 5% of budget, and in 2013/14 it consumed a mere 3.6% of government's budget. Utilising this so-called democracy dividend, the fiscal authorities were able to reallocate government expenditure away from defence and other related activity to key social services, including the provision of education, healthcare and welfare. For example, in 1993/94 the government allocated 8.2% of the budget to social security and welfare. This rose to 9.3% in 2000/01, but has since escalated dramatically to 14.6% of total government spending. In addition, the proportion of government spending on housing has more than doubled in the twenty years since 1994.

Interestingly, although government's budget allocation to education and healthcare rose fairly noticeably in the first few years after the 1994 elections, these allocations have since fallen back and are now similar to the proportion of government spending that prevailed in 1994. This is not because government is fully satisfied with the current outcomes in public healthcare and public education. Instead, it reflects the fact that simply allocating more money to these departments will not necessarily yield a better result. Rather, many government departments, including those responsible for health and education, need to significantly improve the efficiency of their operations within their current budget allocations. This argues in favour of reprioritising expenditure, rather than merely allocating additional funds to underperforming departments.

This point was highlighted by the Auditor General in November 2013 in the consolidated general report on the national and provincial audit outcomes. The report noted that approximately R2.3 billion of unauthorised expenditure was incurred by thirty-two departments and that 'little progress has been made in decreasing the extent of this unauthorised expenditure'. In addition, irregular expenditure of R26.4 billion was incurred, while R2.1 billion was incurred in 'fruitless and wasteful expenditure'. The extent of wasteful expenditure had risen by 43% compared with the previous year.

Concerns about wasteful government expenditure have been high-lighted by many entities. For example, the Financial and Fiscal Commission, an independent entity responsible for advising Parliament on government finances, stated that 'more effort must be made to improve the effectiveness of public finances, through greater and more rigorous oversight to ensure the elimination of fruitless, wasteful and unauthorised expenditure, and corrupt practices in managing public finances'. In addition, the 2013 government report on national expenditure made the point that 'poor service delivery and wasteful expenditure are a major deterrent to economic growth and development', while finance minister Pravin Gordhan reiterated in his 2014 budget speech that 'in some instances, governance has been weak, corruption has taken hold, and service delivery has faltered'.

In 2013/14, total government expenditure represented 33.2% of South Africa's GDP. This is well below the proportion that prevailed in 1993/94. However, government expenditure has been trending higher since the 2000/01 fiscal year, when spending was recorded at only 26.7% of GDP. The current level of government spending is also relatively high compared with the average for emerging economies of 29.7% of GDP. For example, government spending in Peru represents 20.1% of GDP, in Indonesia 20.3%, Chile 23.7%, Thailand 24.2% and India 28%. In contrast, government expenditure in developed economies is on average significantly higher than in South Africa, at 41.8% of GDP. In particular, government spending in the Euro Area is exceptionally high at 49.8% of GDP, with France at 56.9%, Finland 57.9% and Denmark 58.3%. Many of the Euro Area economies are now experiencing a fiscal crisis, reflecting the fact that the respective governments have systematically increased the depth and breadth of spending on social services, which have now become unaffordable.

It seems clear that the National Treasury has been thoughtful and consistent in allocating taxpayers' money to various parts of government, and that the minister of finance has responded reasonably fairly to the country's wide range of social and economic demands over the past twenty years. However, many government departments and provinces have not used these funds efficiently or effectively over a number of years, leading to a suboptimal outcome, as well as an increase in wasteful expenditure.

Another area of concern has been government's persistent lack of spending on fixed investment activity, especially infrastructural development. Over the past five years, the government has allocated only 6% to 7% of total expenditure to fixed capital formation. This includes spending by provincial authorities. The remaining 93% to 94% of government spending has been allocated to consumption-related expenditure, including salaries. This mix of spending is inappropriate given South Africa's infrastructural shortfall as well as the need to upgrade existing infrastructure. This situation has been exacerbated by a general tendency for government to overshoot its budget on consumption-related activities, but to underspend its capital investment budget.

In the five years from 2009 to 2013, fixed investment spending by general government has grown by a paltry annual average rate of only 0.6%, after adjusting for inflation, and amounts to less than 8% of GDP. This is shockingly low given the need to uplift the country's infrastructure as well as the fact that the cost of finance for government has been at its lowest level in decades. This would suggest that the government has attempted to keep the fiscal deficit in check by cutting back on capital expenditure.

Fortunately, an increasingly larger component of government infrastructural development is being undertaken by large state-owned companies including Eskom, Transnet and SANRAL. In comparison with government investment, over the five-year period from 2009 to 2013, fixed investment spending by state-owned companies averaged 2.9% of GDP, increasing by an average of 6.1% a year, after adjusting for inflation. While this is still relatively low given the urgent need to enhance South Africa's economic infrastructure, including electricity, port, rail and water capacity, it is significantly better than general government's investment in capital improvements. Over the next three years, commencing in 2014, capital expenditure by major state-owned companies is anticipated by the National Treasury to reach R381.9 billion, or the equivalent of just over 3% of projected GDP. While the increase in fixed investment spending by state-owned companies is encouraging, it is less than ideal given the general lack of public sector investment over the past twenty years.

SOUTH AFRICA ACHIEVED FISCAL DISCIPLINE

In the early 1990s, the government's annual fiscal deficit regularly exceeded 5% of GDP, and total government debt rose steadily from 31.8% of GDP in 1990/91 to a peak of 49.5% of GDP in 1995/96. This largely reflected the previous government's lack of fiscal discipline and the perceived need to spend a disproportionate share of the budget on national defence. At the same time, the cost of servicing government debt (interest) increased from 14% of total government spending, which at the time was considered relatively high, to a peak of over 21% of government spending in 1998/99. The increase in debt, combined with the rise in debt-servicing costs, raised significant concerns that the South African government was heading towards a debt trap. More specifically, the worry was that the interest cost would ultimately overwhelm the budget, dramatically undermining government's ability to finance basic services.

Fortunately, shortly after Trevor Manuel was appointed minister of finance, he embarked on a process of transforming the government's persistent and substantial fiscal deficit into sustained fiscal discipline, ensuring that the annual deficit remained at less than 3% of GDP for the ten years from 1999 to 2008. This included the two-year period from 2007 to 2008 when the government was able to generate a fiscal surplus.

This outstanding improvement in fiscal discipline allowed government's gross domestic debt to ease from almost 50% of GDP to a low of 27.3% of GDP in 2008/09, while at the same time more than halving the government's debt service ratio from over 20% of the national budget to well below 10% of budget in the mid-2000s. This is a truly outstanding set of policy achievements.

This success was partly reflected in glowing endorsements from the IMF and the credit-rating agencies. Furthermore, in 2012 South Africa was ranked second in the world in the International Open Budget Index, after having been ranked first in 2010.

The international Open Budget Survey is produced every two years by the International Business Partnership, which was formed in 1997 in order to improve governance and reduce poverty, and covers 100 countries. The survey is subject to an extensive review process, including two anonymous peer reviewers who are unaffiliated to the relevant governments. The bulk of the survey's questions focus on the amount of budget information that is available. The answers to these questions create an Open Budget Index score of between 0 and 100, with a score of 100 being perfect transparency. The survey is designed to provide an understanding of the current state of budget transparency and accountability in each country, with a score above 60 regarded as acceptable.

According to the 2012 Open Budget Survey, the state of budget transparency and accountability around the world 'is generally dismal'. Only 23 countries provide significant information or better, which is reflected in a score that exceeds 60. The average score among the 100 countries studied is just 43. Worryingly, 26 countries provide scant or no budget information, with scores of 20 or less, while 15 countries provide only minimal budget information, with scores between 21 and 40. The countries that are regarded as providing extensive information on the budget are South Africa, New Zealand, the UK, Sweden, France and Norway, with South Africa receiving a score of 90.

There is no doubt that South Africa's budget process has improved dramatically over the past twenty years, especially under Trevor Manuel's tenure. In particular, the documentation has become consistent, transparent and rich in detail, qualities that were completely lacking prior to 1994.

Unfortunately, a transparent budgeting process is a necessary but not sufficient condition for effective government. Once the National Treasury has allocated the funds and set the key expenditure priorities, it is up to each government department to deliver an acceptable outcome using the funds available. That is clearly not happening, especially in key areas, such as education and healthcare, but also within many provinces and municipalities.

During the period from 1996 to 2008, there was some criticism of the National Treasury that it was being far too zealous in reining in the fiscal deficit, and that this stunted the development of South Africa's economic infrastructure. While this criticism has some validity, it assumes that had the minister of finance allocated more funds towards infrastructural development in the late 1990s and early 2000s, the money would have been spent effectively. In reality, government has consistently underspent its capital expenditure budget, with a portion of funds earmarked for infrastructural development being misallocated or simply wasted. This largely reflects a lack of institutional capacity, especially within provincial and local government, including a shortage of skilled personnel. Indeed, it is entirely feasible that had the minister of finance embarked on a more expansionary fiscal policy, the additional funds would not have been efficiently utilised, leading to an increase in government debt without a commensurate improvement in infrastructure.

THE SOUTH AFRICAN GOVERNMENT ADOPTED A COUNTER-CYCLICAL FISCAL POLICY

Economic recessions occur fairly regularly, and for a wide variety of reasons. These could include a sharp and perhaps unexpected increase in interest rates, a fall-off in exports, an external shock that destroys confidence, a surge in bank bad debts or perhaps something as simple as a sustained rise in the global oil price.

Ultimately, all recessions reflect a pull-back or decline in overall spending. Stated differently, an increase in economic activity is dependent on an increase in spending, irrespective of whether that spending emanates from consumers, businesses or the government. Conversely, an economic slowdown or recession implies that the rate of growth in spending is slowing or actually declining.

A risk associated with a fall-off in economic activity is that the slowdown starts to feed off itself. When the economy slows, unemployment rises; as unemployment rises, incomes fall; as incomes fall, spending falls; and as spending falls, unemployment rises. Without an appropriate policy response, this fall-off in activity can quickly become self-reinforcing, leading to a severe recession, or even a depression that is difficult to correct.

Typically, most countries respond to an economic slowdown by first cutting interest rates. This was certainly the response during the global financial crisis in 2008/09. Over a period of sixteen months from August 2007 to December 2008, the US cut its official interest rate from 5.25% to an all-time low of 0.25%. Similarly, the UK and the Euro Area also moved rates sharply lower.

Unfortunately, at the onset of the 2008 crisis, many governments (especially in the developed world) were already highly indebted, with their debt-to-GDP ratio well above the internationally accepted guideline of 60%. As the crisis worsened, the level of government debt deteriorated significantly, partly hurt by a sharp reduction in tax revenue. Consequently, the ratio of government debt to GDP in the US quickly rose above 100%, while in the UK it moved up to over 75% and in the Euro Area to more than 85%.

Faced with rising government debt, many analysts and policy officials clamoured for governments to reduce spending and raise taxes. This was especially evident in the UK as well as in most parts of Europe. Unfortunately, if a government reduces its spending (introduces fiscal austerity) at the same time that the private sector is in decline or contracting, the combination will certainly worsen the country's overall economic performance, leading to a more severe recession that is likely to start to feed off itself. This certainly occurred in the UK and the Euro Area.

Fascinatingly, the response from the US fiscal authorities to the recession in 2008/09 was significantly different from that of the UK and most European governments – at least initially. Instead of invoking a policy of fiscal austerity, the US government continued to increase spending, leading to a significant rise in the government debt. This, combined with other fiscal measures, ultimately contributed to the US losing its AAA credit rating for the first time ever. However, the increase in government spending undoubtedly helped limit the extent of the economic contraction as well as assist with the pace of economic recovery. Within twelve months the US economy had recovered from the worst point in the recession, with GDP surpassing the level of activity that existed prior to the start of the crisis, after adjusting for inflation. In contrast, by the end of 2013 the UK and the Euro Area had still not regained their previous peak level of economic output. Then, having mostly recovered from the crisis, the US government introduced an element of fiscal austerity, which together with increased tax revenue has significantly improved the government's financial position.

This argument in favour of increased spending at a time of economic difficultly is counter-intuitive when applied at a household level. Most households, when faced with an unsustainably high level of debt, would introduce an element of fiscal austerity in their own monthly budgets. In other words, households that have become highly indebted due to an exorbitant lifestyle are wise to reduce their spending until they are 'living within their means'. While this is sound advice at a household level, it makes little sense at a country or national level. The reason is that in making the decision to reduce spending, the household automatically assumes that its monthly income remains unchanged. But at a national level, cutting spending reduces income levels, which aggravates the economy's financial position, leading to lower growth. This is what fiscal austerity tends to do at a national level. As Paul Krugman, the Nobel Prize-winning economist, has highlighted on numerous occasions, 'One person's spending is another person's income.' So by cutting your spending, you are effectively hurting someone else's income and, by implication, their spending. If this happens on a grand scale, the economy would experience a recession.

This does not mean that the level of government debt is irrelevant. Instead, it highlights a number of key policy issues. First, governments should regularly maintain a low and sustainable level of debt since policy officials never know when the economy is going to need a significant increase in government spending. Second, introducing fiscal austerity at the start of an economic slump must be carefully considered as it is likely to substantially worsen the downturn. Third, while a country's existing level of debt may already be extremely high, making fiscal stimulus prohibitive, it should still be possible to reprioritise spending in favour of initiatives that cushion the downturn and help to restore confidence within the private sector.

In response to the 2008/09 financial market crisis, the South African government decided to embark on a policy of counter-cyclical fiscal policy, which focused on increasing government expenditure rather than cutting taxes. While the idea of stimulating economic activity at a time when the private sector is in recession is to be applauded, government chose to dramatically increase spending on government salaries. This included a rise in both employment as well as salary increases. Consequently, the public sector's salary costs doubled over a period of five years, which equates to an average annual increase of around 15%. Unfortunately, using the government as an unemployment sponge rapidly undermines the viability of the state. Crucial to the capacity of the state to deliver is the soundness of its financial structure.

The situation was compounded by the fact that because of the prevailing economic recession, tax revenue became significantly constrained in 2009/10. This translated into a revenue shortfall of over R60 billion in 2009/10, which was equivalent to over 9% of total revenue.

The combination of an increase in salary payments and a revenue shortfall meant that the budget deficit expanded dramatically to over

6% of GDP in 2009/10, attracting the attention of the international credit-rating agencies. Since then the fiscal authorities have endeavoured to reduce the deficit to around 3% of GDP, but the combination of high levels of consumption spending, coupled with sluggish economic growth, has meant that the fiscal deficit has remained stubbornly high. This eventually contributed to South Africa having its credit rating downgraded in late 2012.

Ideally, instead of boosting salary payments, government should have tried to stimulate economic activity through an increase in infrastructure-related projects. While implementing infrastructure projects can require a long lead time, the government could have adopted a 'ready-to-go' approach to infrastructure development, as outlined in Chapter 9 of this book. This could have included fast-tracking projects that were already at an advanced stage of preparation, projects that had stalled due to changes in personnel, or smaller projects that did not require extensive planning and environmental approval.

RISKS HAVE INCREASED

Over the past twenty years the financial demands on the South African government have been extensive and relentless. On reflection, the fiscal authorities have done a remarkable job in establishing a credible policy of fiscal discipline while at the same time improving the process of tax collection. However, the combination of relatively subdued economic growth and high unemployment has meant that the tax base has remained relatively constrained. At the same time, above-inflation increases in government salaries and other consumption-related activities over the past five years, combined with a rise in wasteful expenditure, have meant that the fiscal deficit has remained uncomfortably elevated.

The rise in South Africa's fiscal deficit from 2009 to 2013 has come at a high cost. Government debt has risen from a low of 27.3% of GDP in 2008/09 to 45.8% of GDP in 2013/14, and is projected to rise to 48.3% of GDP in 2016/17. This is the largest debt level as a ratio of GDP that South Africa has experienced in almost twenty years.

The higher the debt, the higher the interest cost associated with that debt. In South Africa's case, the interest cost of state debt is projected to rise to almost R114.9 billion in 2014/15, or 9.7% of total government expenditure. Over the three years from 2011 to 2013, the cost of state debt has risen by an average of 15.2%, making it one of the fastest-rising expenditure items in the budget.

Fortunately, although the cost of state debt is rising sharply, it remains manageable within the context of the national budget. For example, the interest cost of government debt is still below 3% of GDP. As a comparison, many European countries have a debt-to-GDP ratio of well over 100%, with the interest cost of that debt above 5% of GDP.

Nevertheless, while South Africa's public sector debt parameters remain very acceptable by world standards, the total debt as well as the cost of servicing that debt is clearly on the rise. If left unchecked, government debt will quickly become a major hindrance to achieving many vital policy objectives. For example, already the cost of debt exceeds the total budget allocation to police services.

Looking forward, policy officials will increasingly need to focus on implementing measures that ultimately encourage employment growth in order to broaden the tax base. Without a rapid and sustained rise in tax revenue, it is going to become increasingly difficult for the South African government to satisfy the demands of the population.

INFLATION TARGETING HAS BEEN A RESOUNDING SUCCESS

The South African Reserve Bank has had great success in substantially and sustainably reducing the country's inflation rate over the past twenty years. A key component of the Reserve Bank's monetary policy has been the introduction of a 3% to 6% inflation target in February 2000. Remarkably, despite regular bouts of currency weakness, a rapid increase in electricity prices, above-inflation increases in salaries and wages, and relatively large increases in education and water costs, South Africa's consumer inflation rate has been inside the range most of the time since the target was introduced. Lowering the inflation rate has been extremely beneficial for the country. Households, businesses and the government have benefited significantly from the substantial reduction in interest rates. However, monetary policy has its limitations and cannot be used to solve all of South Africa's economic ills. Instead, monetary policy should remain focused on keeping inflation inside the target range in a stable financial environment. In addition, a greater emphasis should be placed on coordinating and sequencing the goals of various other key economic policies in order to meet the country's broader economic objectives.

A sustained high level of inflation is extremely harmful to the economy. Inflation erodes or discourages savings; inhibits growth by undermining spending power; exacerbates the income and wealth divide, which can lead to social tension or even civil unrest; stimulates capital outflows as households and businesses try to protect themselves against likely currency weakness; discourages investment into productive assets; and makes economic planning and budgeting extremely difficult.

Once inflation starts to rise, there is a tendency for it to quickly spiral higher and potentially become unmanageable. Consequently, the monetary authorities need to react early to an anticipated broad-based build-up of inflationary pressure. Delaying an inevitable tightening of monetary policy usually means that when interest rates are finally increased, they have to rise far more than would have been the case had the authorities acted more promptly.

HISTORY OF INFLATION IN SOUTH AFRICA

Over the twenty-year period from 1994 to 2013, South Africa's consumer inflation rate, which is calculated monthly and measures the rate of increase in prices of a wide range of consumer goods and services across the country, averaged a very respectable 6% a year. This compares with an average of 13.4% during the preceding twenty years, and a peak of almost 22% in the beginning of 1986. During the 1980s and early 1990s, it was very common for economists working in South Africa to adopt a baseline inflation forecast of around 15%.

Historically, much of South Africa's consumer inflation has emanated from an increase in state-administered costs, especially in the water, electricity, telecommunications, transport, health and education sectors. In addition, increases in the cost of doing business, such as the cost of labour or raw material (sometimes due to a weaker exchange rate), which are then passed on to the consumer, also explain a significant portion of the upward pressure on prices. This type of inflation is normally referred to as cost-push inflation. In contrast, it is very unusual for South Africa to experience a sustained rise in demand-pull inflation, where the growth in household demand outpaces the supply of goods and services, creating capacity constraints within the business sector and thereby forcing prices higher.

In general, monetary policy is more effective in combating demand-pull inflation than cost-push inflation. For example, increases in interest rates will have very little impact on the cost of electricity in South Africa, but higher interest rates will certainly dampen the demand for motor vehicles, forcing prices to remain competitive.

In South Africa a number of components of consumer inflation are relatively sticky and tend to remain comparatively high most of the time. This has certainly been the case for electricity cost inflation in recent years, given Eskom's need to fund its long-overdue capacity expansion. In the five years to end 2013, electricity inflation averaged 18.1% a year. Water inflation has also been under pressure, given the increasing strain on storage capacity and the cost of distribution that is plagued by an ageing infrastructure. Water inflation has averaged 8.7% per year in the five years from 2009 to 2013. Education inflation has also tended to remain high, reflecting partly the shortage of tertiary education facilities but also the systematic increase in salaries. In the five-year period from 2009 to 2013, education inflation averaged 9.2% a year. Added to this, the cost of labour in South Africa has tended to rise at an average of at least 2% above the prevailing inflation rate. These and other factors make it extremely difficult for the Reserve Bank to keep overall consumer inflation under control.

Fortunately, some key aspects of consumer inflation have been consistently relatively low, including new-vehicle prices, which have increased on average a mere 0.8% per year from 2009 to 2013, as well as the prices of household furniture and appliances, which have increased on average by only 2.5% in the same five-year period.

INFLATION TARGETING HAS BEEN DECISIVE

A key component of the Reserve Bank's monetary policy management over the past fifteen years has been the introduction of a 3% to 6% inflation target in February 2000. Remarkably, despite regular bouts of currency weakness, a rapid increase in electricity prices, above-inflation increases in salaries and wages, and relatively large increases in education and water costs over these fifteen years, South Africa's consumer inflation has been inside the target range for more than 65% of the time, ending 2013 at 5.4%.

Success in substantially and sustainably reducing the inflation rate over the past twenty years has been largely due to the astute monetary policy management of the South African Reserve Bank, under the leadership of Tito Mboweni (Reserve Bank governor from 1999 to 2009) and Gill Marcus (Reserve Bank governor from 2009 to present).

Prior to the introduction of the inflation target in 2000, monetary policy in South Africa was based on an eclectic mix of policies, including the formal targeting of the M3 money supply (the broadest measure of the amount of money in the economy), which was introduced in the mid-1980s to serve as an anchor for monetary policy. This policy was based on the argument that by controlling the amount of money in the economy, the central bank can control inflation. While targeting money supply had some success in controlling inflation, the policy failed to anchor inflation expectations since the demand for money is relatively unstable (partly due to the dynamics of the financial markets). The anchoring of inflation expectations is critical to maintaining a low inflation rate. If most households and businesses expect inflation to be inside the target range, then they will tend to act accordingly, which means there is a greater chance that inflation remains range-bound.

The inflation target in South Africa is set not by the Reserve Bank but by the government, more specifically the minister of finance in consultation with the Reserve Bank. Having set the target, the finance minister then instructs the Bank to achieve the target on a sustainable basis using any monetary policy the Bank feels is necessary. Obviously, the attainment of the inflation target is most effectively achieved when key economic policies, especially monetary, fiscal and industrial policy, are well coordinated. Ideally, this coordination should include discussions with business and the trade union movement.

The Reserve Bank governor is required to report periodically to Parliament on the success of the Bank's inflation-targeting efforts and must be prepared to answer any questions relating to the setting of monetary policy. If the inflation target has not been met, the governor has to explain what went wrong. In most countries, including South Africa, there is no explicit action taken against the governor if the central bank misses the target. However, if the Reserve Bank misses the target regularly, and by a very wide margin, the government, through the minister of finance, would presumably request that the governor resign. This process of reporting back to Parliament, together with the release of a prepared statement following each bimonthly Monetary Policy Committee meeting as well as a biannual Monetary Policy Forum, leads to a better understanding on the part of the public as to how monetary policy decisions are made.

South Africa's decision to set an inflation target of 3% to 6% was carefully considered. In the eighteen months prior to the introduction of the target, the inflation rate was trending in a range of around 6% to 9%. However, setting the target at that level would have served little purpose, since it was well above the internationally accepted level of inflation. In addition, setting a relatively high target would have given the impression that the central bank was not serious about combating inflation. Equally, setting a target of 1% to 3% would have been too demanding, requiring punitively high interest rates. Consequently, a compromise target of 3% to 6% was adopted.

When South Africa's inflation target was first announced, there was some discussion that the 3% to 6% range would be an interim measure and that the target would ultimately be reduced. This has not transpired, since keeping inflation below 6% has itself been challenging. Furthermore, it could be argued that over the past few years the inflation target has really become 6%, with some tolerance on either side. An IMF research paper titled *Estimating the Implicit Inflation Target of the South African Reserve Bank*, published in July 2012, concluded that 'although the official inflation target range is 3% to 6%, in practice, the South African Reserve Bank seems to have aimed for the upper segment of the band (4.5% to 6%)'. In addition, the IMF highlighted that the Reserve Bank's implicit inflation target has 'shifted toward the upper limit of the inflation target range. This perhaps suggests that since the outbreak of the financial crisis in 2008, the South African Reserve Bank's tolerance for higher inflation has somewhat increased to better support economic activity.'

Initially, South Africa opted to target a measure of consumer inflation known as CPIX. CPIX is essentially the consumer price index (CPI, which measures the monthly price increase across a very diverse group of consumer goods and services) excluding interest rates on mortgage bonds. This target measure was adapted from the inflation-targeting process in the UK. The advantage of excluding mortgage interest rates is that the remaining inflation rate is much more stable, easier to forecast and consequently more suitable as an inflation target.

However, on 21 October 2008, Minister Trevor Manuel announced that the CPI for all urban areas (known as 'headline inflation') would replace CPIX as the inflation-target measure of the Reserve Bank. This change came into effect from January 2009.

In making the change, the finance minister argued that the alignment of the inflation target with the headline measure of inflation would make the use of inflation data simpler for all participants. The change in the targeted measure of inflation was also made possible by Stats SA's decision to bring South Africa's CPI in line with international standards. This meant dropping interest rates on mortgage bonds as the indicator of change in housing costs. Instead, they included 'owners' equivalent rent', which is based on rentals paid for similar dwellings as those found in the owner-occupier market, as an indication of the cost of housing.

The introduction of an inflation target has meant that South Africa's monetary policy has become far more transparent. In prior years, monetary policy was shrouded in mystery, with the public having very little understanding of how interest rates were determined. With a policy of inflation targeting, the Reserve Bank forecasts inflation (the forecast is regularly updated and freely available) and compares its forecast with the target inflation rate. The difference between the forecast and the inflation target effectively illuminates the central bank's likely interest-rate outlook, reducing the uncertainty about the future course of monetary policy. This helps to improve planning and budgeting in the private sector.

The Reserve Bank has to be willing to react pre-emptively to a build-up of inflationary pressure. This means not necessarily waiting for inflation to move outside the target range before increasing interest rates, which is sometimes extremely unpopular. The decision to raise interest rates will normally only fully impact inflation around twelve to eighteen months later (in some countries the time lag is even longer). Consequently, the inflation target can be achieved only if the Reserve Bank is forward-looking. This means the Bank has to have a very reliable and robust system for forecasting inflation. Fortunately, the Bank has devoted a significant amount of resources to constructing and maintaining its inflation forecast model.

The adoption of an inflation target does not mean that the central bank has no discretion. Rather, if the economy is hit by a significant supply shock – for example, a dramatic increase in the global oil price – the Reserve Bank can apply a certain amount of discretion in deciding on the most appropriate policy response. In some instances, even though the inflation rate is above the target, simply increasing interest rates can prove counterproductive, as an increase in rates will not necessarily bring inflation down, and at the same time the higher rates will weaken economic activity.

A major advantage of inflation targeting is that it combines elements of both 'rules' and 'discretion' in the setting of monetary policy. This framework allows the Reserve Bank to focus on achieving a numerical target range for inflation in the medium term, but also to devise an appropriate policy response to economic shocks in the short term.

REDUCING THE RATE OF INFLATION

In order to reduce South Africa's inflation rate on a sustainable basis, the Reserve Bank had to pursue a number of different strategies, including constantly reiterating its adherence to inflation targeting, especially when the inflation rate moved outside the target band. This was done in order to shape inflation expectations. The Bank also had to make it clear that it was focused on achieving the midpoint of the inflation target in order to dispel any ideas that the top end of the target range was good enough. The Bank also used, and continues to use, every opportunity, including the Monetary Policy Committee press conferences, to repeatedly explain the merits of inflation targeting, as well as to explain every interest-rate decision with direct reference to achieving the inflation target. This repetitive and consistent communication has been extremely effective not only in establishing the Reserve Bank's inflation-fighting credentials, but also in ensuring that as many businesses, households and labour unions as possible understand exactly what the inflation target is and that the Reserve Bank is adamant in achieving the target on a sustainable basis. An inflation-targeting framework can be successful only if the public is convinced that the central bank is serious about containing inflation. This is because expectations play a major part in sustainably controlling inflation. As mentioned earlier, if most participants in the economy expect inflation to be inside the target range, then they will tend to act accordingly, which means there is a greater chance that inflation will remain contained.

During the first few years following the introduction of the target, the Reserve Bank also had to maintain a relatively high level of real interest rates, measured as the difference between inflation and the

Bank's repurchase rate (repo rate), which is the interest rate commercial banks pay to borrow money from the South African Reserve Bank. For example, in the four-year period from 2003 to 2006, South Africa's level of real interest rates averaged 6%, which was similar to the average in the preceding four years. However, once the inflation target had been achieved, the Bank was able to systematically lower the level of real interest rates, thereby reducing the cost of capital.

Economic conditions since the global financial market crisis in 2008/09 dictated that the Reserve Bank needed to maintain negative real interest rates (that is, an inflation rate above the repo rate). This can be considered extremely unusual. This exceptionally low level of interest rates cannot be maintained indefinitely as it will systematically distort economic decision-making, as well as discourage savings. As some point in the near future, the Bank will most likely try to normalise interest rates by increasing the repo rate to above the inflation rate. Nevertheless, looking forward, the level of real interest rates will most likely remain well below the historical average as long as the inflation target is mostly achieved.

One of the key reasons why the Reserve Bank has been able to implement inflation targeting so successfully is the sophistication of the country's financial system. In general, the policy instruments used by monetary authorities work best if there are effective money, capital and foreign exchange markets. If financial markets do not react quickly to policy changes made by the Reserve Bank, this reduces the effectiveness of monetary policy and leads to a delay in the Bank's ability to impact inflation. The sophistication of financial markets depends in part on having the right regulatory and institutional framework to channel funds to their most productive use. South Africa has been consistently applauded for its financial market regulation. In the *Global Competitiveness Report 2013–2014*, South Africa was ranked first out of 148 countries in terms of 'regulation of securities exchanges' and third out of 148 countries in terms of 'soundness of bank'. Consequently, the achievement of price stability in the country is underpinned by the stability of the financial system and financial markets.

It also has to be acknowledged that South Africa benefited from lower global inflation, especially following the 1997/98 financial crisis in emerging markets. In 1998 inflation in emerging economies averaged over

13%, but by 2004 the average had dropped to 6.1% as more and more countries introduced an inflation target and the monetary authorities in each country made a concerted effort to bring inflation down. At the same time, South Africa's trade with emerging markets started to rise significantly, exposing the country to more competitive prices and helping to subdue its own inflation rate.

Looking back at the introduction of the Reserve Bank's inflation-targeting policy, four factors contributed meaningfully to its success. First, the policy adopted was internationally accepted and endorsed by numerous analysts, credit-rating agencies and the IMF. Second, the policy was made very simple so that as many people as possible could easily understand the objective. Third, the policy was extensively and repeatedly communicated in a consistent fashion. Finally, the Reserve Bank never wavered in its adherence to achieving the inflation target, even when that meant an unpopular and significant increase in interest rates. Consequently, the process followed by the Reserve Bank is an extremely valuable example for policy initiatives developed elsewhere in the public sector.

INFLATION TARGETING HAS BECOME INTERNATIONALLY ACCEPTED

Many countries around the world make use of an inflation target to guide monetary policy and the setting of interest rates. This is partly in response to the relative failure of other monetary policy regimes, such as those that target money-supply growth or the value of the currency.

The choice of the inflation target varies across countries. Some countries have opted for a point target (for example, 3%), while other countries have a point target but allow for some leeway each side of the target. The decision to adopt a point target or a target range is essentially a trade-off between the simplicity of a point target versus the increased monetary policy flexibility of a target range. A target range seems appropriate for South Africa, given the regular number of supply shocks that impact inflation and that are outside the control of the monetary authorities.

The first country to adopt inflation targeting was New Zealand, in December 1989, setting a target of 1% to 3%. Since then a total of twenty-eight additional countries have introduced some form of an inflation target, including Japan, which set an initial inflation target of

1% in February 2012 but then raised it to 2% in January 2013.

The countries that have adopted a formal inflation target comprise both developed and emerging economies, including Canada, the UK, Australia, Brazil, Mexico and Turkey. The Euro Area has also set an inflation target of 2%, which applies across the region. (The EU has no inflation target because it has no central bank. The Euro Area has a central bank, which is known as the European Central Bank.) Although the US does not have an inflation target, the members of the Federal Reserve regularly refer to an optimal inflation rate of 2%. The country with the highest inflation target is Ghana, which set a target of 8.5% in 2007, with a leeway of two percentage points either side of the target.

At the risk of oversimplification, most developed economies (for example, the US, the Euro Area and the UK) try to maintain their inflation rate at around 2%, while many emerging economies are comfortable with an inflation rate of around 4% to 6%.

MONETARY POLICY HAS ITS LIMITATIONS

Lowering the rate of inflation has been extremely beneficial for South Africa, especially because of the associated reduction in the cost of finance (lower interest rates). In 1994, South Africa's prime interest rate, which is the interest rate banks charge their top clients, averaged 15.5%, but in October 1998 it rose to a record high of 25.5% as the Reserve Bank tried to respond to the impact on the rand of the 1997/98 emerging market financial crisis. On reflection, lifting interest rates so dramatically appears to have had little impact on stemming the weakness of the rand. Instead, it caused significant damage to the domestic economy by dampening the overall growth rate and pushing the housing market into recession.

However, as inflation was reduced to below 6%, the Reserve Bank was able to systematically lower the prime interest rate. The Bank, under the guidance of Tito Mboweni, also developed a more constructive and measured policy response to supply shocks, such as the rapid depreciation of the rand exchange rate, thereby avoiding a dramatic hike in domestic interest rates every time the rand weakened.

By the end of 2004, the prime interest rate had fallen to 11%, and it has averaged 10.9% over the last ten years to the end of 2013, and a mere 9.6% over the past five years. At the end of 2013, the prime interest rate was 8.5%, its lowest level since 1974.

The lower cost of finance has benefited not only the household and business sectors but also the public sector. In 1994, the government's ten-year bond was trading at an average yield of around 16%. This effectively meant that the South African government could borrow over a ten-year period at a cost of 16% a year, which is extremely high by global standards. However, in 2004 the cost of government debt had fallen to an average of 9.5% a year, and has been below 10% for the past ten years. At the end of 2013 the cost was 8%.

Unfortunately, there has been a tendency in South Africa, and in other parts of the world, to assume that changes in monetary policy, principally changes in interest rate, can be used to solve almost every economic problem, including a weakening exchange rate, subdued growth, high inflation, excessive credit demand and a lack of savings. This is unfair and unrealistic. While monetary policy has a role to play in helping South Africa achieve a broad range of economic objectives, its primary function remains achieving the inflation target in a stable financial environment.

SCORING THE SECOND PUZZLE PIECE

Ahead of the 1994 elections, South Africa's fiscal and monetary policy environment was less than ideal. The inflation rate had been allowed to spike to almost 20%, and the prime interest rate was regularly above 15%. This distorted many investment decisions and made the purchase of a house or a car extremely expensive.

Immediately following the 1994 elections, there was a great deal of scepticism that South Africa's monetary and fiscal authorities would have the political will to control the fiscal deficit as well as bring inflation down through an extended period of relatively high real interest rates. However, that is exactly what happened. The fiscal balance was systematically brought under control and then maintained at less than 3% of GDP. This allowed government debt to fall to a mere 27% of GDP. At the same time, the introduction of an inflation target in 2000 and the Reserve Bank's unwavering commitment to achieving the target on a sustained basis resulted in consumer inflation becoming anchored in a range of 5% to 6%. Once the inflation target had been achieved, the Reserve Bank could systematically lower interest rates, thereby reducing the cost of capital.

Unfortunately, in recent years the fiscal deficit has widened again and the debt level has increased to well over 40% of GDP, raising concerns among the credit-rating agencies. In particular, the agencies are concerned about government's rapid increase in consumption expenditure, as well as their persistent underspending of infrastructural budgets. Nonetheless, the National Treasury and the South African Reserve Bank have exceeded expectations in instilling fiscal and monetary discipline. This piece of the puzzle is assigned a subjective score of 4 out of 5.

7

THE THIRD PIECE OF SOUTH AFRICA'S ECONOMIC PUZZLE

OVERVIEW

South Africa's high income inequality and its enormous shortfall of social goods and services in 1994 needed to be redressed as quickly as possible following the first democratic elections. Although the government and various academic researchers tried to estimate and articulate the extent of the backlogs, most of these estimates tended to understate the true extent of the social deficit. Furthermore, although the government was able to reprioritise government spending away from defence and other apartheid-related expenditure towards the upliftment of social services and increased welfare payments, they faced two very significant constraints.

First, the tax base was relatively small, with a high incidence of tax evasion. The minister of finance, together with the South African Revenue Service (SARS), was able to systematically improve the incidence of tax collection. However, the sustained high level of unemployment meant the tax base continued to be constrained and demands for increased expenditure remained exceptionally high. Balancing the need for fiscal discipline against the need to address the massive socio-economic backlogs and high income inequality required exceptional skill on the part of the finance minister.

The second constraint was that government had an obligation to transform the racial composition of government departments and institutions to more appropriately reflect the demographics of the country. This meant that most government institutions undertook a fairly rapid process of transformation. While this significantly improved the level of legitimacy of each government department, it also meant the average level of relevant work experience in each government institution fell sharply. This initially reduced the institutional capacity of the state, at a time when the government was under enormous pressure to address the socio-economic deficit.

Remarkably, despite these constraints, the government has made meaningful progress in addressing a number of key deficiencies in the delivery of social goods and services as well as increasing the provision of welfare payments.

ALLEVIATING THE SOCIO-ECONOMIC BACKLOGS

South Africa's current level of income and wealth distribution is extremely unequal by global standards. This partly results from the legacy effects of apartheid, but also reflects the lack of job creation in the past twenty years. The government has initiated a number of social policies, including a substantial increase in income grants, to try to alleviate the pressure. In addition, the provision of basic social services, such as electricity, housing, water and sanitation, has improved measurably. Unfortunately, significant backlogs remain, but ultimately a meaningful narrowing of the income divide is highly dependent on sustained job creation.

Although South Africa is classified as an upper-middle-income country by the World Bank, and the growth in income per person has easily outpaced inflation over the past twenty years, the distribution of household income in the country remains extremely unequal by global standards.

According to a World Bank report released in July 2012, 'South Africa stands as one of the most unequal countries in the world', while an Oxfam report released in January 2013 concluded that South Africa is 'now the most unequal country on earth and significantly more unequal than at the end of apartheid'. Clearly, income inequality remains one of South Africa's most important economic, political and social challenges.

If personal income is evenly divided across all households, then each quintile (each 20%, or one-fifth) of the population would account for 20% of total income. Conversely, household income would be considered unequal if one or more quintile of households accounted for less (or more) than 20% of total household income.

According to World Bank data, the lowest 20% of households in South Africa earn a mere 2.7% of total household income, while the top 20% earn just over 68%, with the top 10% accounting for almost 52% of income. The remaining 60% of households receive a disproportionately small share of the country's total household income at 29%. Shockingly, over 60% of working people earn less than the tax threshold of about R5 000 a month.

South Africa's current level of income divide is fairly similar to the level of income inequality that prevailed twenty years ago. In 1994, the bottom 20% of households accounted for only 3% of income, while the top 20% represented 64%.

More positively, the size of South Africa's middle class has increased measurably since 1994. Estimates from Stats SA suggest that the number of households classified as middle class has increased from around 2 million in 1998 to approximately 5 million in 2012, representing around a third of the total number of households in the country. In addition, the percentage of the population living on less than $1.25 a day (adjusted for inflation) has fallen from 24.3% in 1994 to 13.8% in 2009.

Despite these gains, the level of income inequality remains extremely high, mainly because high-income earners have pulled further away from people in the lower-income brackets. Consequently, even though South Africans are getting richer, there is still a very high level of inequality across and within population groups.

The overall extent of income inequality in a country can be calculated using the Gini coefficient, which calculates the extent to which the distribution of income or expenditure among individuals within a country deviates from an exactly equal distribution. A Gini coefficient of 0 represents exact equality: that is, every person in the society has the same amount of income. A Gini coefficient of 1 represents total inequality: that is, one person has all the income and the rest of the society has none.

According to the World Bank, South Africa's Gini coefficient measured 0.63 in 2009, compared with an estimate of 0.59 in 1994. This compares with 54.7 for Brazil and Colombia at 55.9. At 0.63, South Africa has one of the most unequal levels of income and expenditure distributions in the world and the highest among the countries for which the World Bank compiles data. Furthermore, income inequality has either remained relatively unchanged or worsened in the past twenty years. According to the Conference Board of Canada, the Gini coefficient for the world is currently around 0.52, which is actually below the peak of 0.55 recorded in 2001, but well above the 1980 level of 0.47.

Typically, as countries become more developed, they first experience more inequality and then progressively less inequality. In other words, as countries move up the development ladder, there is a tendency for the level of income inequality to expand. (This has certainly been the case in China.) Consequently, middle-income countries are most likely to have relatively high inequality, while high-income countries are more likely to have lower income inequality.

South Africa's official estimate of income inequality is compiled by Stats SA every five years and published in the Household Income and Expenditure Survey. Since 1994, three household surveys have been compiled, with the most recent being published in November 2012. This particular survey highlighted the large income divide that remains between the various race groups.

According to this survey, black African households, which represent more than 75% of the total numbers of households in the country, earn less than half (44.6%) of the total annual household income. In contrast, white households make up 12.4% of households but earn 40.1% of the total income. Coloured households (8.5% of the total households) earn 9.9% of the total income, while Indian/Asian households (2.5% of all households) earn 5.4% of annual household income.

There has been some narrowing of the income divide between the various race groups over the past twenty years. For example, the most recent Household Income and Expenditure Survey indicates that over the past five years, Indian/Asian-headed households recorded a 36.8% increase in income, after adjusting for inflation. This was closely followed by black African-headed households, with income growth of 34.5%. Households headed by coloureds saw a 27.7% increase in income, while white-headed households saw only a 0.4% real increase. Despite this significant growth in income in non-white households, there is still a significant income gap between the various race groups. White-headed households, on average, earn more than 5.5 times the income of the average black African-headed household.

Estimates of total household income, the distribution of income across households and the size of the middle class are typically based on fairly limited survey data that is not always comparable over time or between countries. Consequently, the Gini coefficient and the data on distribution of income among households should be viewed as broad, not exact, measures of income disparity.

DISTRIBUTION OF WEALTH IN SOUTH AFRICA REMAINS DEEPLY DIVIDED

According to the Credit Suisse *Global Wealth Report 2013*, published in October 2013, global wealth reached another all-time high of $241 trillion during 2013, up 4.9% compared with 2012. Global household wealth, which is the difference between household assets (mostly houses and pension funds) and household debt (mostly mortgages), passed the pre-crisis peak in 2010, and has set new highs each year since then. As expected, the US accounted for 72% of the latest annual rise in wealth, and has recorded five consecutive annual increases in personal wealth. This has been fuelled mostly by the bull market in equities and some recovery in house prices. Over long periods, trends in household wealth are strongly related to economic growth, saving rates and demographic factors.

Interestingly, Japan's household wealth suffered very little during the 2008/09 financial crisis. In fact, personal wealth in that country actually grew by 21% between 2007 and 2008. This is partly because equities account for only around 10% of the financial wealth of Japan's household sector. However, in marked contrast to recent performance in the US, total personal wealth in Japan is now just 1% above the 2008 level, mainly as a result of recent currency weakness.

The global average wealth per adult reached a new all-time high of $51 600 in 2013, with wealth per adult in Switzerland rising to an amazing $512 562. This compares with $301 140 per adult in the US, $243 570 in the UK, $192 232 in Germany, $35 872 in Mexico, $22 230 in China and only $19 613 per adult in South Africa.

Wealth per adult in China is significantly higher than in the other major emerging economies, and is actually fairly evenly distributed. China has relatively few adults at the bottom of the global wealth distribution, but also relatively few at the top. Instead, China dominates the upper-middle section of global household wealth. This standing reflects not only the country's population size, but also its sustained high economic growth, rampant job creation, rising asset values and currency appreciation.

China now has more people in the top 10% of global wealth holders than any country except for the US and Japan, having moved into third place in the ranking by overtaking Italy and Germany. This is one of the key reasons why China is likely to exhibit sustained high economic growth as it endeavours to boost consumer activity. In contrast, residents of India are heavily concentrated in the lower wealth brackets, accounting for a quarter of people in the bottom half of global wealth distribution.

Africa remains extremely poor by global standards. For example, the average wealth per adult amounted to an estimated $4 929 in Africa during mid-2013. This compares with $103 712 per adult in Europe and a massive $296 004 per adult in North America. Stated differently, Africa has 11.79% of the world's adult population but only 1.13% of world household wealth. In contrast, North America has 5.71% of the global adult population, but a staggering 32.75% of world wealth. The average wealth per adult in China, which has a larger population than Africa, is $22 230.

Household wealth in Africa remains well below the peak in 2007 of $6 489 per adult. This reflects not only the relative weakness of the various exchange rates in Africa (wealth data is measured in US dollars), but also the fact that the relatively high level of economic growth enjoyed by the continent in recent years has not resulted in broad-based job creation and a broadening of household income.

Household wealth remains extremely uneven in Africa. For example, although the average level of household wealth per adult is measured at $4 929, the median level (the middle number of a set of values) of wealth per adult is a mere $680. Half of all African adults are found in the bottom quintile (20%) of the population. At the same time, some individuals are found among the top 10% of global wealth holders, and even among the top 1%.

Africa appears to have very low wealth mobility. In other words, it appears fairly difficult for individuals to move into a higher wealth bracket, with almost two-thirds of Africans remaining in the same wealth range after one generation. In contrast, China is classified as the most mobile wealth region in the world, mainly because the risk of a downward move in wealth is relatively low. North America and Europe record the highest chance of moving from the bottom wealth levels to the millionaire class, but equally there is a greater chance of downward mobility in these regions.

Data on the household sector's balance sheet is notoriously difficult to construct and maintain. However, back in June 2006, the South African Reserve Bank released a relatively comprehensive assessment of the South African household sector's assets and liabilities. This information is updated annually, with data stretching back to 1975. The Bank also provides quarterly updates on the ratio of household wealth to disposable income. Thus, South Africa is one of the few emerging economies that publish an official estimate of the household sector's balance sheet, thereby providing a consistent and fairly reliable basis for research into wealth trends in the country.

According to the Reserve Bank, the value of the country's household assets amounted to R7 751 billion at the end of 2012. Unusually for a developing country, household wealth in South Africa is largely comprised of financial assets (R5 609 billion), including, for example, bank deposits, pension funds and unit trusts. This reflects a vigorous stock market and sophisticated life insurance and pension industries.

The value of residential buildings in South Africa rose by a relatively modest 5.9% in 2012 (up R101 billion) to R1 808 billion, or 28.9% of total assets. Nevertheless, this is the largest value ever attributed to residential property in South Africa, and is well above the mortgage debt outstanding on residential property, which totalled R812 billion at the end of 2012. Correspondingly, the net equity in residential property reached an all-time record high of R996 billion at the end of 2012. This suggests that overall the banking sector has been extremely cautious in how it approaches mortgage finance (with, perhaps, the exception of financing luxury golf estates, which has resulted in increased bad debt). Furthermore, the banking sector appears well insulated against a meaningful decline in residential property prices, unless the decline in prices is accompanied by a sharp fall in employment.

The value of South Africa's household debt totalled R1 494 billion at the end of 2012, which equates to a ratio of total debt to annual household disposable income of 75.4%, well above the early 1994 ratio of 55.4%. Most of this debt is in the form of mortgages (R812 billion). The remaining debt is represented by items such as car finance, overdrafts, personal loans, student loans and credit cards (R682 billion). In South Africa, as in many other countries, the increase in the household debt-to-income ratio over the past two decades can largely be attributed to three factors: financial deregulation during the 1980s, the introduction of many new financial products and the systematic reduction in interest rates.

Correspondingly, South African households were worth a net R6 257 billion at the end of 2012. This is up R941 billion or 14.9% relative to the end of 2011 and the highest ever recorded. If durable consumer goods (such as cars and furniture) are included, household wealth rises to R6 718 billion.

The gain in wealth during 2012 was relatively broad-based, although the largest improvement was in the value of the household sector's financial assets, including pension funds, unit trusts and other financial assets. The total value of financial assets rose by an impressive 17.2% (R823 billion) in 2012, and except for a decline of R236 billion in 2008, they have increased in value each year since 1994, recording a compound average annual increase of 11% over the past nineteen years.

Household net wealth, which is household assets less household debt, expressed as a ratio of disposable income (household income after tax) increased from a low of 292% in the first quarter of 2009 to 314% at the end of 2012 and 326% in mid-2013. The current ratio of wealth to income is well above the long-term average of 305%. This means that household wealth has risen faster than household income, indicating that the gain in wealth has easily outperformed the broader economy and that households have experienced a meaningful uplift in their financial well-being. The rise in wealth is even more impressive considering that disposable income has risen well above inflation for most of that time.

Globally, there is a broad but positive relationship between increases in household wealth and increased consumer activity. In South Africa, this relationship is fairly weak, with consumer spending much more dependent on changes in consumer income and employment conditions than on an increase in household wealth. This is partly because household wealth is extremely unevenly distributed.

According to Credit Suisse, to be among the wealthiest half of the world, an adult needs only $4 000 in assets, once debts have been subtracted. However, a person needs at least $75 000 to belong to the top 10% of global wealth holders, and $753 000 to be a member of the top 1%. The bottom half of the global population together possess less than 1% of global wealth. In sharp contrast, the richest 10% own 86% of the world's wealth, with the top 1% alone accounting for 46% of global assets. Together, North America and Europe represent more than 64% of world household wealth, but have less than 20% of the world's adult population.

South Africa's distribution of wealth is fairly similar to the distribution for the world as a whole, although as a proportion of the total adult population, it has fewer individuals with wealth above $100 000. Credit Suisse estimates that around 62 000 South Africans are included in the top 1% of wealthy individuals globally, and that around 43 000 South African adults are dollar millionaires. In total, the country accounts for only 0.25% of world household wealth, but has 0.67% of the world's adult population. This is aggravated by the fact that although South Africa's average level of household wealth per adult is $19 613, the median level of wealth per adult is a mere $3 051.

WHAT CAUSED SOUTH AFRICA'S HIGH LEVEL OF INEQUALITY?

The extremely high level of income and wealth inequality in South Africa cannot be blamed on one single factor, although it is clear that the legacy of the apartheid system, which denied non-whites (especially Africans) the chance to accumulate capital in any form, including land, education and finance, has played a very significant role. The impact of apartheid is still evident in the current level of income and wealth distribution, despite the advent of affirmative action and broad-based black economic empowerment. In fact, some recent studies have suggested that black economic empowerment has worsened the income divide in South Africa over the past twenty years, as only a relatively few individuals have benefited meaningfully from the initiative.

Importantly, the legacy of apartheid is not the only factor impacting the country's income distribution. Globally, income inequality rose sharply from the early 1980s to the early 2000s. The factors that caused this increase – in particular the impact of globalisation and increased wages paid to high-skilled workers – have also influenced South Africa's income distribution.

After 1994, under the guidance of Trevor Manuel as minister of trade and industry, South Africa embarked on an aggressive process of reducing its extremely high level of import protection that existed during most of the apartheid era. At the same time, China began to experience a rapid acceleration in economic activity, resulting in a dramatic increase in global trade. The combination of reduced trade restrictions and increased global trade meant that as the country internationalised its economy after 1994, an increasing number of less-skilled South African workers became extremely vulnerable to competition from abroad. So, as South Africa increased its demand for imported goods, especially basic consumer goods, including clothing and footwear, there was an effective widening of the income divide between low- and high-skilled workers.

Moreover, technological advances during the past twenty years have been biased in favour of those jobs requiring higher levels of education and training. Consequently, technological progress has affected household income distribution in two important ways. First, increased use of technology quickly became a substitute for low-skilled workers, leading to increased capital intensity in business. Second, many technology advances increased the need for high-skilled workers, which has effectively raised demand for and the relative wages of these workers.

This increased use of technology is also polarising the labour market by reducing the demand for middle-management skills. In other words, the demand for high-skilled workers who perform non-routine cog tasks (for example, engineers and lawyers) remains relatively high, a the demand for low-skilled workers who perform non-routine n tasks (for example, truck drivers and waiters). In contrast, the dem many medium-skilled workers who perform routine tasks (admini support and factory workers) is diminishing. This is because it is e replace these jobs with new technologies (for example, robotic ass

These technological changes have produced substantial earnin s among workers in the top income groups, while workers in the n brackets have also improved their earnings (partly with help from trade unions). Importantly, wage growth of the bottom- and top-income earners has exceeded that of workers in the middle of the earnings distribution.

WHY IS INEQUALITY A PROBLEM?

A certain level of income inequality is very beneficial to economic growth by rewarding risk taking, innovation, skills development and hard work. Without a sense of financial reward, many individuals would simply not be willing to undertake the effort required to move an economy forward.

However, the current level of income inequality in South Africa is far too high, leading to increased social instability, high levels of crime, labour market unrest and inefficiency. As inequality rises, people at the bottom of the income scale tend to borrow more in order to keep up, which in turn increases the risk of a credit crisis. It also impedes the progress of health and education (through a lack of available finance) and increases the chance of widespread civil unrest as people become more and more unhappy with their economic situation. Together these factors are having a detrimental effect on South Africa's business environment and investment potential.

A growing volume of research highlights the fact that inequality is bad not only for the poor, but also the rich. In general, recent studies have shown that richer people are happier and healthier if they live in more equal societies.

At the 2011 World Economic Forum in Davos, income inequality and corruption were singled out as the two most serious challenges facing the world. Zhu Min, a special adviser at the IMF, told delegates that 'the increase in inequality is the most serious challenge for the world ... I don't think the world is paying enough attention.' This certainly applies to South Africa.

Another important consequence of South Africa's uneven income distribution is that the tax base of the country is highly concentrated, with a relatively small share of the population paying the bulk of the taxes.

According to a recent report jointly published by the National Treasury and the South African Revenue Service, titled *2013 Tax Statistics*, there were 13.7 million individual taxpayers registered in the 2012 tax year. Of these 13.7 million individuals, only 5.881 million are liable to submit tax returns, and in total 5.108 million individual taxpayers were assessed. The assessed taxpayers recorded taxable income of R1.023 trillion and a tax liability of R206.7 billion.

Personal income tax represents roughly 34% of the country's total tax revenue, making it the single biggest component of the tax base. However, in the 2012 fiscal year, 2.181 million registered taxpayers contributed less than 2.25% of total personal income tax. In contrast, among the high-income earners, a mere 859 000 taxpayers paid 53% of the country's total personal income tax. This means that less than 5% of South Africa's labour force pays more than 50% of personal income tax.

Moreover, less than 1.75% of the country's entire population pays more than 50% of personal income tax, and clearly a substantial portion of VAT, excise duties, import duties and the fuel levy.

It is critical that South Africa expand its tax base through increased employment, and not through higher taxes, in order to meet the increasing demands of the country. High-income earners are already highly taxed when the incidence of tax is measured against the social benefits these earners receive from government. Without a broadening of the tax base through job creation, the government's debt level will tend to rise in relation to the size of the economy and public sector service delivery will tend to disappoint due to a lack of financial resources.

There is always the risk that in trying to meet vital social objectives, government either increases taxes to the point where they become a disincentive to work; takes on an excessive amount of debt, which will quickly become unsustainable; or endeavours to forcefully redistribute wealth, which will undermine confidence and investment.

HOW TO REDUCE INEQUALITY IN SOUTH AFRICA

Over the past twenty years the South African government has introduced a number of policies aimed at reducing income and wealth inequality and 'redressing the wrongs of the past'. These have included affirmative action, black economic empowerment, minimum wages, land restitution, worker-friendly labour legislation, unemployment insurance, a school nutrition programme, capital gains tax and the provision of almost 3 million low-cost houses. There has also been a significant expansion of no-fee schools, from 13 912 schools in 2007 to 20 688 schools in 2012, helping over 8.5 million learners afford an education.

While these policies have had some success in helping to broaden the middle class, they have not led to a meaningful reduction in income inequality, and instead have had some significant unintended consequences. In particular, the labour legislation has led to a relatively inflexible labour market and a general reluctance by business to expand employment. The labour legislation has proved especially onerous for small and start-up businesses.

Perhaps the most successful and vital income distribution policy has been the introduction and expansion of social grants. At the end of 2013, around 16.5 million people were eligible for social grants, up substantially from only 2.5 million in 1998. The number of people receiving social grants has expanded dramatically in recent years, mainly as a result of the systematic extension of the child-support grant to age 18. In addition, the eligible age for an old-age grant has been reduced from 65 to 60.

In number terms, most of the social grants are paid out in the form of child support (71% of the total number of grants). This is followed by old-age grants (18% of total). There has been a significant reduction in the number of disability-grant beneficiaries in recent years, largely as a result of an improved assessment process.

In value terms, the government spent more than R113 billion on social grants in 2013/14. This has risen by well in excess of inflation for almost fifteen years and now represents almost 10% of total government spending, more than 5.5% of household disposable income and a little more than 3% of GDP.

Sadly, the 16.5 million people that receive a grant represent almost a third of South Africa's entire population and exceed the number of people that have a job. Given that most people receiving a grant are unlikely to have much other income, this means that 33% of South Africa's population receive a mere 3% of the country's total annual income. That reflects extreme income inequality. The situation is even worse when one considers that there are many unemployed people that receive no assistance from government.

The rapid increase in social grant payments has led to a great deal of policy debate. The main negative argument is that the government is effectively paying people not to work and that social grants could act as a disincentive to work. However, the grant system remains relatively modest by world standards, and the amount paid out each month (the child-support grant is R300 per month, while the disability and old-age grants are each R1 260 per month) is extremely low relative to the poverty line. The poverty line is based on the amount of money required to afford the minimum food needed to survive as well as essential non-food items such as shelter.

The level of income inequality in South Africa would have been morally indefensible without the rapid growth in social grants. According to the World Bank, financial transfers from the national budget account for more than 70% of the income of the bottom 20% of the population (up from 15% in 1993 and 29% in 2000). Stated differently, without the social grants as part of income, 40% of the population would have seen their income decline in the first decade after apartheid.

In 1995 it was estimated that 48% of the population were living below the estimated poverty line. Since then the country's income per capita has risen steadily, there has been a sizeable increase in the number of middle-income households, and the roll-out of basic and social services has significantly improved the lives of millions of South Africans. Consequently, the number of people living below the poverty line has fallen meaningfully. A report titled *Poverty Trends in South Africa*, published by Stats SA in April 2014, argues that the percentage of the population living in 'extreme poverty' has declined from 26.6% in 2006 to 20.2% in 2011, and that there has been a 21% reduction in the levels of poverty among adults from 2006 to 2011. Unfortunately, measuring the exact reduction in poverty is difficult because South Africa does not have a single official measure of the poverty line that dates back to 1994. Nonetheless, the reduction in the proportion of the population living below the poverty line is closely linked to the massive increase in welfare payments.

Access to quality basic services, such as education, healthcare and essential infrastructure (like water and sanitation), provides an individual, irrespective of background, the opportunity to advance and reach his or her potential. In many developed countries, knowing that if you get sick you will receive adequate healthcare, regardless of your income, is one of the greatest benefits afforded the population. Knowing that if you lose your job there is a social safety net to help you and your family is key to tackling inequality. Similarly, access to good-quality education is critical in the fight against inequality.

Remarkably, despite numerous constraints, the government has made meaningful progress in addressing a number of key deficiencies in the provision of social goods and services. For example, in 1994/95 only 51% of all households in South Africa had direct access to electricity – a substantial deficiency. However, by 2011/12 the percentage had increased to 77%. This means that more than 5.5 million households have been electrified in the past twenty years, which is the equivalent to electrifying 23 000 houses a month.

In the early 1990s, South Africa had a very significant shortage of formal housing. The 1996 census reported that 1.5 million households were living in informal houses in urban areas, and a further 1.6 million households were living in informal/traditional housing in rural areas. In October 1994, the government had signed a National Housing Accord, in conjunction with the RDP, to deliver 1 million new houses in five years. The project quickly became known as RDP housing. Although the five-year target was not met, government was able to provide the 1 million houses in a period of seven years and has subsidised or built a total of 3.384 million houses since 1994/95. In addition, the government has announced further initiatives to assist with the funding of housing development, including a R1 billion guarantee for the granting of housing loans to people that earn less than the minimum required to qualify for a housing mortgage from the formal banking sector but who also earn more than the threshold to qualify for RDP housing.

The government's initiatives to improve living conditions have been supported by increased access to water and sanitation. The proportion of households with access to sanitation has risen from 50% in 1993/94 to 83% in 2011/13. This progress meant South Africa met the Millennium Development Goal of halving the proportion of people without sustainable access to improved sanitation in 2008, seven years before the 2015 global target. Moreover, the number of households with piped water, either inside their house or inside their yard, has increased from 5.47 million in 1996 to 10.6 million in 2011. This still represents only 73% of all households. However, the percentage of households with access to water (defined as a minimum of 25 litres of water per person per day within at least 200 metres of the household) has risen from 62% in 1993/94 to 96% in 2011/12.

These improvements in the provision of basic social goods and services are not the only successes government has achieved in lifting living conditions. For example, the government has also dramatically improved access to education. This does not mean that the socio-economic backlogs have been completely erased, or that there are no longer significant numbers of people struggling to survive, or even that most people are satisfied with the level of service delivery. Nevertheless, the South African government has made significant progress in attending to some principal areas of historical social neglect, especially given the country's financial constraints.

Fundamentally, public services such as education, healthcare and unemployment insurance are extremely expensive and require a large and growing tax base to make them affordable. Without employment growth, provision of these services is simply not sustainable. As the National Treasury highlighted in its 2013/14 national budget, 'state-funded services cannot fully meet either social and development challenges or all the needs of households and communities'. Economic growth, employment and rising wages are the main determinants of social progress and poverty reduction.

SCORING THE THIRD PUZZLE PIECE

In 1994, South Africa faced an enormous backlog of essential social goods and services. Within residential areas this included a shortage of formal housing, clean water, sanitation and electricity. Within the broader community there was a shortage of transport facilities, as well as access to education and healthcare.

The government had to try to balance the need to rapidly increase the provision of essential goods and services against the obligation to implement and maintain fiscal discipline. Ultimately, the compromise the government chose resulted in a respectable increase in a range of essential services, especially the electrification of homes, increased access to water, reduced levels of malnutrition, improved access to education and a dramatic rise in welfare payments.

Despite these successes, the government neglected a number of key areas of society. In particular, the crime rate escalated to alarming levels, with some international newspapers arguing that South Africa had become the 'murder capital of the world' in the mid-2000s. Since then various areas of crime have improved, but crime remains extremely high by global standards. The government also failed to respond promptly and effectively to the AIDS epidemic. In particular, the roll-out of awareness campaigns and ARV drugs was unnecessarily delayed, thereby exacerbating the epidemic.

Overall, this piece of the puzzle is assigned a subjective score of 2.5 out of 5, suggesting that although mistakes were made, there was also a great deal of progress in the provision of essential services, especially considering that the extent of the backlog in basic services was probably greater than most people anticipated in 1994.

8

THE MISSING PIECE OF SOUTH AFRICA'S ECONOMIC PUZZLE

OVERVIEW

The fourth and final piece of South Africa's economic puzzle, and the area of greatest concern, is the inadequate support and encouragement of the business sector. Expanding and strengthening the business sector requires a relatively wide range of support measures. These include the availability of skills, access to appropriate economic infrastructure (especially energy, road, rail, port and airport systems), the rule of law, a consistent policy framework and equal opportunity to compete for business. Unfortunately, some of the most critical ingredients needed to expand the business sector have been absent. These include a shortage of electricity capacity, ageing port and rail infrastructure, a rapid rise in the cost of logistics, a complex set of industry regulations that makes it increasingly difficult to do business, a lack of technical skills, and a relatively volatile labour market.

While it is extremely common for businesses around the world to encounter operational difficulties, the combination of factors negatively impacting South Africa's business sector has led to a general reluctance to expand and increase employment. Furthermore, initiatives to encourage new business ventures have struggled to gain momentum.

SOUTH AFRICA'S NEGLECT OF KEY INFRASTRUCTURE AND BUSINESS SUPPORT

An adequate and well-maintained infrastructure is critical to the growth and development of the country. This is reflected in the economic damage caused when there are electricity outages, a railway line used for exporting mineral products is damaged or there are delays in the loading or offloading of cargo ships. More importantly, deterioration in infrastructure tends to dent business confidence, leading to a general reluctance to expand. Of course, problems with inadequate infrastructure are compounded if at the same time an increase in regulation is making it more difficult to do business, the level of corruption is distorting the granting of contracts or the skills needed to get the job done are not available. All of this undermines the competitiveness of the country and ultimately the economy's ability to grow and provide the job opportunities the population desperately requires.

Shortcomings in the country's economic infrastructure have become a major constraint to economic growth and development. This applies in particular to road and rail transport services as well as the supply of electricity. For example, in January 2008, South Africa experienced a significant electricity supply crisis, resulting in widespread load-shedding. Since then, the inadequate level of electricity-generating capacity has been exacerbated by the fact that some power stations are approaching the end of their lifespan, resulting in substantial operational inefficiencies. This meant the country had to introduce a number of measures to deal with the electricity crisis, including the reduction of supply to electricity-intensive users such as mines and smelters. Yet there is a relatively high correlation between access to electricity, by both businesses and households, and economic growth, including the willingness of the business sector to expand production capacity.

Another example of South Africa's underdeveloped infrastructure is the fact that the demand for rail services easily exceeds the current supply. While the railway-track infrastructure does have the capacity to accommodate more trains, especially in the case of the general freight network, the shortage of rolling stock is the main constraint to greater utilisation of available infrastructure. This has constrained the country's ability to export but, together with the deregulation of the road transport industry, has also led to an increase in the use of road transport, which has subsequently weakened the road network due to over-utilisation. Unfortunately, South Africa has also underinvested in its road network, which is reflected by the fact that some 81% of the national road system is older than the original twenty-year design life. Consequently, many provincial and municipal roads are in very poor condition and are deteriorating exponentially.

The lack of rail investment has also meant that the infrastructure has not kept up with population growth and the rate of urbanisation. On the busiest corridors of the Passenger Rail Agency of South Africa – such as Khayelitsha to Cape Town, Soweto to Johannesburg, and Mabopane to Pretoria – maximum hourly capacity is in the region of 25 000 passengers per hour, whereas many modern mass-transit rail systems can carry 60 000 passengers per hour. This suggests that even if current infrastructure were fully restored, demand could not be met. The reason for this is that the original rail network was not designed for the current levels of line capacity, let alone the much higher passenger numbers that modern commuter rail systems in other countries achieve.

The maintenance of economic infrastructure in South Africa does not receive a high enough priority, thereby undermining the reliability of a wide range of public services. In some instances, the lack of infrastructure, or the lack of adequately maintained infrastructure, is due to insufficient funding for maintenance, or to tax revenue not being used for the intended purpose. In other instances, it reflects a lack of institutional capacity for maintenance, due to skills shortages or poor labour relations. In general, many municipalities lack capacity, skilled resources and funding to efficiently and effectively manage their infrastructure. Weak institutional capacity and the shortage of skills ultimately impact on planning capacity for infrastructure development, operation and maintenance.

Improperly maintained infrastructure can negatively impact the logistics in the economy, including the transport of passengers as well as goods. This leads to increased inefficiency and a fall-off in productivity, with vehicles stuck in the traffic for hours or passengers left stranded on railway platforms. Equally, old railway carriages and faulty signalling systems will negatively impact the reliability of rail freight. Goods are not able to reach their destinations at desired times, or customers may cancel orders due to costly delays, all of which impact negatively on the economy's ability to grow. Poor maintenance leads to acceleration in the degradation of the infrastructural asset, and if there is no investment in refurbishment, the infrastructure will ultimately reach a state of complete collapse.

In general, South Africa's lack of infrastructure development partly reflects government's emphasis on addressing basic needs rather than ensuring that the bulk infrastructure capacity is able to meet the increase in demand. This is highlighted by the Development Bank of Southern Africa's (DBSA) 2012 report titled *The State of South Africa's Economic Infrastructure: Opportunities and Challenges*. In the report, the DBSA states that 'given the imperative of addressing basic needs, the focus of the democratic government in the first fifteen years [of democracy] was to roll out social infrastructure. Consequently, the focus for the next ten years is to also redress economic infrastructure backlogs and inadequacies which have become a constraint to economic growth.' This decision to focus on 'access' infrastructure without a concomitant development of 'bulk' infrastructure is reflected in the fact that numerous houses have been electrified since 1994, but South Africa's fundamental shortage of electricity-generating capacity was completely overlooked. It is also reflected in the development of water services infrastructure without due consideration for the availability of water resources. Consequently, many water-treatment works have been operating at full capacity or beyond, and are now starting to collapse due to an increase in demand and a lack of maintenance and capacity. According to the DBSA, 'South Africa's infrastructure portfolio is not only ageing; there has also been significant deterioration as a result of insufficient maintenance and lack of ongoing capital renewal.'

South Africa's lack of infrastructural development is compounded by increasing levels of corruption. The International Corruption Perceptions Index is compiled by the Transparency International Institute, which is based in Berlin, and evaluates corruption in 177 countries. The survey was first published in 1995, using data sourced from independent institutions specialising in governance and business-climate analysis, and is updated once a year.

The corruption index is based on how corrupt the public sector is perceived to be. A country's score indicates the perceived level of corruption on a scale of 0 to 100, where 0 means that a country is perceived as highly corrupt and 100 means it is perceived as very clean. While no country has a perfect score, 69% of countries score below 50, including South Africa, indicating a serious corruption problem.

In 2013 South Africa was ranked as the 72nd most corrupt country in the world, with a score of only 42 out of 100. This is worse than South Africa's ranking of 69th in 2012, 64th in 2011 and 54th in 2010. Sub-Saharan Africa is still ranked as one of the most corrupt regions in the world, with 90% of the countries scoring below 50. The most corrupt countries in Africa are Zimbabwe, Burundi, Democratic Republic of the Congo, Nigeria, Chad, Sudan and Somalia. In 2013, Botswana ranked as the least corrupt country in sub-Saharan Africa. The least corrupt countries in the world include Denmark, New Zealand, Finland, Sweden, Norway, Singapore, Switzerland, the Netherlands, Australia and Canada.

Corruption destroys lives and communities, and undermines the development of countries and institutions. It generates popular anger that threatens to further destabilise societies and exacerbate violent conflicts. It leads to failure in the delivery of services such as housing, healthcare and other basic household services.

Rising levels of corruption, combined with increased and onerous levels of business regulation, exacerbate the normal difficulties businesses encounter on a daily basis. This applies especially to small- and medium-sized enterprises. Corruption also makes it far more difficult to start a new business.

Each year the International Finance Corporation, together with the World Bank, publishes an assessment of the ease of doing business around the world. In particular, the report highlights how easy or difficult it is for a local entrepreneur to open and run a small- to medium-sized business when complying with relevant regulations. The report provides a quantitative measure of ten indicators with the specific aim of measuring the regulation and red tape relevant to a business. The main goal of the report is to provide an objective basis for understanding and improving the regulatory environment for business. However, the analysis also provides a comparison and ranking of 189 countries, including South Africa, according to the ease of doing business.

In the *Doing Business 2014* report, South Africa was ranked 41st overall out of 189 countries. This is two places down from 39th position in 2013 and six places below the 2012 ranking of 35th. Unfortunately, South Africa's ranking has dropped steadily from 28th position in 2006.

More positively, the country ranks well in four of the ten indicators measured: 'protecting investors' (10 out of 189), 'paying taxes' (24 out of 189), 'dealing with construction permits' (26 out of 189) and 'getting credit' (28 out of 189). Unfortunately, these positives are more than offset by key areas of concern for business. Two indicators, in particular, are a serious hindrance to South African business – namely, 'getting electricity' (150 out of 189) and 'trading across borders' (106 out of 189). In terms of the ease of starting a business, South Africa is ranked only 64th in the world. In recent years, many economies around the world have actively taken steps to make it easier to start a business. This has included streamlining procedures by setting up a one-stop shop, making procedures simpler or faster by introducing technology, and reducing or eliminating minimum capital requirements. Many countries have undertaken business registration reforms in stages, and these reforms are often part of a larger regulatory reform programme.

The combination of poor infrastructure, rising levels of corruption, increasing difficulty in doing business or starting a business, and a range of other factors, such as skill shortages, poor productivity and variable industrial policies, has systematically reduced South Africa's competitiveness.

In the *Global Competitiveness Report 2013–2014*, compiled by the World Economic Forum, South Africa was ranked 53rd out of 148 countries. This ranking is down from 52nd in 2012/13 and 50th position the year before. In general, South Africa's global competitiveness ranking has declined steadily over the past few years. As recently as 2009/10, South Africa was ranked 45th, and 40th in 2005. In 2013, the top five places went to Switzerland, Singapore, Finland, Germany and the US. The key change at the top of the rankings in 2013 was that Germany moved up from 6th to 4th, while the US improved from 7th place to 5th place. Last place went to Chad. Interestingly, China's ranking remained unchanged at 29th.

The breakdown of South Africa's competitiveness ranking highlights the dichotomy of the economy. For example, South Africa ranks near the top of the global ratings in a number of important areas. These mostly relate to the development of the financial sector (ranked 3 out of 148 countries) and financial markets including the availability of financial services (2 out of 148), soundness of banks (3 out of 148) and regulation of securities exchanges (1 out of 148). There has also been a welcome improvement in quality of air transport infrastructure (11 out of 148) as well as the effectiveness of anti-monopoly policy (8 out of 148). In contrast, South Africa ranks last in cooperation in labour-employee relations and in the quality of maths and science education, and very poorly in quality of electricity supply (101 out of 148), hiring and firing practices (147 out of 148), pay and productivity (142 out of 148), and business costs of crime and violence (141 out of 148). Unfortunately, the rankings in various aspects of healthcare also remain poor.

These extremes reflect an economy that is able to compete with the best in the world in some sectors, but is ultimately held back by crucial factors, including an outdated rail transport system, a shortage of electricity, a depleted public sector healthcare system, insufficient technical skills and ongoing labour market inflexibility. The main risk for the South African economy is that the factors at the bottom of the ranking drag the other, better-ranked factors systematically lower.

SCORING THE FINAL PIECE OF THE PUZZLE

The development of the business sector is critical to the success of the South African economy. This is because, as the NDP highlights, a growing and vibrant business community is likely to create the jobs the country so desperately needs. Government cannot act as a sponge in the labour market, absorbing more and more workers. The tax base alone will not support such an endeavour.

However, private sector job creation requires that the business community is willing to invest either through starting new businesses or expanding existing businesses. This is simply because the level of investment determines the level of employment. In order to invest, many entrepreneurs need at least three critical components: a sufficiently skilled workforce, a consistent and transparent set of rules, and the necessary economic infrastructure needed to facilitate their business. Unfortunately, South Africa has neglected all three of these critical components. In particular, the economic infrastructure of the country has been allowed to age without undertaking the necessary maintenance or expansion. A good example is the fundamental shortage of electricity that has hampered business development for a number of years. The country has also not developed the appropriate supply and mix of skills required to compete internationally, such as mathematical skills. Lastly, industrial policy, including labour policy, has become incredibly complex and uncertain.

Over the past twenty years, the government has launched numerous growth strategies to help lift South Africa's economic performance and inspire job creation. Unfortunately, these have not always been consistent with previous strategies and have largely failed to be fully implemented.

All these shortcomings have led to deterioration in business confidence and a lack of expansionary investment and employment. Consequently, the final puzzle piece is assigned a subjective score of only 1 out of 5.

More positively, there are a number of promising infrastructural initiatives that, given the right economic policy environment, could encourage private sector investment. These include the development of additional electricity supply as well as the upgrading of rail and port capacity. It is critical that these and other developments are completed timeously. Overall, proper attention to business-sector development is necessary in order to avoid a serious negative feedback loop developing in which the already high level of unemployment further aggravates an already difficult social environment, leading to increased demands on the state, a further credit rating downgrade and a dearth of investor confidence.

PART III
SOLVING SOUTH AFRICA'S
ECONOMIC PUZZLE

INTRODUCTION

Looking back over the past twenty years, there is little doubt that the South African economy has made impressive progress in three of the four key building blocks needed to lift growth and employment, and to meet the aspirations of the population. Furthermore, in some instances the achievements have far exceeded what could realistically have been expected in 1994, especially in the areas of monetary and fiscal policy.

Unfortunately, the distinct lack of progress in developing the fourth piece of the puzzle has meant that South Africa's economic growth has ultimately been below expectations. Employment growth, in particular, has been staid. The economy had to move forward in all four key areas of policy to achieve the goals outlined in the 1996 GEAR strategy as well as subsequent growth initiatives. More importantly, this lack of development has now started to undermine the other three puzzle pieces, creating a negative feedback loop. If left unchecked, this can derail the South African economy, leading to increased unemployment, an outflow of foreign investment and rising social tension.

This negative feedback loop is evident in a number of sectors of the economy. For example, the shortage of electricity capacity has stunted private sector expansion; the neglect of water-treatment facilities is now undermining the delivery of water in many municipalities, leading to increased service-delivery protests; the ageing of the municipal road infrastructure is limiting domestic tourism, leading to increased frustration and declining confidence as well as a rise in road accidents; and the increase in business regulation is restricting small-business development and job creation. Unfortunately, this negative feedback loop is also starting to impact monetary and fiscal policy. For example, the rising level of corruption is hindering infrastructural development and undermining the efficacy of public sector spending. This increases the strain on government finances, which in turn persuades the credit-rating agencies to either downgrade South Africa or place the country on a negative credit watch. A lower credit rating accentuates the pressure on the rand exchange rate, which increases the risk of inflation, necessitating a rise in interest rates.

South Africa urgently needs to improve a number of microeconomic components of the economy. These include key aspects of the country's economic infrastructure, such as the lack of infrastructure maintenance within many municipalities, the shortage of critical technical skills, the over-regulation of business, the unacceptably high level of corruption, an overly complicated set of industrial policies and the need to more fully embrace technology in the development of the business sector.

In outlining the way forward, there is a tendency to set numerous economic and social goals that are to be achieved simultaneously through multiple policy initiatives across most sectors of the economy. While this type of strategy approach appears comprehensive, it also tends to be complex, unwieldy and largely unattainable. Under these circumstances, there is the risk that attention and resources are diverted away from alleviating the economy's most crucial constraints.

There is also a tendency to ignore the importance of sequencing or prioritising policy initiatives. For example, an appropriate port, rail and energy capacity is needed before a policy to expand industrial production can be successful. Furthermore, South Africa has limited skills, especially engineering and other technical skills. This suggests that crucial infrastructural projects need to be coordinated to make sure the resources are available when required and that vital projects are not unnecessarily delayed.

It seems sensible to narrow the number of policy objectives to a few key initiatives that can be successfully implemented and that are critical to stimulating business investment and job creation. These initiatives can be divided into realistic short-term goals and longer-term structural changes. This is the approach outlined in Chapters 9 and 10.

There is a risk that policy efforts are weakened by trying to address the symptoms and not the cause of South Africa's economic difficulties. At the heart of the country's economic underperformance, especially the lack of job creation, is policy uncertainty combined with poor levels of education, a deficiency of appropriate economic infrastructure and a lack of innovation.

9

SHORT-TERM IMPROVEMENTS

SIMPLIFY INDUSTRIAL POLICY

Since 1994, South Africa's industrial policy ambitions have included the promotion of labour-intensive industry, increased beneficiation or further processing of raw materials, growth in manufactured exports, development of small business, formulation of favourable trade agreements, an increase in competitiveness and an increase in employment.

However, despite these policy intentions, the reality is that the depth and breadth of the manufacturing sector has diminished since 1994, the country has become relatively more import-intensive and industrial production has become more capital-intensive. In addition, there has been little success in growing South Africa's manufactured exports, the unemployment rate has stayed exceedingly high, and the beneficiation of mineral products and the formation of small business remain underdeveloped.

One of the reasons for this lack of success in transforming industry is that over the past twenty years the country's industrial policy has gone through many iterations. These have included the launch of numerous policy documents, each with its own set of ambitious objectives supported by a multitude of financial incentives and lofty policy goals. Unfortunately, these variations have meant that South Africa's industrial policy has tended to lack consistency, which has led to a lack of acceptance and understanding. Many businesses struggle to fully understand the numerous policy initiatives, leading to relatively low awareness and limited uptake of the proposed industrial support measures.

Simply reading through a list of programmes that South Africa has initiated to support industry is daunting and relatively confusing. The language used is strikingly inaccessible, especially for many businesses unfamiliar with policy documents. There is also the challenge of trying to follow the various additions and deletions, as well as keeping track of which programmes have expired or have been substantially revamped.

Ironically, a basic analysis of the government's financial assistance programmes reveal that many of them have merit and could help to encourage industry as well as promote small- and medium-sized business. However, the programmes face a number of significant constraints. First, the schemes are not well publicised and awareness levels are extremely low. Second, many of the schemes are modified on a regular basis, or simply scrapped. This leads to confusion and increases the complexity of the support initiatives. Third, in trying to support small business, the agencies responsible for promoting small business have themselves changed, leading to a lack of consistency. And while there are a plethora of initiatives available to help small business, they appear to have had limited success.

One of government's more recent policy initiatives that has proved to be reasonably successful, albeit on a relatively small scale, is the Jobs Fund. The Jobs Fund was launched by President Zuma in his State of the Nation Address on 10 February 2011 and was established by the National Treasury in June 2011. It is administered by the DBSA and aims to 'support innovative approaches and initiatives that create employment'. The fund has a specific focus on addressing youth unemployment, although it is acknowledged that it cannot provide a long-term solution for this problem.

At the end of 2013, the National Treasury reported that the total value of job-creation projects approved by the Jobs Fund was R6.1 billion, with a target job creation of 143 914 new, permanent jobs over the next five years. In addition, approved projects are expected to place 55 989 individuals into existing vacant jobs by providing training and placement services. This is reasonable progress in a relatively short period, but it is clear that job creation can take time and probably costs more than most people anticipate.

INDUSTRY NEEDS CONSISTENCY

A consistent, relevant and well-articulated industrial policy that is easily understood by everyone is critical to South Africa's economic success.

Simply formulating or articulating a long list of policy objectives, no matter how desirable, dilutes the overall message, and potentially leads to conflicting or contradictory policies that are not fully embraced by business or labour. This means that to be effective, industrial policy needs to have a clear and relatively simple goal that is easily understood by business, labour and government, and one that is not regularly revised or altered depending on changes in the hierarchy of the DTI. It also needs to be a goal that can be easily and regularly measured, in order to instil confidence.

In the South African context, it is sometimes argued that industrial policy is inherently complex, and therefore defining an overarching goal that business can relate to is simply not possible. This is not the case. For example, the primary goal could be to increase exports, as measured by South Africa's annual trade data, or it could be to enhance the productivity and efficiency of business as measured by the country's annual competitiveness ranking. Both these goals would entail achieving many of the current objectives outlined by the DTI, but with a lot more focus and understanding.

Ideally, industrial policy should be a growth strategy and not a process to try to restructure industry. This is partly because governments are notoriously poor at selecting winning business sectors. For example, there is little benefit in government actively encouraging a particular industry to develop at the expense of an existing industry. Under these circumstances, the policy approach is simply switching one industry for another, with no real gain and no guarantee the new industry will survive. Instead, it would be more beneficial if the policy encouraged the development of all business sectors without choosing sides or favouring one industry over another. This does not argue against the validity of equity goals or other transformation objectives. However, these goals are probably best achieved through mechanisms that are specifically designed to efficiently attain the appropriate targets rather than through measures that force an existing industry to restructure.

MANUFACTURING IS IMPORTANT, BUT DON'T UNDERESTIMATE THE SERVICES SECTOR

Developing a strong manufacturing sector holds a number of advantages for South Africa, as it does for any economy. In general, manufacturing activity has strong forward and backward linkages with the rest of the economy, especially transport, finance and mining. A robust performance in the manufacturing sector can boost the rest of economy, including employment. In addition, the economies of scale in manufacturing can allow for robust growth in productivity and a higher return on capital invested, but also encourage innovation and an improved level of R&D. There is also the prospect that a vibrant domestic manufacturing base will lead to a systematic rise in exports, which is vital to sustain economic development.

In the South African context, growth in labour-intensive manufacturing is especially attractive, given the country's persistently high rate of unemployment. However, this typically requires a relatively high degree of labour market flexibility and an extremely productive workforce, which has been difficult to achieve in South Africa, given the regular strike activity and other labour market disruptions. Nevertheless, a sustained increase in manufacturing activity as well as in manufactured exports would be extremely beneficial to the country's economy.

Industrial support policies should not be confined to the manufacturing sector. Over the past twenty years, output and employment in South Africa's services sectors have strongly outperformed the production sectors, especially mining and manufacturing. In fact, the cumulative growth in services output from 1994 to 2013 was 108%, compared with only 64% for manufacturing and a shocking decline of 4% for mining.

The forward and backward linkages within the service economy are not inconsequential, including the impact on employment and income growth. This applies especially to various forms of transport and retail trade, including online retailing. Furthermore, the development of the communications and technology sectors can provide many start-up investment opportunities in areas of activity that have remained relatively underdeveloped in South Africa. This includes fixed, mobile, wireless and satellite telecommunications networks. Of particular importance is the widespread availability of broadband infrastructure at competitive prices.

The country has an especially weak presence in the production of high-technology products and limited areas of meaningful R&D, yet product innovation is critical to successful manufacturing in value-added products, as well as in the creation of new services. In total, South Africa spends much less than 1% of GDP on R&D, with many relatively large companies undertaking no R&D at all. In comparison, the developed economies spend an average of around 2.4% of GDP on R&D, with Denmark, Finland, Israel, Japan, Korea and Sweden all above 3% of GDP. Over the last decade, R&D intensity in the EU rose from 1.7% to 1.9% of GDP, in the US from 2.7% to 2.9% of GDP, and in Japan from 3% to 3.3% of GDP. In the same period, R&D intensity in China almost doubled, increasing from 0.9% to 1.8% of GDP. China's average annual real growth in R&D spending has been close to 20%, making it the world's second fastest R&D performer, surpassing Japan in recent years. It does appear that South Africa needs a much more comprehensive strategy for building technological competitiveness. This would include a closer link between universities, government research agencies, private sector research facilities and product innovation and development.

BUSINESS NEEDS TO ACCEPT SOME OF THE BLAME

In South Africa there still appears to be a relatively high degree of mistrust between business, government and labour. While industrial policy cannot guarantee the success of the business sector, a transparent and collaborative approach to the formation and implementation of industrial policy can help to build trust, and provide vital support in a highly competitive global environment.

In the South African context, many research initiatives have identified a lack of skills as one of the key constraints holding back new investment, including infrastructural development. However, this is not solely the responsibility of government. Private sector companies also have a responsibility to develop their own skills, either at a firm level or as a sector initiative. It is also somewhat naive for business to argue that they are uncompetitive simply because of a skills shortage, poor productivity or increased labour costs. There are many other factors that combine to determine a company's ability to compete, especially in the manufacturing sector, including the cost of raw materials, logistical costs (which have risen sharply in South Africa), the availability of appropriate economic infrastructure and the cost of capital.

Key factors that are sometimes overlooked in the competitiveness debate are the skills level, efficiency and cost of senior management as well as the distinct lack of product innovation. Many of the world's most successful companies are constantly innovating. This includes design enhancements of existing products and services, but also improvements in how the company interacts with its customers, and in how senior management treats its employees. There is a tendency in South Africa to generously reward senior management for a 'business as usual' approach. This tends to suppress innovation and competition, and ultimately leads to mediocrity and stagnation.

A successful industrial policy requires a number of ingredients: a clear and overarching goal that is relevant and easily understood by all participants in the economy; a policy approach that business trusts; regular interaction between business and government in order to evaluate and understand any changes in policy; and a high level of coordination across a range of government departments to provide the necessary support. This support includes vital economic infrastructure that is modern yet still affordable; an appropriate education system that can generate the array of skills, including technical skills, required to compete; and a focus on building a culture of innovation within the business sector.

INITIATE READY-TO-GO-PROJECTS

Over the past ten years, government has announced various initiatives to increase the level of infrastructural development. These initiatives have usually been articulated in the national budget, and are always a welcome component of the budgeting process. Unfortunately, while these plans have appeared extensive, covering most areas of public sector infrastructure, they have seldom differentiated between maintenance spending and capacity-building investment, which can be deceptive. In addition, many of these projects have either been delayed, are still in the early stages of planning or have been altered due to changes in budget priorities, leading to an under-utilisation of the public sector's capital expenditure budget and disappointment in the private sector. Over the years, this disappointment has to some extent become entrenched within the private sector. Correspondingly, the business sector is likely to first wait for infrastructure upgrades to be completed before initiating large investment projects that are dependent on the upgraded infrastructure for success. This applies especially to the provision of bulk electricity supply.

The key exception was the build-up to the Soccer World Cup in 2010. During this phase, government was able to delivery on a fairly wide range of investment projects, exceeding the rigorous demands of the Fédération Internationale de Football Association (FIFA). These investments included upgrading key airports, building and enhancing soccer stadiums, developing the necessary communications and media facilities, and improving public transport. The investments were highly visible, which substantially boosted business and consumer confidence. Consumer confidence moved from a low of –6 index points in the second quarter of 2008 to a high of 16 index points six months before the World Cup started in 2010.

In an effort to fast-track and boost confidence in South Africa's infrastructural development, the government could embrace the concept of 'ready-to-go' projects. These are relatively straightforward infrastructure-related projects that can start reasonably quickly (ideally within six to nine months), can be funded through existing budgets, will meet local infrastructure needs and can be completed within two years. Typically, these projects don't require extensive engineering design or a protracted environmental assessment. They are also likely to contribute to local economic development goals, encourage business and household confidence, and generate some increase in employment.

Obvious examples of ready-to-go projects include cleaning up litter and urban decay; improving storm-water drainage; repairing traffic lights; improving road signage; repairing broken water pipes, potholes and road barriers; enhancing refuse removal; upgrading emergency response services; improving the collection and recycling of scrap metal in order to reduce theft; further enhancing taxi services; and upgrading various forms of public transport. In addition, cities could consider unique initiatives that capture the imagination of the residents, such as free wireless Internet, car-free zones, open-air markets, dedicated bicycle lanes, adult education facilities, and so on.

MUNICIPALITIES CAN PLAY A VITAL ROLE

The initiative for support of ready-to-go projects should ideally be launched at a municipal level. South Africa has 8 large metropolitan municipalities (each has over 500 000 voters), 44 district municipalities and 226 local municipalities. Using the municipal structure increases the opportunity to broaden the scope of the initiative. Obviously, not all municipalities will be in a position to identify and launch these types of projects within the time frames outlined. However, such an approach would help the authorities recognise those municipalities that require additional assistance and guidance. More positively, it could also lead to healthy competition between those municipalities that are more dynamic, especially if the successes are publicised and the process is tracked and reported on regularly.

South Africa's unemployment rate varies quite considerably between provinces. For example, at the end of 2013, the national unemployment rate was measured at 24.1%. However, the unemployment rate in the Eastern Cape was at 27.8%, followed by North West at 27.3% and Mpumalanga at 27.2%. If discouraged work-seekers are included, the unemployment rate in the Eastern Cape jumps to a staggering 43.3%, and is well over 60% for people younger than 25 years old. This would suggest that key municipalities in the Eastern Cape, and elsewhere, could benefit enormously from targeted infrastructural developments, especially if they are linked to long-term initiatives to increase regional economic activity.

PROJECT SELECTION IS IMPORTANT

In selecting projects, the emphasis should be on those that facilitate business development or that have been identified by local residents as being crucial to their environment. There could also be an emphasis on fast-tracking projects that are already at an advanced stage of preparation or projects that have stalled due to changes in personnel. The focus is not solely on community development, but also on encouraging local business to expand and employ more workers. Boosting both household and business confidence on a sustained basis is critical to economic success.

Another important project guideline to consider is the value of imports required to undertake the project. While it is not always possible to rely exclusively on domestic supplies, the higher the local content the larger the multiplier effect in the domestic economy. Typically, capital invested in this type of stimulus programme generates economic activity to the value of 1.5 times or more per rand spent, potentially assisting a broad range of industries, such as building materials, steel production, construction, engineering, commercial transport equipment and logistics. That could provide a very welcome boost to economic growth in underperforming areas while at the time improving the country's base of capital stock. Ultimately, though, the greatest economic benefit and boost to confidence comes from completing the project on schedule, within budget and according to design specifications.

Ready-to-go projects are not a new initiative. Many countries have successfully utilised similar concepts to boost urban development or achieve predetermined objectives. In some instances, the ready-to-go projects have involved both the private and public sectors. In South Africa it seems clear that most development initiatives would benefit from increased use of private–public partnerships, but with final control and oversight remaining within the public sector. These partnerships could be utilised in almost every sector of the economy, with government identifying the projects and then contracting with the private sector to build and maintain the infrastructure. A very good example is the Renewable Energy Independent Power Producer Procurement Programme, which is soon to enter its fourth phase and has successfully built numerous solar- and wind-power plants to supplement South Africa's energy production. Other private–public partnerships that could be implemented fairly easily include water and waste-water treatment plants. It is important that all projects are independently verified and evaluated in order to reduce levels of corruption, as well as to ensure that projects are completed timeously and within budget. Ideally, the ready-to-go projects can ultimately be linked to and complemented by the longer-term development of South Africa's economic infrastructure.

ENCOURAGE SMALL BUSINESS

A diversified, confident and growing business sector is critical for economic success. This is because a vibrant business community is able to generate the employment and tax revenue needed to sustain the development of the economy. Boosting business confidence is the key to unlocking a country's potential. This includes the encouragement and support of new business ventures.

Internationally, there is a great deal of research that demonstrates how important small-business development is to the performance of the economy, especially job creation. This is partly because new companies create the majority of new jobs in the economy, while existing large companies tend to focus on increasing output but with a more modest increase in employment. This is due to a global tendency towards the increased use of technology in the workplace, as well as a focus within many large companies on constantly improving productivity in order to boost profitability.

Correspondingly, the development of South Africa's small-business sector is critical to the government's aim of increasing employment and sustainably lifting the country's economic growth rate. The NDP states that looking forward, 'small and expanding firms will become more prominent, and generate the majority of new jobs created'. This view, the NDP argues, is supported by the fact that '90% of jobs created between 1998 and 2005 were in micro, small and medium size firms'.

Unfortunately, there is little detailed information available on the size and performance of the South African small-business sector. In addition, much of the information that is available is somewhat dated. Nevertheless, the DTI estimated that in March 2007, there were 1.87 million enterprises, both big and small, listed in the Stats SA Integrated Business Register. This register covers only the formal economy and excludes sole proprietors and partnerships. Amazingly, only about 556 000 of the 1.87 million enterprises were regarded as economically active, and of these a total of 536 000 operated as small, medium or micro enterprises (SMME), up from 422 000 in 2004. Furthermore, in 2007, a breakdown of South Africa's business sector revealed that 36% were micro enterprises, 46% very small enterprises, 11% small enterprises and 4% medium enterprises; only 3% were large enterprises with more than 200 employees.

This data reveals how few large companies there are in South Africa, and indicates that the bulk of the business sector is comprised of mostly small businesses. However, large companies dominate South Africa's business activity. This is reflected in the fact that although there are hundreds of thousands of small businesses in South Africa, in 2007 they accounted for only around 27% to 34% of total GDP. Large enterprises, which equate to around 3% of all businesses, represent roughly 70% of the country's economic activity, excluding the public sector. Yet some estimates suggest that SMMEs are responsible for about 60% to 70% of all new jobs created annually in South Africa, including within the informal sector. Informal business ventures, although largely subsistence in nature, provide a safety net for many dependants that would otherwise not have any alternative source of income.

South Africa's small-business sector is plagued by a number of constraints. These include limited access to finance, high levels of crime and increased incidences of corruption, extensive and time-consuming regulation, high cost of transport and energy, regular 'dumping' of goods in the country by foreign suppliers and a shortage of technical skills. In addition, most policy negotiations are conducted between government, organised labour and big business. Small business is largely excluded from the policy debates. The result is that small business simply has to accept and comply with onerous industry-wide agreements. These include aspects of South Africa's labour legislation, which have become a major hindrance to job creation. In many instances the agreements reached are seldom beneficial to small business and add substantially to the cost of doing business, yet small-business development is critical to job creation.

The 2012 Global Entrepreneurship Monitor (GEM) report on South Africa highlighted that although there is sufficient finance available in the country, 'the available finance (from both the public and private sector) is not made easily accessible for new and growing firms, and that which is available comes at very high costs'.

The World Bank and International Finance Corporation (IFC) report titled *Doing Business 2014: Understanding Regulations for Small and Medium-Size Enterprises* assesses regulations affecting domestic companies in 189 economies. The document ranks economies in regulations affecting ten areas of business. These include aspects such as starting a business, getting electricity, registering property, getting credit, protecting investors, paying taxes and enforcing contracts. The 2014 report is the 11th edition of the *Doing Business* series.

As noted earlier, the *Doing Business 2014* report ranked South Africa 41st in the world in terms of the overall ease of doing business. This is two places down from 39th position in 2013 and six places below the 2012 ranking of 35th. Unfortunately, the country's ranking has dropped steadily from 28th position in 2006. The top five economies in 2014, in descending order, were Singapore, Hong Kong, New Zealand, the US and Denmark.

A breakdown of South Africa's ranking reveals a number of areas of weakness, including the ease of 'starting a business', which is ranked only 64th out of 189 countries; 'enforcing contracts', which has a rank of

80th; 'resolving insolvency', ranked 82nd; registering property, ranked 99th; 'trading across borders', ranked 106th; and 'getting electricity', ranked 150th. More positively, 'getting credit' is ranked 28th, 'paying taxes' is ranked 24th and 'protecting investors' has an impressive ranking of 10th.

A broader analysis of the *Doing Business* report reveals that over the past few years many countries have recognised that there is a need to reduce the level of bureaucracy encountered by the business community, and that simplifying the process of doing business helps to encourage business development. Unfortunately, most of South Africa's competitors have made more progress in their efforts to encourage business, and consequently the country's overall global ranking has fallen.

Another important insight from the *Doing Business* report is that the economies that are ranked the highest in the survey are not those countries with no regulation. Instead, those governments that have managed to create a regulatory system that protects public interests without unnecessarily hindering the development of the private sector have the highest ranking. There is also no evidence to suggest that countries that rate highly in the *Doing Business* survey tend to have a 'smaller government' philosophy. Instead, the data suggests that it is generally the bigger governments that are able to promote business more efficiently. This is because larger governments are able to play a more constructive role in developing the private sector through the establishing and enforcing of rules. It is the enforcing of rules in a consistent manner that clarifies key issues and reduces the cost of resolving disputes. This process also tends to increase the predictability of doing business, providing participants with a high degree of protection against abuse or misconduct. Without good rules that are consistently applied, entrepreneurs have a hard time growing their business, especially small- and medium-sized firms.

However, it is critical that the culture adopted in enforcing rules is one that looks to encourage, nurture and educate business rather than a culture of enforcement that makes businesses feel they are the enemy. Stated differently, the authorities need to facilitate business development rather than police business development.

Currently, small-business owners in South Africa are trying to survive in an environment that is not especially conducive to entrepreneurship. This environment tends to inhibit people from venturing into business or from taking calculated risks in expanding their existing business. Furthermore, many individuals who do start a business do so out of necessity and not because it is a particular passion or calling.

Given these circumstances, it is not surprising that South Africa has a very high rate of business failure. It is estimated that 40% of all new businesses in the country fail in their first year, 60% in the second year and 90% within the first ten years. This poor survival rate is confirmed by the 2012 GEM report, which highlights that the survival rate for local start-up businesses in South Africa is low by global standards. It is also no surprise that the GEM report suggests that entrepreneurial 'capacity' is one of the most underdeveloped areas in the South African entrepreneurial landscape. In particular, business owners require four skills to be successful: technical knowledge, an understanding of business operations, management ability and interpersonal skills.

EFFORTS TO ENCOURAGE SMALL BUSINESS

Since 1994 the South African government has introduced various initiatives to support the SMME sector. These have included efforts to reduce the tax rates and tax-compliance burden for small enterprises, set up dedicated credit facilities, establish agencies to provide support, and diversify public sector procurement towards small business. While these initiatives are welcome and are not without merit, they remain relatively modest.

A key set of factors inhibiting the promotion of small business in South Africa has been the fact that policy formulation has been fragmented, support measures have been frequently revised, government agencies have varied and initiatives have been very poorly promoted. This means that although many government support programmes have the potential to provide valuable assistance, they have not reached the small-business sector effectively. Fortunately, in 2012 the various national small-business finance agencies were consolidated into the Small Enterprise Financing Agency (SEFA), while the Small Enterprise Development Agency (SEDA) provides business-related information, advice, consultancy, training and mentoring services to small business. Hopefully, this will result in a consistent set of measures to support the small-business sector.

It is especially encouraging that the Tax Review Committee appointed by the minister of finance in July 2013 investigated the impact of the tax system on SMMEs and made some recommendations to encourage the promotion of small business. This includes tax relief to organisations involved in small-enterprise development. In addition, according to the 2014 national budget, the 'government aims to create an environment that supports both informal traders and entrepreneurs who seek to develop small businesses into larger enterprises. Policies are designed to promote the development of basic entrepreneurial skills and facilitate a greater degree of self-determination for those lacking formal opportunities. Red tape and bureaucracy are hindrances to doing business, especially for small- and medium-sized firms. Government aims to streamline the regulatory regime.'

INNOVATION IS NEEDED

The successful promotion of small business probably requires three broad strategies. The first is the systematic development of an entrepreneurial culture that demystifies starting a business, but also explains the accompanying responsibility, risks and rewards. Developing this culture could include the use of institutions such as schools, universities and research facilities, but also the promotion of small business in the media, the participation of international organisations and the use of competitions. Interestingly, the 2012 GEM report concluded that 'South Africa's culture does not make entrepreneurship a highly desirable career choice', but that education in general, and more specifically entrepreneurship education, can change the culture.

Encouragingly, SEDA successfully ran a business plan competition during 2011/12. The competition encouraged over 5 500 aspiring and existing entrepreneurs to submit their business plans. Hopefully this type of encouragement will be augmented by a broad range of relatively high-profile initiatives that inspire young people to consider starting their own business.

The second strategy is to make it as easy as possible to do business. This requires thoughtful regulation that does not overburden the business owner, a simpler system of taxation, efficient and cost-effective infrastructure, leniency in complying with industry-wide agreements, as well as cheaper and faster access to the Internet.

The Internet plays a unique role in the small-business environment as it potentially allows many companies direct access to a very broad base of consumers at a fraction of the cost of more traditional forms of marketing. It also allows small businesses to compete directly with larger, more established businesses, since an effective Internet strategy is not dependent on the size of the business.

Many business owners highlight South Africa's complex labour legislation and the relatively hostile labour market as key obstacles to expanding their business. The 2012 GEM report stressed that the country rates among the worst in the world in terms of labour market efficiency. South Africa's dismissal requirements are expensive and inflexible, constraints which small business cannot afford. Labour market inefficiency, together with uncompetitive minimum wages, centralised collective bargaining and unnecessary bureaucracy, significantly hinder a business's chances of survival and growth. While some of the points highlighted by the GEM report might be exaggerated, especially the level of minimum wages given South Africa's high cost of living, labour market regulation and the hostile labour environment clearly discourage many small businesses from expanding their level of employment.

Most importantly, the authorities need to recognise that government institutions are not there merely to enforce regulations, but rather to enable and assist business development within the confines of the law.

The third strategy is to provide avenues of support corresponding to the stage of business development and to ensure that small-business owners are aware of these programmes. The 2012 GEM report indicated that 'where government programmes are concerned, the majority of entrepreneurs in numerous surveys have stated that they are not aware of any programmes'.

During the early stages of starting a business, many aspirant entrepreneurs might need help transforming a good idea into a product or service. This could include guidance on formulating a solid business model, developing a business plan or marketing strategy, as well as starting to establish a network of possible suppliers and sources of finance. It may also entail assistance in registering a business.

Once the business starts to operate, the entrepreneur might need help building a client base and securing financing to cover start-up costs and expansion. Unfortunately, most small businesses in South Africa don't move much beyond this stage of development, and are largely regarded as subsistence enterprises that struggle to survive from month to month.

The third stage of business development is the critical phase for sustainable business success, and includes developing a product or service that has a niche in the market and a growing customer base. As the company grows, the entrepreneur needs to be able to delegate authority to managers to handle more staff and increased production. Funding for expansion is likely to become far more challenging and regulation more demanding. It is this phase of development that has the potential to substantially boost economic growth and employment.

The support offered by government needs to be tailored to provide the level of expertise the business venture requires at the time. Initially, support could simply be to help the entrepreneur examine the feasibility of a business idea and provide the resources to register the business. The second stage should focus on trying to ensure that the business survives. This may include mentoring and assistance in improving the business plan or building a local customer base. The third stage requires targeted assistance in expanding the business into markets across the country, accessing opportunities to network with the broader business community, understanding financing opportunities, and keeping abreast of new legal and regulatory changes.

Once the business has reached the third stage of development, it would be useful to introduce a broader range of finance options beyond the array of financial support offered by SEFA. This could include equity finance in terms of a venture capital initiative funded and administered by the private sector, but dedicated exclusively to assisting small but fast-growing businesses. Alternatively, a loan finance initiative could be offered that is jointly funded by the public and private sectors, but is administered by the private sector with the exclusive goal of developing small business as determined by the DTI. This initiative could also try to radically simplify and speed up the process of granting finance. There is still a tendency to over-complicate this process. Furthermore, instead of basing the qualifying criteria for financing entrepreneurs on maximising profits, the focus could be on harnessing inherent entrepreneurial talent.

The success of this loan finance initiative would be determined by the growth in the companies funded rather than the return on capital invested. This would require big business to voluntarily provide funding with no specific return objective, although they could claim a tax benefit. In addition, the funding could also contribute towards the company's transformation score. Ultimately, however, a growing business sector is to the benefit of all companies since each new business would be adding employment as well as purchasing goods and services from other businesses. This would certainly help with establishing a culture of entrepreneurship.

Entrepreneurial activity should be regarded as one of South Africa's major economic strengths. Unfortunately, the data and surveys suggest that the country is neglecting this opportunity. According to the 2012 GEM report, only 2.3% of South African adults (aged 18 to 64) are currently owner-managers of an established business that has been operating for more than forty-two months. This is well below the percentage recorded in most other emerging economies, including Thailand (30%), Nigeria (16%), Brazil (15%), South Korea (10%), Malaysia (9%) and Chile (8%). It would appear that 'not enough is being done to enable the discovery, creation and exploitation of business opportunities in the marketplace'. This is partly because the 'education system is not effectively developing individuals with the skills and confidence required to consider entrepreneurship as a valid career'. Helping to develop a vibrant small business sector is not a quick and easy option. It takes time, money and perseverance, with many failures along the way. But the rewards – in terms of increased employment, reduced social tension, an uplift in consumer and business confidence, and higher tax revenue – are well worth the effort.

THE INTERNET CAN BOOST ECONOMIC GROWTH

Advancements in technology, if utilised correctly, tend to boost economic activity. This includes the development of the Internet and associated services and applications. Unfortunately, South Africa's connection speed is well below the global average, and has significantly underperformed that of many African countries in the past five years. Recent international research as well as South Africa's own Planning Commission supports the view that access to the Internet can boost job creation, business development and competitiveness. This includes small-business development in particular. While most policy documents envisage South Africa making greater use of information and communications technology (ICT) services to boost economic activity, there is very little specific detail on how this is going to be achieved.

GLOBAL ACCESS TO THE INTERNET ON THE RISE

The Internet has had a profound impact on households, businesses and government, and on the way in which the global economy functions. It has changed the way we shop, work, source inputs, collect and transfer information, communicate, educate, think and meet people.

Since the year 2000, Internet access has risen by more than 600%, to an estimated 2.7 billion users, or almost 40% of the world's population. Internet access is expanding by roughly 200 million new users a year. In some parts of the world, Internet penetration is already extremely high. This is especially evident in North America and Japan, where an estimated 80% of the population has access to the Internet. Europe is not that far behind, with an Internet penetration ratio of around 75%. Some countries within Europe have a penetration rate of over 90%, including Norway (95%), Sweden (94%), the Netherlands (93%), Denmark (93%) and Finland (91%). In contrast, only 16% of individuals in Africa have access to the Internet, although Nigeria's penetration ratio is 33% and Kenya's is 32%.

South Africa's Internet access has grown rapidly from a mere 8.5% of the total population in 2008 to an impressive 41% in 2012. This explosive growth is largely due to adoption of mobile broadband technology and the advent of smartphones. Unfortunately, fixed-line (wired) Internet access remains extremely limited in South Africa, and is effectively still a niche industry rather than a standard feature in most homes.

Globally, there is a significant performance and cost difference between fixed-line (wired) and cellular (wireless) Internet access. For example, in 2013 the average fixed-line Internet speed in South Africa was around 170% faster than the average mobile (wireless) connection, and also significantly cheaper.

The faster the Internet connection, the more useful it becomes. The scope and complexity of tasks that can be performed over the Internet increases dramatically as the speed of connection rises. This includes the transfer and download of data, the ability of institutions and organisations to collaborate on research projects, and the effectiveness of remote education (including real-time teaching and library access). There are also a growing range of business services, including entertainment, design, weather, transport and healthcare, that require a relatively fast Internet connection to be effective.

While the growth in South Africa's access to mobile Internet is very encouraging, the usefulness of the service is limited by the speed and consistency of access. The current speed of mobile Internet in the country is sufficient to allow for the growth in social media, but is not really satisfactory to facilitate the growth of numerous potential business applications. Additionally, the cost of mobile Internet access remains relatively expensive.

GLOBAL INTERNET SPEEDS CONTINUE TO INCREASE

Globally, the speed of access to the Internet has grown dramatically over the past decade, and it continues to increase. The global average fixed-line peak Internet connection speed was recorded at 18.4 megabits per second (Mbps) in the beginning of 2013, up an impressive 36% over the past year.

In the US, the average peak connection speed was 36.6 Mbps in the first three months of 2013, up 27% over the previous year. The latest speed rating in the US is more than 200% faster than the speed recorded at the end of 2007.

Remarkably, Hong Kong achieved an average fixed-line peak connection speed of 63.6 Mbps in early 2013, which is the fastest in the world. Although some high-end users in Hong Kong have access to mind-boggling speeds of 500 Mbps, 2012 marks the first year that a country's average peak connection speed exceeded 50 Mbps. Japan also reached an average peak connection speed of 50 Mbps in early 2013, making it only the second country in the world to reach that threshold.

South Africa's fixed-line Internet system achieved a very modest and disappointing average peak connection speed of only 7.6 Mbps in the first few months of 2013. While South Africa's connection speed has increased by an impressive 25% over the past year, the country is ranked as having only the 25th fastest average peak connection speed in Africa, and the 126th fastest Internet in the world. Within Africa, countries with relatively fast average peak connection speeds include Ghana (21.3 Mbps), Morocco (16.6 Mbps), Seychelles (10.7 Mbps) and Nigeria (9.7 Mbps).

Unfortunately, very few people in South Africa have access to high-speed Internet. Currently, broadband fixed-line Internet is classified as a connection speed in excess of 4 Mbps. On this basis, only 8% of South Africa's population has a broadband Internet connection, placing

South Africa 69th in the world. This low ranking appears to be due to a combination of outdated telecommunications infrastructure and the high cost of connection.

Given the rapid growth in global Internet speeds, a further classification of speed has evolved, namely 'high-speed broadband'. High-speed broadband is currently regarded as a fixed-line connection in excess of 10 Mbps. Only 1.5% of South Africa's population has this speed of Internet connection. This compares with 50% in South Korea, 43% in Japan, 34% in Hong Kong and 25% in the US.

Understandably, average Internet speeds are significantly slower than peak speeds. During the first few months of 2013, South Africa's average fixed-line Internet speed was only 2.1 Mbps. In practice, this means the average fixed-line Internet user will struggle to access many of the Internet's value-add services that have been developed in the past few years and that continue to expand at an extremely rapid pace.

SOUTH AFRICA HAS EMBRACED CELLULAR TECHNOLOGY

Data released in 2013 by the International Telecommunications Union estimates that the global number of mobile-cellular users has increased to a staggering 6.83 billion in 2013, up from only 2.2 billion eight years ago. This means that worldwide, the number of mobile-cellular users is almost equivalent to the global population, which was estimated at 7.2 billion in 2013.

As the global mobile-cellular penetration rate approaches 100%, when market saturation will be reached, growth rates have fallen off measurably in both developed and developing countries. For example, the annual growth rate in the number of mobile-cellular users worldwide is currently around 5.4%, down dramatically from around 25% growth eight years ago.

Globally, the mobile-cellular penetration rate is estimated at 95%, with 128% penetration in developed countries, where it is relatively common for people to have more than one mobile subscription, and 89% in developing countries. In Africa the penetration percentage is 63%, making it the region of the world with the lowest cellular penetration. South Africa's cellular penetration rate is up at an amazing 135%, compared with 17% in 2000. This means the number of cellular users in South Africa has grown by an annual average of around 20% over the past thirteen years, but the market is considered relatively saturated, with almost every adult now having a cellphone.

The current boom in the telecommunications industry is the adoption of mobile broadband technology, which is effectively a high-speed cellular connection that allows for greater use of data services. Worldwide, the number of mobile broadband users has increased from 268 million in 2007 to 2.1 billion in 2013. This reflects an average annual growth rate of 40%, making mobile broadband the most dynamic part of the telecommunications market. In developing countries, the number of mobile broadband users more than doubled between 2011 and 2013 (from 472 million to 1.16 billion) and surpassed those in developed countries in early 2013.

Interestingly, Africa has experienced the highest growth rate in mobile broadband over the past three years, with the penetration rate rising from only 2% in 2010 to 11% in 2013. Unfortunately, for those in many African countries a high-speed mobile broadband connection remains largely unaffordable.

ACCESS TO THE INTERNET CAN BOOST ECONOMIC PERFORMANCE

An accepted economic principle is that advancements in technology, which facilitate the development and adoption of new ideas, tend to boost economies. This principle became evident following the introduction of various types of public infrastructure, including telephones. However, while the telephone infrastructure has more of a coordination function that improves productivity, the development of high-speed Internet accelerates the distribution of ideas and information, encouraging the development of new products, business processes, entrepreneurship and job matching. Simply stated, the development of high-speed Internet boosts the innovative capacity of a country, which is good for growth and development.

Over the past few years, a number of international research reports have investigated the effect of the Internet on economic growth. In general, these reports have concluded that access to the Internet plays a positive and significant role in stimulating economic activity.

Three pieces of research are worth highlighting. The first was undertaken in 2009 by the Department of Economics at Myongji

University, South Korea, using panel data from numerous countries between 1991 and 2000. The second was also compiled in 2009, by the Ifo Institute for Economic Research at the University of Munich, Germany, using data from 25 Organisation for Economic Co-operation and Development (OECD) countries between 1996 and 2007. Lastly, in 2011 the McKinsey Global Institute researched the Internet's impact on growth, jobs and prosperity, focusing on thirteen countries that account for more than 70% of global GDP.

The 2009 University of Munich research into the relationship between access to broadband Internet and economic growth reached two very important conclusions. First, after introducing broadband Internet, countries achieved 2.7% to 3.9% higher GDP per person. Second, every 10% increase in broadband Internet penetration brings a 0.9% to 1.5% increase in the growth of GDP per person.

The McKinsey report is equally impressive in its conclusions, highlighting that the Internet has been a major driver of economic growth in many major economies. Remarkably, in the thirteen countries selected by McKinsey, the Internet has contributed 10% of their growth over the past fifteen years, and 21% of their growth in the past five years. Consequently, the Internet now represents 3.4% of GDP in the thirteen countries selected. Around 53% of this contribution to GDP is in the form of consumer spending (on-line retailing), while private investment in Internet-related technologies and the use of the Internet to facilitate foreign trade accounts for an impressive 31%, with the public sector accounting for the remaining 16%. This means that in these countries the Internet has a greater share of GDP than the agriculture, utilities, communication, education or mining sectors.

As would be expected, the economic impact of the Internet varies widely, even among countries at the same stage of development. For example, the Internet represents around 6.4% of GDP in Sweden and 5.4% of GDP in the UK, but only 3.1% in France and 2.7% in Canada. Within the BRICS, the role of the Internet is much smaller than in the developed world, especially Brazil (1.5% of GDP), Russia (0.8% of GDP) and South Africa (0.3% of GDP). Interestingly, within China (2.6% of GDP) and India (3.2% of GDP), the facilitation of foreign trade comprises between one-third and one-half of the Internet's contribution to GDP.

At a more micro level, McKinsey surveyed more than 4 800 small/ medium enterprises and other entrepreneurial activities, and found that those companies utilising the Internet grew more than twice as fast as those with a minimal Internet presence. This applies across all sectors of the economy, including manufacturing. Furthermore, Internet-friendly companies created more than twice the number of jobs as companies that don't make use of the Internet. While some jobs have been lost by the growth of the Internet, many more have been created, including jobs directly linked to the development of the Internet, such as software engineers and online marketers, but also more traditional jobs such as logistics to deliver online purchases.

SOUTH AFRICA CAN USE THE TELECOMMUNICATIONS INDUSTRY TO ENCOURAGE SMALL BUSINESS

It is clear from the prevailing global research that South Africa has fallen well behind in the development and use of information and communications technology and is missing out on a major opportunity to grow the economy. This is highlighted by the country's low level of high-speed Internet penetration relative to many emerging economies and most developed economies. Building an extensive broadband capability would provide many small businesses with a more effective way of competing with larger and more established businesses. This is because an effective and dynamic presence on the Internet is dependent not on the size of the company, but rather on the creative flair of the web designer and the imagination of the business leaders. The development of the Internet could also create many direct and indirect job opportunities for the youth, as well as provide numerous emerging entrepreneurs with a platform to launch new business initiatives.

A substantial increase in the Internet penetration rate over the next couple of years, especially high-speed fixed-line Internet access, has the potential to raise the country's average growth rate by roughly 1% a year. This is very meaningful in the South African context, and would tend to boost the communication, logistics, information technology and retail sectors. It would also promote a larger uptake of youth employment and encourage related skills training and development.

The 2011 NDP highlights the importance of the ICT sector to the growth and development of South Africa. In broad terms, the

NDP suggests that 'ICT can be used to fight poverty, [and] increase employment, education and entrepreneurship' and that 'a country that seeks to be globally competitive must have an effective ICT system'. It also points out that the link between ICT development and economic growth takes effect only when the country reaches a certain critical mass in the penetration of cellular services (40% penetration is regarded by the World Bank as a sufficient critical mass in cellular communication to positively influence the broader economy) and access to Internet services (20% is regarded as a sufficient critical mass).

Unfortunately, the last full policy review of the ICT sector in South Africa was completed in 1995. That is shocking given the extensive advancements in telecommunications technology, products and services. Consequently, it is no surprise that the sector struggles with a number of constraints, including a lack of skills, extensive and restrictive regulation, lack of private sector competition, lack of affordability and a general lack of policy direction.

The NDP envisages that there will be 100% broadband penetration in South Africa by the year 2020. That is a laudable target, although the NDP appears to focus on the advancement of mobile broadband and not high-speed fixed-line access. Also of concern is that the NDP lacks meaningful detail on how the improvements in ICT usage will be achieved. Simply stating that South Africa should regain its position as the leader, in both quality and cost, of ICT services in Africa is not nearly sufficient to achieve the target.

Given the potential uplift to small-business development, employment and growth, a detailed timeline and set of measures to significantly boost the role of the Internet and the broader ICT sector is urgently required.

10
LONGER-TERM SOLUTIONS

SKILLS DEVELOPMENT IS CRITICAL

Over the past twenty years, the South African government's spending on education as a percentage of the national budget has ranged from a low of 17.7% in 2009/10 to a high of around 22% in 1996/97. This roughly equates to between 5% and 7% of the country's GDP, which means education spending has increased in line with economic growth. The size of South Africa's education budget compares very favourably with that of other emerging economies. For example, in 2012 Brazil spent 18.1% of its budget on education, Peru 18.1%, Chile 17.8%, Botswana 16.2%, Indonesia 15.2%, the Philippines 15%, Russia 11.9% and India 10.5%.

Access to education has also increased meaningfully over the past twenty years. For example, in 1996 only 49.1% of South African children aged six were enrolled in school, while 73.1% of children aged seven attended school. In 2011 this had increased to 92.7% for children aged six and an impressive 96.1% for children aged seven. It would appear that these percentages have increased further since 2011, suggesting that the country is approaching a position were almost all children are able to enrol in an education facility at a relatively young age.

A number of factors have combined to improve the level of school attendance in South Africa, including an effective reduction in the tuition fees paid by many families. For example, the percentage of children paying no school fees has increased from a mere 0.8% in 2002 to an impressive 56.2% in 2012. It is morally unacceptable to exclude a child from obtaining a basic education simply because his or her parents are poor. The improvement in the affordability of education has mostly occurred since 2007, despite a reduction in the number of public schools, which has dropped from 26 644 in the late 1990s to 24 282 in 2012. In contrast, the number of independent schools has increased significantly, from 817 in the late 1990s to 1 544 in 2012.

Unfortunately, despite a significant increase in access to education facilities and the improved subsidisation of school education, South Africa is not achieving the type of educational outcomes that would be commensurate with the amount of money spent, especially within the school system.

THE SCHOOL DROP-OUT RATIO IS FRIGHTENING

In 2002, a total of 1 286 591 children started Grade 1 in South Africa. Twelve years later, in 2013, only 562 112 wrote matric and a mere 439 779 passed matric. While this represents a Grade 12 pass rate of 78.2%, which is up significantly from a low of 60.9% in 2009, it means that only 43.7% of the total number of children that started school actually wrote matric and a mere 34.2% passed Grade 12. The minister of education has argued that this calculation is misleading because a large number of children drop out of school during Grade 1 for a variety of reasons, but then enrol later. Adjusting for this objection, in 2003 a total 1 087 933 children started Grade 2, which is 198 658 (or 15.4%) less than the number of children that enrolled for Grade 1 in 2012. Despite this adjustment, it still means that only 51.7% of children in Grade 2 during 2003 wrote the Grade 12 year-end exams eleven years later, and only 40.4% of these children matriculated. This is a truly shocking outcome.

More disturbing, however, is the fact that only 241 509 students (22.2% of the total number of students that enrolled in Grade 2 eleven years previously) wrote the Grade 12 final mathematics exam. Furthermore, only 142 666 students (13.1% of Grade 2 enrolment) obtained more than 30% for mathematics, a mere 97 790 pupils (9% of Grade 2 enrolment) obtained more than 40%, and a paltry 19 802 received more than 70% (1.8% of Grade 2 enrolment). While the number of schoolchildren passing mathematics has actually increased in recent years, the pass rate as well as the number of students studying mathematics is still extremely low by international standards, and is well below the level required for the country to develop its economy and compete internationally.

It is also troubling that a very small percentage of students (15.8%) who enrolled in Grade 2 eleven years previously obtained a bachelor's pass, which effectively means they can attend university. More positively, the annual bachelor pass rate has risen steadily from 18% in 1994 to 30.6% in 2013. In addition, the percentage of students who obtained more than 70% for science increased from 3.4% in 2008 to 7.4% in 2013, while 9.7% of accounting students achieved more than 70% in 2013, compared with only 4.5% in 2008. Unfortunately, the number of students who studied accounting fell by 17.5% from 2008 to 2013, while the number of science students also declined by 15.1% over the same period.

HIGHER EDUCATION IS ALSO PROBLEMATIC

In 2013, there were 23 public higher education institutions (HEIs) in South Africa. Of these, 11 can be regarded as traditional universities; 6 are universities of technology, which were formerly known as technikons; and 6 are comprehensive universities, which were established through the merger of traditional universities and former technikons. Together, these institutions offer approximately 198 000 first-year enrolment opportunities, and have almost one million registered students.

In addition to the public HEIs, South Africa has around 50 further education and training (FET) colleges in the public sector and approximately 344 registered private FET colleges. The FET colleges in both the private and public sectors have around 410 000 registered students, with the bulk of these students (360 000) registered with public sector FET colleges. There are also 109 private sector HEIs, with around 90 000 students, and over 3 000 public and private sector adult education and training centres.

Most students within the 23 public sector HEIs are enrolled in humanities-related programmes (around 40% of the total), while 30% are enrolled in programmes associated with the business field, with another 30% enrolled in the science, engineering and technology fields.

Unfortunately, the graduation rate, as measured by the number of graduates in a particular academic year as a percentage of the total enrolment for that year, was recorded at a mere 15% in 2011, and has averaged around 16% since 2005. The University of South Africa (UNISA), which is the largest HEI in the country with a total enrolment of about 328 000 students, has a graduation rate of only 7%. This is largely because most UNISA students are part-time learners, and it is generally recognised that part-time learning is a more difficult context in which to complete a degree.

Overall, it seems clear that many students who enrol at university are simply unprepared for the challenge, and either drop out or fail. South Africa's education process is thus an extremely expensive and inefficient process.

The performance of the FET colleges is also less than ideal. This is partly because their programmes do not involve enough practical training that is aligned to the needs of industry. In addition, many colleges create an oversupply of graduates in fairly specialised fields, leading to frustration on the part of students as they are unable to find employment in their area of study. Added to this, many of the courses are extremely expensive, while the pass rate varies between 34% and 38%, depending on the year of study. Many of the FET colleges have also been accused of maladministration.

In 2013 the government signed into law the FET Colleges Amendment Act, which effectively moves the administration of the colleges from the provinces to the national Department of Higher Education. This only came into effect in October 2013, and will hopefully lead to an improved performance by the colleges, providing training and coursework that is better aligned to the needs of industry and coordinated with other educational programmes.

EDUCATIONAL REFORMS REQUIRED

At the end of 2013, the unemployment rate among South Africans younger than 25 years was a staggering 48.9%. While this is lower than the 50.7% recorded at the end of 2012, it is still extremely high by historical as well as international standards. If the number of discouraged work-seekers is included, then the unemployment rate for people younger than 25 jumps to a massive 62.6%. The combination of a tremendously high youth unemployment rate, an extremely significant school drop-out rate, a poor matric pass rate and the fact that more than a million children start school each year suggests that

South Africa has a crisis in youth education and employment that needs to be addressed extremely urgently.

Although many countries are plagued with a high rate of youth unemployment, including most of southern Europe, it is clear that Germany has achieved great success in educating and employing its young people. The youth unemployment rate in Germany has systematically fallen from a high of 16.5% in early 2005 to a record low of 7.8% at the end of 2013. This is a remarkable achievement considering that youth unemployment around the world has moved noticeably higher over the same period.

One of the key factors that led to Germany's success is that many decades ago the country created a 'dual' system to blend schooling and apprenticeship training. The system was revamped in 1981, with the main idea being that after a few years at a conventional school, students, together with their parents, can choose the type of schooling they wish to pursue, based in part on the student's academic ability. Students then enrol in a school that provides the type of education they require, with a clear focus on preparing students either for university study or for some form of vocational education or apprenticeship training. This means that for many students, practical apprenticeship training is supplemented by theoretical instruction in vocational schools. Consequently, around 60% of all young people learn a trade of some kind and will more easily find employment once they are certified. In addition, and very importantly, German chambers of commerce and industry associations ensure that work opportunities are matched to vocational teaching. This is done through regular market or industry surveys.

The structure of the German school system brings future job applicants in much closer contact with the job market and generates a more fairly reliable qualification standard. This effectively limits the risk incurred by employers when they hire young workers. The practical nature of the education system is a significant advantage as it allows for a mutual screening of potential employers as well as employees during the training process.

There are many lessons South Africa can learn from the German system of education. Among these are the recognition that not everyone should endeavour to obtain an academic qualification, that providing vocational training is critical to ensuring young people are more employable, and that there needs to be ongoing coordination between industry and the various educational institutions in order to ensure that the country is producing the right mix of skills.

In 1997, South Africa introduced an outcomes-based education (OBE) system, with the hope of addressing some of the complexities in transforming the education system to meet the needs of all students as well as the demands of the economy. There is much debate about the effectiveness of the OBE system, although the weight of argument suggests that the process did not achieve the desired results. Consequently, the OBE system was dismantled in 2010 and several policy changes have since been introduced to shift the education system in a different direction. Although some improvements have occurred, especially the Grade 12 pass rate, the school drop-out rate remains far too high.

There are at least five key steps to improving South Africa's education and skills development. First, to tackle the high drop-out rate, it seems clear that a relevant form of schooling should be developed to provide an alternative for learners who are considering dropping out of school in Grade 10. As it is, the education system tends to force all students to follow an academic route of study, rather than recognising that many individuals are simply not inclined towards a purely academic education. Instead, many young adults would benefit from a vocational or apprenticeship form of learning. This form of education combines some theoretical instruction with practical guidance and a large element of industry-based experience. Students would attend formal lectures for a portion of the year, but then gain on-the-job training for the remainder of the year. The system could be applied across all sectors of the economy, guided by industry forums and feedback from potential employers. This would hopefully provide students with a greater understanding of industry as well as possible career choices.

Second, students need to be much better prepared for tertiary education. Although access to basic (primary and secondary) education has improved dramatically over the past twenty years, the quality of South Africa's schooling system appears to have declined, as evidenced in various international surveys. There are still schools without electricity, textbooks and basic equipment, and many schools are overcrowded. However, a greater concern is the regular disruptions to the teaching day, which partly result from labour unrest – in particular, strike activity by the South African Democratic Teachers Union, the country's largest trade union for teachers. In addition, there appears to be a significant shortage of skilled teachers, especially in mathematics and science.

Third, although much of the research into the education system and labour market indicates that the country has a skills shortage, there is not a lot of detail on exactly what the skills shortage implies. Furthermore, the country has a mismatch of skills, with an oversupply of some skills and a shortage of others. It is not sufficient simply to suggest that South Africa has a shortage of technical or engineering skills. In particular, it is important to know what specific skills the country lacks, as well as the mix of skills likely to be needed over the next ten to twenty years. Such determinations would require an initial skills audit, and then a detailed projection or estimate of possible future requirements. While these estimates are unlikely to be extremely accurate, they could provide at least basic guidelines for many schools, tertiary institutions and households on how to direct future studies.

Fourth, the advances in telecommunications and increased access to the Internet provide an opportunity to enhance the learning process. This enhancement could include video seminars, increased student interaction, access to a broader range of source material and practical examples from within industry. However, this type of education requires that the country substantially improve the speed of access to the Internet, while at the same time reducing the cost of access.

Finally, it is clear from the 2012 GEM report that the higher the level of education, the more likely it is that individuals will perceive that they are capable of becoming entrepreneurs. This seems most applicable to individuals who have attained a post-matric or university qualification. Unfortunately, because less than 1% of the country's population have attained a tertiary education, which is well below the world average of around 4%, many young South Africans lack the confidence and knowledge to consider starting their own business. This is one of the key factors holding back small-business development, which in turn places a huge strain on the public sector as well as the business community to create employment opportunities or provide welfare support. Instead, the secondary and tertiary education system could be doing a lot more to encourage a vibrant culture of small-business development. As the 2012 GEM study suggested, the introduction of entrepreneurship education within the school system is important for inculcating a positive attitude towards entrepreneurship and self-employment as a viable future career choice. Business studies as a school subject has been shown to have a positive correlation with entrepreneurial attitudes and aspirations to start one's own business.

In April 2014 Stats SA published a report titled *Poverty Trends in South Africa*, which highlighted that there are significant differences in levels of poverty among the adult population depending on the level of education attained. In 2011, only 5.5% of individuals with an education level higher than matric were living in poverty. In contrast, 66% of adults with no formal schooling remained impoverished in 2011. Not surprisingly, the report concluded that 'the relationship between education and poverty appears strong, as the poverty measures reflect [that] the lower the level of education attained, the more likely adults were to be poor and experience more intense levels of poverty'.

IMPROVE SOUTH AFRICA'S ECONOMIC INFRASTRUCTURE

There is a clear and positive relationship between infrastructural development, economic growth, industrial competitiveness and social well-being. The higher the level of investment spending, the higher the level of economic activity. This is especially evident if investment activity has been sustained for a number of years, since a sustained rise in investment activity leads to an increase in employment, which in turn boosts economic activity.

For example, from 1994 to 2013, fixed investment spending by developed economies averaged 20.7% of GDP, while economic growth was measured at an average of only 2.2% a year. In comparison, investment activity in emerging economies averaged a substantial 27.6% of GDP over the same period, helped by the fact that investment spending in China comprised 39.5% of GDP. Not surprisingly, GDP growth in emerging economies averaged a very respectable 5.4% over the same twenty years.

As the DTI highlighted in their framework for a national industrial policy, sufficient, reliable, modern and competitively priced infrastructure and logistics systems are essential for a modern industrial economy. Effective infrastructure is required for production efficiencies, to move goods and people, and for the cost-effective linking of people and businesses.

There is also the possibility that endeavours to significantly develop South Africa's economic infrastructure will encourage the country to develop its skill base. This is exactly what happened during the building programme ahead of the 2010 Soccer World Cup. Once South Africa was awarded the right to host the event, there were many sceptics who suggested the country would not have enough skilled labour to complete the projects on time. These sceptics were proved wrong, partly because industry responded to the demands of the World Cup, and fast-tracked various initiatives to develop additional skills or enhance existing skills.

Historically, South Africa's level of fixed investment spending averaged a respectable 21.1% of GDP in the 1960s, rose to a substantial 26.4% of GDP in the 1970s and then eased to 23.1% of GDP in the 1980s. At its peak, in the final quarter of 1975, fixed investment spending represented 31.1% of GDP.

Unfortunately, the country's level of fixed investment activity began slowing in the mid-1980s, after an escalation in domestic political unrest and a dramatic fall in investor confidence that culminated in the US introducing the Comprehensive Anti-Apartheid Act in 1986. This deterioration in investment spending continued into the early 1990s, with investment activity averaging a mere 16.7% of GDP and reaching a low of 14.6% of GDP just ahead of the 1994 elections. At the end of 2013 it was a more encouraging 19.3% of GDP, but still well below the minimum target of 25% of GDP.

Since 1994, despite many promises to the contrary, South Africa has largely neglected its economic infrastructure, which has now become a major constraint to economic growth and business development.

RATING SOUTH AFRICA'S INFRASTRUCTURE

In 2006, the South African Institution of Civil Engineering (SAICE) compiled the country's first ever report card on the state of built environment infrastructure. The report was significantly extended and updated in 2011 and is a respected assessment of South Africa's infrastructural strengths and weaknesses.

The SAICE system of evaluating the country's infrastructure uses a grading system that ranges from A to E. An A rating represents world-class infrastructure, comparable to the best internationally in every respect, with capacity to endure unusual events. A B rating refers to infrastructure that is fit for the future, satisfying current demands and sufficiently robust to deal with minor stresses. A C rating represents infrastructure that is satisfactory for now, although it might be stressed at peaks and will require investment to avoid serious deficiencies. A D rating is assigned to infrastructure that is at risk, not coping with demand and poorly maintained. This is infrastructure that might subject the users to inconvenience and possibly danger without prompt attention. An E rating is given to infrastructure that is unfit for the intended purpose and that has failed or is on the verge of failure, exposing the public to health and safety hazards. This infrastructure requires immediate attention.

In 2006 South Africa's infrastructure was assigned an overall D+ rating, with skills shortages and a lack of maintenance spending highlighted as the two main concerns across all sectors. However, in 2011 the rating was upgraded to C−, mainly as a result of the infrastructural developments associated with the 2010 World Cup. These developments included airport upgrades, as well as some improvements to national roads and ports.

The airports received the best overall infrastructure rating of B+. This is not surprising, as South Africa has developed a world-class aviation capability at most of its airports in the past few years. In addition, the commercial port infrastructure is rated at a respectable B−, helped by a number of upgrades that have already been completed at the major harbours. In addition, the development of the Ngqura port in the Eastern Cape has provided the region with a modern and relatively efficient commercial harbour. Unfortunately, South Africa still has some of the most expensive container ports in the world, according to the Ports Regulator of South Africa. This clearly hurts the business sector, stunting its ability to compete. Although Transnet reduced the cost of the container ports in 2013, they remain extremely expensive by global standards.

In contrast, the sanitation infrastructure in rural areas as well as smaller towns received a shocking E− rating, while the Department of Water Affairs infrastructure received a rating of only D−. The SAICE noted that 'there has been a further deterioration in the ageing bulk water infrastructure portfolio as a result of insufficient maintenance and neglect of ongoing capital renewal'. It is also deeply disturbing that the hospitals (mostly government hospitals) received a D+ grade, while public schools were also rated only D+.

A SHORTAGE OF ELECTRICITY-GENERATING CAPACITY

In January 2008, South Africa experienced a significant electricity supply crisis, resulting in widespread blackouts that dented economic growth and stunted private sector investment. Since then, the country's shortage of electricity-generating capacity has been exacerbated by the fact that some power stations are approaching the end of their lifespan, resulting in substantial operational inefficiencies. Power stations, like other infrastructure components, require ongoing maintenance and regular upgrades to meet growing demand.

Consequently, since 2008 South Africa has had to introduce a number of measures to deal with the electricity crisis, including a significant increase in electricity prices as a way of rationing the available supply. At the same time, the supply of electricity to highly intensive users, such as mines and smelters, has regularly been reduced on both a voluntary and involuntary basis.

Subsequently, Eskom, the country's main electricity supplier, has embarked on an extensive campaign to expand electricity-generating capacity. This campaign includes the renewal of existing power stations, the building of two new large power plants (Medupi and Kuseli), and a highly successful partnership with the private sector to develop alternative energy supplies, primarily wind and solar power.

Unfortunately, the building of the two new power stations has experienced numerous disruptions, including poor workmanship by some of the subcontractors as well as labour unrest. This has led to extensive delays and massive cost overruns. As of April 2014, neither of the power stations had been completed, although Medupi is expected to come online in late 2014 or early 2015.

Globally, there is an extremely high correlation between access to electricity, by both businesses and households, and economic growth, including the willingness of the business sector to expand production capacity. Needless to say, the shortage of electricity generation in South Africa is a critical concern.

RAILWAY CAPACITY HAS DIMINISHED

Another example of South Africa's underdeveloped infrastructure is the fact that the demand for rail services easily exceeds the current supply. While the railway-track infrastructure does have the capacity to accommodate more trains, especially in the case of the general freight network, the shortage of rolling stock is the main constraint to greater utilisation of available infrastructure. Theft and vandalism is another major concern and safety remains a significant issue.

All of this has constrained South Africa's ability to export. Moreover, deficient railway capacity, along with the deregulation of the road transport industry, has led to an increase in the use of road transport, which has subsequently weakened the road network due to over-utilisation.

Brian Molefe, the chief executive officer of Transnet, indicated in early 2014 that the average age of train locomotives in South Africa is 32 years, with some as old as 45 years. The railway carriages are of a similar age. Consequently, the rolling stock is unreliable, resulting in substantial delays, higher maintenance costs and an erratic railway service. This applies to the transport of goods as well as passengers.

Consequently, Transnet has embarked on a relatively ambitious programme to increase the number of locomotives by 1 064 units over the next few years. Under the terms of the contract, CSR Zhuzhou Electric Locomotive Company of China and Bombardier Transportation South Africa will supply 599 electric locomotives, while General Electric South Africa Technologies and CNR Rolling Stock South Africa will build and supply 465 diesel locomotives. Nearly all the locomotives will be built in Transnet's plants in Pretoria and Durban and are expected to be completed within three and a half years.

This initiative forms part of Transnet's R307 billion 'Market Demand Strategy' that was first announced in 2012. The plan aims to substantially upgrade South Africa's port and railway capacity over the following seven years, with coal capacity scheduled to increase by 44%, iron ore capacity by 57%, general freight by 57% and port container capacity by 76%.

ROAD SYSTEM HAS DETERIORATED

The country has also underinvested in its road network. Paved roads in South Africa are typically built with a structural design life of approximately twenty years, with the assumption that the roads are adequately maintained over this period. Unfortunately, according to information provided by the South African National Roads Agency (SANRAL), 81% of the country's paved roads are older than twenty years, with almost 70% older than twenty-five years. In addition, a significant proportion of the network, especially the provincial and municipal roads, has not been correctly maintained. Consequently, many roads have deteriorated to the point of needing urgent attention, and now represent a safety concern for motorists. This has led to higher road transport costs through an increase in vehicle maintenance costs as well as transport delays.

It appears that a shortage of skilled personnel in many provincial departments, misdirected funding, and the lack of routine and periodic maintenance have contributed to the current state of the provincial and municipal road system.

In contrast, the national road network, under the jurisdiction of SANRAL, is in mostly good to excellent condition. This network includes a fairly extensive system of toll roads as well as much of the metropolitan road network. Fortunately, SANRAL demonstrates expert knowledge and world-class management, and has excellent monitoring and maintenance systems. This is likely to result in SANRAL's responsibilities and network allocation expanding further to include some of the provincial roads.

WASTE- AND WATER-TREATMENT PLANTS

South Africa has serious problems with the management of many waste-water (sewage) treatment works as well as water-treatment facilities. According to the Department of Water Affairs, in 2012, 44% of the country's municipal waste-water treatment plants were regarded as either 'high risk' or 'critical'. In contrast, only 27% of treatment plants were regarded as 'low risk'. These statistics reflect a relatively high level of waste-water leakage and spillage into major rivers, which leads to significant health risks and increases the costs associated with providing reasonable-quality drinking water.

In 2011, SAICE assigned South Africa's sanitation infrastructure in the major urban areas a rating of C–, while all other areas of the country received an E– grade.

South Africa's water-treatment plants are not in much better shape. In 2012, only 10.5% of the country's water system received 'Blue Drop' status, which is a measure of water quality. Within many municipalities, especially outside the major metropolitan areas, the quality of the water has deteriorated to the point that it is undrinkable, largely as a result of the ageing of the bulk water infrastructure, compounded by insufficient maintenance. Acid mine drainage is also a serious concern, especially surrounding gold and coal mines. In addition, water wastage as a result of leaks remains extremely high, while large dams have capacity constraints and require urgent attention. Unfortunately, because of the long lead times required for the development of new water- and waste-treatment facilities, the situation is likely to get worse before it becomes better – assuming the funds that have been allocated for infrastructure maintenance are used for their intended purpose.

Overall, SAICE assigned the Department of Water Affairs a D– grade, which is of extreme concern given the critical importance of clean running water in the functioning of any economic system.

A LACK OF POLITICAL WILL TO DEVELOP INFRASTRUCTURE

In almost every policy document, the South African government has repeatedly referred to the need to invest in infrastructure. Moreover, the government has established several institutions to strengthen the state's capacity to improve infrastructure delivery. For example, the National Planning Commission, located in the Presidency, was tasked with developing a long-term vision and strategic plan for the country, which is now called the National Development Plan (NDP). Infrastructure is one of the key issues that feature in the NDP. In addition, the Department of Performance Monitoring and Evaluation in the Presidency is tasked with facilitating delivery agreements for all infrastructure departments and monitoring their implementation. The relatively newly created Presidential Infrastructure Coordinating Commission, headed by the president, is tasked with coordinating and overseeing the implementation of strategic infrastructure projects that stimulate social and economic growth. Lastly, the Presidential Review Committee on State-Owned Enterprises (SOEs) aims to align SOEs with the government's development agenda, including that of infrastructure development.

Despite all these initiatives, South Africa's infrastructure is ageing and overloaded. Municipal infrastructure, in particular, is below standard and poorly maintained. It also has to be recognised, as was highlighted in the 2011 SAICE report, that 'once infrastructure has been developed it is unrelenting in its demand for maintenance and it will increase this demand the longer it is ignored'.

In the February 2014 national budget, the minister of finance highlighted that an impressive R847.3 billion has been allocated to public sector infrastructural development over the next three years. This is 25% more than what was estimated to have been spent on public sector infrastructure in the preceding three years. Most of the R847.3 billion has been earmarked for transport and logistics (41% of the total of the next three years) and for energy (22% of the three year total).

There has, however, been a tendency in South Africa for the public sector to budget for a substantial increase in infrastructure, but then underspend the allocation. In other words, the promise of widespread infrastructural development is proving difficult to implement. For example, in 2012/13 the government allocated R255.6 billion for public sector infrastructure spending. However, according to the 2014 national budget, the public sector spent a total of R217.7 billion, which is effectively only 85% of budget.

WHY HAS THE PUBLIC SECTOR STRUGGLED TO EXPAND THE COUNTRY'S INFRASTRUCTURE?

It is evident from various reports on South Africa's infrastructure, including the SAICE reports in 2006 and 2011, that the maintenance of the country's economic infrastructure does not receive a high enough priority, thereby undermining the reliability of a wide range of public services. In some instances, the lack of infrastructure, or lack of adequately maintained infrastructure, is due to insufficient funding for maintenance or to tax revenue not being used for the intended purpose. In other instances, it reflects a lack of institutional capacity for maintenance, due to skills shortages or rising levels of corruption. In general, many municipalities lack capacity, skilled resources and funding to manage their infrastructure efficiently and effectively – all of which is compounded by increasing levels of corruption.

South Africa's lack of infrastructure development also reflects the government's emphasis on providing access to infrastructure rather than ensuring that the bulk infrastructure capacity is able to meet the increase in demand.

LOOKING FORWARD

Transnet and Eskom are both undertaking relatively substantial expansion programmes. These initiatives are primarily aimed at expanding the country's rail, port and energy infrastructure. Other public sector infrastructural initiatives are also being developed and systematically implemented. Together, these initiatives have the potential to allow for a substantial improvement in the efficiency of domestic business activity. Hopefully, the expansion by Transnet and Eskom as well as other state-owned enterprises and public sector departments will become a trigger that encourages the South African corporate sector to systematically enhance their own expansion plans, providing a vital and sustainable boost to growth and employment.

In the February 2014 national budget, the minister of finance stated that 'increased investment in the economy by both the private and public sector is at the heart of creating jobs and growth'. This is exactly where the emphasis needs to be at this stage of South Africa's economic development, but there appears to be a lack of a sense of urgency on the part of both the public and private sectors. In the meantime, each year more than a million children start school, and they will eventually want to be employed and live a prosperous life. Clearly, much more needs to be done to encourage higher levels of fixed investment spending in South Africa, with special attention to infrastructural development.

A REGIONAL OPPORTUNITY

Sub-Saharan Africa has become one of the world's most dynamic economic regions. Since 2000 the region has achieved an average annual economic growth rate of 5.4% and is forecast by the IMF to grow at over 5% a year during the next five years. Consumer inflation has fallen from over 15% in the late 1990s to under 7%, while government debt has moderated from 71% of GDP in 2000 to less than 35% of GDP in 2013.

This improvement in economic conditions is reflected in rising household incomes, a growing middle class, increased exports and a focus on expanding regional transport and energy infrastructure, including the production of natural gas. This does not imply that every country in the sub-Saharan Africa is prospering. While some countries have clearly made enormous progress over the past ten years, including Nigeria, Ghana, Zambia and Kenya, many others continue to flounder, hampered by internal conflict, poor governance, extremely weak infrastructure and a lack of skills.

Although there is significant interest in sub-Saharan Africa's mining and natural gas resources, the region's real long-term attraction lies is its potential consumer market. This is because there are around 850 million people in the region that have lagged the rest of world in household consumption. However, unlocking this potential requires that the major economies find a way to transition from high economic growth to inclusive economic development that raises the living standards of the broader population. This would include reducing the infrastructure backlogs; raising the enrolment at secondary and tertiary education facilities; improving institutional governance, transparency and accountability; building a diversified productive capacity, with reduced dependence on natural resources; and implementing deep, market-based reforms such as certainly about land rights, uniformity in the granting of permits to operate and the transparent awarding of contracts by the public sector. There also needs to be a focus on lifting inter-regional trade. Currently, there are substantial deficiencies in the transport infrastructure, unnecessary border controls, high levels of corruption and excessive trade restrictions that impede regional trade.

The deepening of financial markets, which ultimately reflects the development of the country's financial system and its ability to help develop the economy, is also critical to sub-Saharan Africa's success. This includes the banking sector and stock market, but will likely require a regional approach, especially when it comes to raising money for large capital projects as well as initiating cross-border infrastructural developments. This will not be easy given the diverse legal and regulatory regimes, an undeveloped financial infrastructure and each country's bias towards satisfying its own national interests.

Despite these limitations, an increasing number of sub-Saharan African economies have caught the attention of international investors who have been looking to diversify their investments and are attracted by the region's high growth rate, an emerging middle class and relatively high investment returns. With the exception of South Africa, the impact of the 2008/09 global financial market crisis on sub-Saharan Africa was relatively modest. Instead, in recent years, the region has benefited from a commodities price boom and a sharp increase in foreign direct investment, including from China and India.

The rapid economic growth in sub-Saharan Africa has also caught the attention of South African companies, an increasing number of which have established commercial links in countries throughout the region. These links include the distribution of goods into the retail sector, the establishment of mining and manufacturing operations, the development of communication networks, and the provision of financial and other business services.

South Africa's exports to the rest of Africa have grown substantially in recent years, rising to a total of R264.2 billion in 2013. This is equivalent to 29% of the country's merchandise exports, making the rest of Africa the second largest regional export destination for South African goods. The largest remains Asia, which consumed 32% of the country's merchandise exports in 2013. South Africa's exports to Europe, which have been hurt in recent years by the exceptionally weak economic performance in the EU, have slipped to only 22% of total exports.

Despite the moderation in exports to Europe, South Africa has managed to establish relatively well-diversified export markets, with Asia consuming mostly basic mining commodities, including iron ore and coal; Africa procuring mainly manufactured goods, especially food products; and Europe purchasing fresh produce and a range of semi-processed goods, including precious stones and metals. South Africa's exports to North and South America comprise less than 10% of total merchandise exports.

NIGERIA IS THE BIGGEST ECONOMY IN AFRICA

In April 2014, the National Bureau of Statistics in Nigeria announced that the size and composition of Nigeria's GDP had been radically revised. This revision was more than a decade overdue, as most countries revisit the measurement of their GDP every five years to take account of new industries that may have emerged. This has certainly been the case in Nigeria, with, for example, the rapid growth in the communications sector. In terms of the adjustment, which followed an extensive review of all economic activity in the country, Nigeria's economy increased from an initial 2013 estimate of $266 billion to $503 billion. This represents a massive increase of 89%. The adjustment to the GDP data was backdated to 2010.

As a result of the rebasing exercise, Nigeria became the biggest economy in Africa, and is 44% bigger than South Africa. (Prior to the revision, South Africa had been Africa's largest economy.) Importantly, Nigeria has a population of around 170 million, making it the fifth most populous country in the world, while South Africa has a population of around 52 million.

Following the revision, Nigeria's GDP is significantly more diverse. In particular, the services sector comprised almost 52% of the economy in 2013, compared with the previous estimate of 29%. Manufacturing activity was revised up from 2% to 7%, while the energy sector was revised down from 32% to 14%. In addition, key high-growth sectors are now more accurately measured. This includes the telecommunications sector, which was revised up from less than 1% of GDP to almost 9%, while the motion picture industry is almost 1.5% of total economy activity, after not having been included in the data under the old estimate of GDP.

From a regional perspective, Nigeria now constitutes 33% of sub-Saharan Africa's GDP, compared with South Africa at 23%. In contrast, South Africa has an investment-grade international credit rating, while Nigeria has a speculative-grade credit rating.

At first glance, the fact that Nigeria's economy is now bigger than South Africa's diminishes South Africa's status in the African and world economy. Furthermore, the adjustment will lead to much debate about Nigeria's possible inclusion in the G20 at the exclusion of South Africa, as well as the legitimacy of South Africa's inclusion in the BRICS formation. However, South Africa is unlikely to be excluded from the G20, since not only was South Africa one of its founding members, but the G20 selection is based in part on each country's importance in the global financial system, and not merely on the size of the economy. Similarly, South Africa's inclusion in BRICS took into account a range of factors apart from the size of the economy and the number of inhabitants. This included the country's level of infrastructural development, its legal and regulatory system, its access to financial markets and its ability to impact global trade.

More importantly, the adjustment in Nigeria sends a clear signal to the rest of the world that sub-Saharan Africa is becoming a more meaningful participant in the global economy and that the region offers investors many diverse opportunities. It also increases Nigeria's as well as South Africa's responsibilities inside and outside of the region given that, on a combined basis, the two countries represent more than 55% of sub-Saharan Africa's economic activity.

A VISION OF SOUTH AFRICA'S ROLE IN AFRICA

Shortly after the 1994 elections, the South African government embarked on a number of initiatives to establish and strengthen economic and political relationships with the rest of Africa. This included South Africa's membership of the Southern African Development Community in August 1994 and the establishment of the African Union in May 2001. However, in the mid-2000s the country focused more purposefully on strengthening financial and trade relationships with Europe and the US, and more recently the government has endeavoured to forge stronger ties with the BRIC economies, especially India and China.

However, the sustained high growth and improving economic fundamentals in many sub-Saharan African countries, coupled with the fact that numerous South African companies have very successfully increased their level of business activity with the rest of Africa, suggests that the South African government should be actively encouraging an increase in regional economic activity. This could include helping to speed up the flow of goods and services between countries, the initiation of regional infrastructural developments, the transfer of skills and technology, and the increased uniformity of business procedures and regulation.

Increased regional integration represents a significant opportunity for all countries. The benefits could include a more efficient flow of goods and services within the region; the ability to attract meaningful foreign direct investment, encouraged by a large potential consumer market; the real possibility of cross-border infrastructure developments; and an ability to exploit up- and downstream linkages associated with the expansion of mining and agricultural activity.

Given South Africa's well-developed financial, communication, logistics and business services sectors, the country has a unique opportunity to become a vital economic hub on the African continent. Already South Africa fulfils this function in a number of ways, but this role could be substantially and actively enhanced to include increased distribution and storage facilities linked to airport, rail, road and port facilities; tourism (including retail tourism, which is already evident in the number of foreign tourists visiting South Africa's major shopping centres); education facilities (especially business schools and executive training facilities); regional conferences and exhibition facilities;

cooperative research and development centres; a regional media hub; and business initiatives linked to specialised engineering and design.

All of this could help to develop the South African economy in sectors that are already relatively well established with a proven level of expertise and competitiveness, and that are going to be increasingly demanded in the rest of Africa.

CONCLUSION

Having appraised South Africa's economic journey over the past twenty years, it is clear that the task of establishing the country as a non-racial democracy with a vibrant and growing economy able to provide for the needs of the entire population was always going to be an immense and arduous task. This task was made extremely difficult by the almost insurmountable shortfall in the provision of basic services, such as sanitation, electricity, healthcare and education, but also by the unfair distribution of land ownership and the unequal distribution of income and wealth.

In order to achieve its goals, South Africa had to focus on simultaneously achieving four key pieces of economic policy. These comprised the integration of the country back into the world economy after years of isolation; the implementation of sound macroeconomic policy, especially monetary and fiscal policy; a vast increase in the provision of social goods and services; and helping the business sector to compete in a modern and dynamic global economy.

Twenty years after the first democratic elections, it is clear that South Africa overachieved in implementing the first two puzzle pieces – namely, successfully integrating the country back into the world economy and instilling sound monetary and fiscal policy. Moreover, the country was reasonably successful at reducing the immense backlog of social goods and services, especially considering the enormity of the task. However, South Africa failed to adequately implement the fourth piece of the puzzle, which required the development and maintenance of key economic infrastructural facilities, including the supply of electricity as well as vital port, rail, road and water systems. It also entailed overcoming the skills shortage, developing key technologies, such as the Internet, and ensuring that business did not become unnecessarily regulated.

Unfortunately, the lack of progress in developing the fourth piece of the puzzle has meant that South Africa's economic growth has ultimately been somewhat disappointing, employment has been staid, and income and wealth have remained largely unequal. This underperformance is evident in the high rate of youth unemployment, subdued economic growth that has been hampered by a shortage of electricity, a scaling back of private sector investment activity, the downgrading of international credit ratings and a spillover of labour market tensions into violence.

Moreover, this lack of progress on the fourth puzzle piece has begun to undermine the other three pieces of the economic puzzle, creating a negative feedback loop that has become more evident in the past five years. If left unchecked, this can derail the remarkable progress achieved in the first fifteen years of democracy, leading to increased unemployment, an outflow of foreign investment and rising social tension.

It is clear that South Africa needs to improve a number of key components of the economy in order to purposefully develop the fourth piece of the puzzle, without jettisoning the many remarkable achievements of the new democracy, especially in the areas of monetary and fiscal policy

When faced with a significant economic challenge, it is always tempting to establish a long list of priorities and economic objectives to try to address the problem. However, these lists can prove unwieldy and daunting. Instead, there are some important initiatives that can be implemented relatively quickly, such as ready-to-go projects or the active promotion of small business, in order to lift confidence and boost the economy, while systematically addressing the longer-term challenges, such as the provision of skills or the development of economic infrastructure. A series of small victories quickly builds confidence, and ultimately leads to greater triumphs.

ACKNOWLEDGEMENTS

First and foremost, I would like to thank Terry Morris from Pan Macmillan for the invite to write *The Missing Piece*, and Andrea Nattrass for expertly guiding the publishing process. This book would not have been possible without Andrea's advice, insights and efficiency, while the sales and marketing team from Pan Macmillan, including Gillian Spain and Laura Hammond, has been hugely supportive.

I would also like to thank Lisa Compton for her insightful editing and meticulous attention to detail. Any errors remaining are, of course, mine alone.

Dr Sibusiso Sibisi kindly agreed to write the Foreword for the book, highlighting the importance of Research and Development in sustainably improving the growth performance of the South African economy. This is a topic that receives far too little attention in the debate on how to move the South African economy forward. Innovation is not purely the domain of hi-tech companies, but can make a valuable difference to every facet of economic development, including within the informal sector.

Early in my career, I was fortunate to have been mentored by one of South Africa's most accomplished economists, Edward Osborn, who taught me so much, and especially to constructively challenge conventional wisdom. While at STANLIB, my ideas and thoughts about the South African economy have been shaped by a large range of factors, including periodic meetings with government officials, labour union members and the South African Reserve Bank, as well as regular visits to the International Monetary Fund. I have also had the opportunity to regularly debate numerous aspects of the country's economy with several of South Africa's leading private sector economists, including Elna Moolman, Azar Jamine, Kim Silberman, Matthew Sharratt, Johan Rossouw, Tertia Jacobs, Bruce Donald, Loane Sharp, Andrea Masia, Marie Antelme, Danelee Masia and Gina Schoeman.

I would like to express my appreciation to Laura Jones for her tenacious efforts in tracking down all source documents, no matter how obscure, and for providing research assistance in helping me to navigate South Africa's somewhat complex education system, and Kganya Kgara for his contribution to explaining the role that Nigeria now plays in the economy of sub-Saharan Africa. I would also like to acknowledge Erica Stuart for helping to compile the presentation that encapsulates the book, and Rachel Lailey and Lebogang Babe for their marketing ideas.

More broadly, I would like to thank STANLIB for its support in writing this book. Over the years STANLIB has encouraged its staff to use their knowledge and passion to make a positive difference within the broader financial community.

Finally, I would like to express my gratitude to my loving, and supportive wife, Kim. Not only was she willing to read the first draft of every chapter I wrote, her suggestions have been invaluable.

SELECT BIBLIOGRAPHY

Adcorp Analytics, 2012. *Adcorp Employment Index*. Johannesburg: Adcorp Analytics.

African Development Bank, July 2010. *Project Implementation Review of the NEPAD Infrastructure Short Term Action Plan*. Johannesburg: African Development Bank.

Akamai, 1st Quarter 2013. The State of the Internet. *Faster Forward*, Vol. 6, No. 1.

Arora, V., and L.A. Ricci, 2005. *Unemployment and the Labour Market*. Washington, DC: International Monetary Fund.

Auditor-General South Africa, 2012 and 2013. *Consolidated General Report on the National and Provincial Audit Outcomes*. Pretoria: Office of the Auditor-General.

Auditor-General South Africa, November 2013. *Presentation to SCOPA: Audit Outcomes of National Departments*. Pretoria: Office of the Auditor-General.

Bhorat, H., C. van der Westhuizen, T. Jacobs and Development Policy Research Unit, April 2009. *Inequality and Economic Marginalisation: Income and Non-income Inequality in Post-apartheid South Africa: What are the Drivers and Possible Policy Interventions?* Pretoria: Trade and Industrial Policy Strategies.

CDE (Centre for Development and Enterprise) Insight, April 2013. *Graduate Unemployment in South Africa: A Much Exaggerated Problem*. Johannesburg: CDE.

CDE Insight, August 2013. *Affordable Private Schools in South Africa*. Johannesburg: CDE.

CDE Insight, December 2013. *Growth in a Time of Uncertainty: Does SA Have a Growth Plan?* Johannesburg: CDE.

Chalmers, R., December 2006. *What is Poverty? Concepts and Measures*. Brazil: United Nations Development Programme International Poverty Centre.

Cilliers, J., and H. Camp, 2013. Highway or Byway? The National Development Plan 2030. *African Futures Paper*, No. 6, pp. 1–16.

Credit Suisse Investment Bank, 2013. *Global Wealth Report 2013*. Zurich: Credit Suisse AG.

CSIR (Council for Scientific and Industrial Research), 2012. *Ninth Annual State of Logistics Survey for South Africa*. Pretoria: CSIR.

Dagut, M., 1991. *South Africa: The New Beginning*. Johannesburg: Euromoney Institutional Investor PLC.

DBE (Department of Basic Education), 2012. *Class of 2013: Information Booklet*. Pretoria: DBE.

DBE, 2013. *Annual National Assessment: 2013 Diagnostic Report and 2014 Framework for Improvement*. Pretoria: DBE.

DBE, 2013. *Annual Performance Plan*. Pretoria: DBE.

DBE, 2013. *National Senior Certificate: Schools Subject Report*. Pretoria: DBE.

DBE, 2013. *National Senior Certificate: Technical Report*. Pretoria: DBE.

DBSA (Development Bank of Southern Africa) and National Treasury, 2014. *Jobs Fund Eligibility and Assessment Criteria*. Pretoria: Jobs Fund.

DBSA Infrastructure Dialogues, 2012. *Municipal Service Delivery: Improving Quality and Quantity: How Do We Square the Circle?* Johannesburg: DBSA.

Deloitte, 2013. *Investors Handbook 2012/13*. Johannesburg: Deloitte and Department of Trade and Industry.

Department of Agriculture, Forestry and Fisheries, 2013. *Abstract of Agricultural Statistics*. Pretoria: Department of Agriculture, Forestry and Fisheries.

Department of Communications, 2013. *Consultation on the Proposed National Broadband Policy for South Africa*. Pretoria: Department of Communications.

Department of Education, 2004. *Education Statistics in South Africa at a Glance in 2002*. Pretoria: Department of Education.

Department of Higher Education and Training, 2010. *Statistics on Post-school Education and Training in South Africa*. Pretoria: Department of Higher Education and Training.

Department of Public Enterprises, 11 October 2011. *SOCs Status of Capital Expenditure*. Pretoria: Department of Public Enterprises.

Department of Sport and Recreation, 2010. *FIFA World Cup Country Report*. Pretoria: Department of Sport and Recreation.

Department of Water Affairs, 2010. *Blue Drop Report*. Western Cape: Department of Water Affairs.

Department of Water Affairs, 2012. *Overview of the Green Drop Progress Report*. Pretoria: Department of Water Affairs.

Directorates within the Department of Education, May 2005. *Education Statistics at a Glance in 2003*. Pretoria: Department of Education.

DTI (Department of Trade and Industry), n.d. *A National Industrial Policy Framework*. Pretoria: DTI.

DTI, 2005–2007. *Annual Review of Small Business in South Africa*. Pretoria: DTI.

DTI, 2011. *Youth Enterprise Development Strategy 2013–2023: Creating New Business Opportunities for Young Women and Men in South Africa*. Pretoria: DTI.

DTI, 2013. *Annual Report 2012–2013*. Pretoria: DTI.

DTI, 2013. *Industrial Policy Action Plan 2013/14–2015/16: Economic Sectors and Employment Cluster*. Pretoria: DTI.

DTI, 2014. *Industrial Policy Action Plan, 2014/15–2016/17: Economic Sectors and Employment Cluster*. Pretoria: DTI.

Esters, C., April 2014. *South African Sovereign Rating – Quo Vadis?* Toronto: Standard & Poor's Ratings Services and McGraw-Hill Financial.

Federal Reserve System, March 2014. *Minutes of the Open Market Committee*. Washington, DC: Federal Reserve.

Finmark Trust, 2010. *FinScope South Africa: Small Business Survey*. Johannesburg: Finmark Trust.

Finmark Trust, 2013. *FinScope SA: Consumer Survey*. Johannesburg: Finmark Trust.

Fukuyama, F., August 2013. *The Role of Politics in Development*. Johannesburg: Centre for Development and Enterprise.

Gatar Financial Centre Authority, March 2014. *The Global Financial Centres Index 15*. London: Gatar Financial Centre Authority.

GlobeScan/BBC/Program on International Policy Attitudes (PIPA), May 2013. Views of China and India Slide While UK's Ratings Climb: Global Poll. London: BBC.

Goldman Sachs, November 2013. *Two Decades of Freedom: What SA is Doing with It and What Now Needs to Be Done*. Johannesburg: Goldman Sachs.

Gordhan, Pravin (Minister of Finance), 2014. *2014 Budget Speech*. Pretoria: Department of Finance.

Hammond, G., 2012. *CCBS Handbook No. 29: State of the Art of Inflation Targeting*. London: Bank of England.

Health Systems Trust, 2013. *South African Health Review 2012/2013*. Durban: Health Systems Trust.

Helliwell, J., R. Layard and J. Sachs, 2013. *World Happiness Report 2013*. New York: United Nations Sustainable Development Solutions Network.

ICT Data and Statistics, 2013. *ICT Facts and Figures*. Geneva: International Telecommunication Union.

IMF (International Monetary Fund), July 2012. *Estimating the Implicit Inflation Target of the South African Reserve Bank*. Washington, DC: IMF.

IMF. 19 July 2013. *South Africa: Staff Report for the 2013 Article IV Consultation – Debt Sustainability Analysis*. Washington, DC: IMF.

IMF, October 2013. *World Economic and Financial Surveys Fiscal Monitor: Taxing Times*. Washington, DC: IMF.

IMF, 2013. *South Africa 2013 Article IV Consultation*. Washington, DC: IMF.

IMF, April 2014. *Fiscal Monitor: Public Expenditure Reform – Making Difficult Choices*. Washington, DC: IMF.

IMF, 2014. *World Economic Outlook*. Washington, DC: IMF.

Institute of International Finance, 13 March 2014. *South Africa: Consolidating the Fiscal Position*. Washington, DC: Institute of International Finance.

International Budget Partnership, 2012. *Open Budget Index 2012*. London: International Budget Partnership.

Jahan, S., 2013. *Inflation Targeting: Holding the Line*. Available at: htcpp://www.imf.org (accessed 12 September 2013).

Kaplan, D., March 2007. *Industrial Policy in South Africa: Targets, Constraints and Challenges*. Geneva: United Nations Conference on Trade and Development.

Kenney, H., and W.D. Reekie, 1992. *Principles of Industrial Economics in South Africa*. Johannesburg: Jonathan Ball Publishers.

Kessides, C., 1993. *The Contributions of Infrastructure to Economic Development*. Washington, DC: World Bank.

Keynes, J.M., 1930. *The General Theory of Employment, Interest and Money*. Available at: http://www.pkarchive.org (accessed 30 August 2006).

Lall, S., 1993. *What Will Make South Africa Internationally Competitive?* London: Institute of Economics and Statistics, Oxford University.

Lall, S., 2004. *Reinventing Industrial Strategy: The Role of Government Policy in Building Industrial Competitiveness*. Working Paper 9. Johannesburg: Trade and Industrial Policy Strategies.

Magana, E., and R. Houghton, 1996. *Transformation in South Africa? Policy Debates in the 1990s*. Johannesburg: Institute for African Alternatives.

Manuel, T., and C. Chibane, 19 February 2013. *Implementation of the National Development Plan – Post-SONA Media Briefing*. Pretoria: National Planning Commission.

McConnell, J.K., C. McFarland and B. Common, n.d. *Supporting Entrepreneurs and Small Business: A Tool Kit for Local Leaders*. Washington, DC: National League of Cities Center for Research and Innovation.

McKinsey & Company, January 2012. *Debt and Deleveraging: Uneven Progress on the Path to Growth*. San Francisco and Shanghai: McKinsey Global Institute.

National Bureau of Statistics (Nigeria), 6 April 2014. *Measuring Better: Rebasing/Re-benchmarking of Nigeria's GDP*. Abuja, Nigeria: National Bureau of Statistics.

National Planning Commission, 2011. *National Development Plan – Vision for 2030*. Johannesburg: National Planning Commission.

National Skills Research Agency, August 2008. *Annual Review of Small Business in South Africa*. Pretoria: Department of Trade and Industry.

National Treasury, n.d. *Jobs Fund Creates Employment through Innovation*. Pretoria: National Treasury.

National Treasury, n.d. *A Primer on Budget Terminology*. Pretoria: National Treasury.

National Treasury, 1994 to 2014. *Budget Reviews*. Pretoria: Department of Finance.

National Treasury and SARS (South African Revenue Service), 2013. *Tax Statistics*. Pretoria: National Treasury and SARS.

National Treasury and SARS, 2014. *How the Employment Tax Incentive Works for You*. Pretoria: National Treasury and SARS.

Nedcor Economic Unit, 1999. The South Africa – EU Trade Agreement: Opportunity Knocks? *Guide to the Economy*, ISSN 1023-7097 (October), pp. 1–8.

NEPAD (New Partnership for Africa's Development), 2012. *Short Term Action Plan for Infrastructure*. Johannesburg: NEPAD.

Nhlapo, M., and B. Anderson, n.d. *Profiling South African Middle Class Households 1998–2006*. Pretoria and Ann Arbor: Statistics South Africa and the University of Michigan.

OECD (Organisation for Economic Co-operation and Development), 2013. Expenditure on R&D. In *OECD Factbook 2013: Economic, Environmental and Social Statistics*. Paris: OECD Publishing.

OECD Economic Surveys, 2013. *China Overview*. Paris: OECD Publishing.

Osborn, E., and K. Lings, 1992. *Capital Intensity in the Manufacturing Sector: EBM Research Conference*. Port Elizabeth: Vista University.

Paton, C., 2013. Job Fund Helps Projects Give the Unemployed a Head Start. *Business Day*, 25 November. Available at: www.bdlive.co.za (accessed 24 April 2014).

PICC (Presidential Infrastructure Coordinating Commission), March 2014. *ASISA Update on PICC*. Pretoria: PICC.

Pickworth, E., 2013. It's Tough in SA When You're Just the Little Guy. *Business Day*, 28 November, p. 21.

Population Reference Bureau, 1962–2012. *World Population Data Sheet – 50 Years*. Washington, DC: Population Reference Bureau.

Ports Regulator of South Africa, 2012. *Global Port Pricing Comparator Study*. Durban: Ports Regulator of South Africa.

Roger, S., 2010. Inflation Targeting Turns 20. *Finance & Development*, March, pp. 46–49.

SAICE (South African Institution of Civil Engineering), May 2011. SAICE Infrastructure Report Card 2011. *Civil Engineering*, Vol. 19, No. 4, pp. 4–6.

SAIRR (South African Institute of Race Relations), 1994–2013. *South Africa Surveys*. Johannesburg: SAIRR.

SAIRR, 25 February 2014. A New Expropriation Bill by Another Name. *@Liberty: The Policy Bulletin of the IRR*, No. 3, pp. 1–5.

SAIRR, 26 March 2014. Delivering on 'Radical' Change If Not on Growth or Jobs. *@Liberty: The Policy Bulletin of the IRR*, No. 5, pp. 1–7.

SARS (South African Revenue Service), 2013. *Revenue Review Chapter 4: Revenue Trends and Tax Proposals*. Pretoria: SARS.

SEDA (Small Enterprise Development Agency), 2011/2012. *Annual Report*. Pretoria: SEDA.

SEDA, 2014. *Annual Performance Plan 2013/2014–2015/2016*. Pretoria: SEDA.

SEFA (Small Enterprise Finance Agency), 2013. *Introducing SEFA*. Pretoria: SEFA.

South Africa: The Good News, 2013. *Fifty Facts about a Remarkable Nation*. Johannesburg: South Africa: The Good News.

South African Reserve Bank, 2007–2014. *Quarterly Bulletins*. Pretoria: South African Reserve Bank.

Stats SA (Statistics South Africa), Q1: 2008 – Q1: 2014. *National and Provincial Labour Market: Youth*. Pretoria: Stats SA.

Stats SA, October 2010. *Survey of Employers and the Self-employed 2009*. Pretoria: Stats SA.

Stats SA, 2010/2011. *Income and Expenditure of Households Survey*. Pretoria: Stats SA.

Stats SA, 16 August 2012. *Recorded Live Births 2011*. Pretoria: Stats SA.

Stats SA, December 2013. *Quarterly Employment Statistics*. Pretoria: Stats SA.

Stats SA, Q4 2013. *Quarterly Labour Force Survey*. Pretoria: Stats SA.

Stats SA, 2013. *GDP Q3 2013*. Pretoria: Stats SA.

Stats SA, 2013. *South African Statistics*. Pretoria: Stats SA.

Stats SA, 2014. *Poverty Trends in South Africa: An Examination of Absolute Poverty between 2006 and 2011*. Pretoria: Stats SA.

The Presidency, 2007. *ASGISA Annual Report*. Pretoria: The Presidency.

The Presidency, 2012. *Development Indicators*. Pretoria: Department of Performance Monitoring and Evaluation.

The Presidency, 2014. *Twenty Year Review*. Pretoria: The Presidency.

The Presidency in conjunction with DBSA (Development Bank of Southern Africa), 2012. *The State of South Africa's Economic Infrastructure: Opportunities and Challenges*. Halfway House: DBSA.

Turton, N., and M. Herrington, 2012. *Global Entrepreneurship Monitor 2012 South Africa*. Cape Town: UCT Centre for Innovation and Entrepreneurship.

United States Conference of Mayors, 2009. *Ready to Go: Jobs and Infrastructure Projects*. Washington, DC: United States Conference of Mayors.

Van der Westhuizen, C., 2006. *Trade and Poverty: A Study of the South African Clothing Industry*. Cape Town: Southern Africa Labour and Development Research Unit, University of Cape Town.

Whiteford, A., D. Posel and T. Kelatwang, 1995. *A Profile of Poverty, Inequality and Human Development*. Pretoria: Human Sciences Research Council.

World Bank, April 2013. *Inequality in Focus*. Washington, DC: World Bank.

World Bank, July 2013. *South Africa: Economic Update – Focus on Inequality of Opportunity*. Issue No. 3. Washington, DC: World Bank.

World Bank, January 2014. *Global Economic Prospects: Coping with Policy Normalization in High-Income Countries*. Washington, DC: World Bank.

World Bank and IFC (International Finance Corporation), 2014. *Doing Business 2014: Economy Profile South Africa*. Washington, DC: World Bank and IFC.

World Bank and IFC, 2014. *Doing Business 2014: Understanding Regulations for Small & Medium Size Enterprises*. Washington, DC: World Bank and IFC.

World Economic Forum, 2013. *Global Agenda Outlook*. Geneva: World Economic Forum.

World Economic Forum, 2014. *The Global Competitiveness Report 2013/2014*. Geneva: World Economic Forum.

Zarenda, H., June 2013. *South Africa's National Development Plan and Its Implications for Regional Development*. Johannesburg: TRALAC.

Zarenda, H., 2013/14. *A Retrospective Briefing on the Industrial Policy Action Plan for South Africa*. Johannesburg: TRALAC.

INDEX